Beyond
Respectability

WOMEN, GENDER, AND SEXUALITY
IN AMERICAN HISTORY

Editorial Advisors:
Susan K. Cahn
Wanda A. Hendricks
Deborah Gray White
Anne Firor Scott,
Founding Editor Emerita

*A list of books in the series appears
at the end of this book.*

Beyond Respectability

The Intellectual Thought of Race Women

BRITTNEY C. COOPER

UNIVERSITY OF
ILLINOIS PRESS
Urbana, Chicago, and Springfield

Library of Congress Cataloging-in-Publication Data

Names: Cooper, Brittney C., 1980– author.
Title: Beyond respectability : the intellectual thought of race
    women / Brittney C. Cooper.
Other titles: Intellectual thought of race women
Description: Urbana, IL : University of Illinois Press, [2017] |
    Series: Women, gender, and sexuality in American history |
    Includes bibliographical references and index. | Identifiers:
    LCCN 2017003605 (print) | LCCN 2017013221 (ebook) |
    ISBN 9780252099540 (ebook) | ISBN 9780252040993
    (cloth : alk. paper) | ISBN 9780252082481 (pbk. : alk.
    paper)
Subjects: LCSH: African American women—Intellectual
    life—19th century. | African American women—Intellectual
    life—20th century. | National Association of Colored
    Women (U.S.) | Terrell, Mary Church, 1863-1954. | Murray,
    Pauli, 1910–1985. | African American women—Biography. |
    African American intellectuals—Biography.
Classification: LCC E185.89.I56 (ebook) | LCC E185.89.I56 C66
    2017 (print) | DDC 305.48/896073—dc23
LC record available at https://lccn.loc.gov/2017003605

For my mother,
Debbie Cooper Hicks,
whose innumerable sacrifices made this work possible.

Contents

Acknowledgments

This book began as a conversation with the late Dr. Rudolph P. Byrd, when he stopped to talk to me one day on the Emory Quadrangle about the ways that I could blend my interests in Black women writers and Black political theory. Invigorated by that conversation, I embarked on a quest to discover race women—who they are, what makes them tick, laugh, cry, and fight for better days. I did not know then that I would be living with these women in one form or another for the better part of a decade. But what I have learned is never to let respectable race ladies fool you—they have taken me on one wild ride!

For their support and encouragement, I thank the incomparable Dr. Byrd; Dr. Kimberly Wallace-Sanders, my first feminist professor and the reason I call myself a feminist today; Dr. Lawrence P. Jackson, my first college professor ever and the reason why I am a college professor today; and Dr. Beverly Guy-Sheftall, the prototype for all of us who have dared to study the rich intellectual legacies of Black women thinkers.

I thank my Emory Crew, colleagues who have supported this book in big and small ways over the years: Robert J. Patterson, Brenda D. Tindal, Keisha Haywood, V. Denise James Kim D. Green, Chante Martin, Worth Kamili Hayes, Yanci M. Baker, Pellom McDaniels, Zeb Baker, Aukje Kluge, Donna Troka, Elizabeth Stice, Aida Levy-Hussen, Lerone Martin, Michelle Purdy, Keisha Green, Regine Jackson, Tracy Smith, and the late Kharen Fulton.

This book received generous financial support from the University of Alabama in the form of a College of Arts and Sciences Research Council Grant and additional financial support from Dean Bob Olin of the College of Arts and Sciences. I could not have asked for better colleagues than Dr. Doveanna Fulton and my friends Jennifer Shoaff and Derrick Bryan.

A Ford Foundation Postdoctoral Fellowship gave me a critical year of time off to devote to this book and afforded me access to one of the most supportive communities of scholars that exists. I am so thankful for Lee Ann Fuji, Salamishah Tillet, Koritha Mitchell, Pier Gabrielle Foreman, David Ikard, Ula Y. Taylor, Monica Coleman, Fox Harrell, Ayesha Hardison, Rashawn Ray, Eric Anthony Grollman and others who have been part of my Ford Foundation mentorship network and community of support. Thanks also to Stephanie Evans for her early support of this manuscript.

The Rutgers School of Arts and Sciences has also supported this book with a critical semester of time off that became critical to my ability to complete the manuscript. I also thank the Rutgers University Research Council for their generous grant in support of publication of this work.

At Rutgers, I have been embraced by the intellectual generosity of so many scholars and colleagues whose gift of time and attention to my professional development fills me with gratitude. Thank you Mia Bay for inviting me to serve my postdoctoral year at the Center for Race and Ethnicity. Thank you to Cheryl Wall and Deborah Gray White for reading drafts of my manuscript. This book is stronger because of you. Thank you to Ann Fabian for always "getting it," and for encouraging me and making me feel like I was on the right path. Thank you to my colleagues in the Department of Women's and Gender Studies, particularly Mary Hawkesworth for her multiple reads of this book and Alison Bernstein for always cheering me on. You are greatly missed, Alison. Thanks also to the Junior Faculty Crew. And thank you to my colleagues in the Department of Africana Studies including Edward Ramsamy, Kim Butler, and Gayle Tate.

Thank you to Martha Jones for affirming the necessity of tangling with the vaunted ideas of the "big boys."

Thank you to each blind reviewer who read the manuscript and gave thoughtful comments that have assuredly made the book stronger. I appreciate Larin McLaughlin for believing in this book when it was in proposal format and for ultimately bringing it to the University of Illinois Press. And thank you Dawn Durante for being a wonderful editor and advocate for this book, for diligently guiding me through the process, and for being patient with me during my many freak-outs along the way.

An earlier version of the information in the prologue was published as "Ain't I A Lady?: Race Women, Michelle Obama, and the Ever-Expanding Democratic Imagination." Thank you to the Journal of Multi-Ethnic Literatures of the United States (MELUS) and to Oxford University Press for permission to include this material. And thank you to the dedicated staff members at the Schlesinger Library, Radcliffe Institute, Harvard University and the Moorland-Spingarn Research Center at my alma mater Howard University.

One of the things I know for sure is that I have one of the baddest crews of homegirls to ever exist. Most of them also happen to be academics. And all of them are brilliance and BlackGirlMagic personified.

Susana Morris, my Wonder Twin and CF, thank you for answering every distressed phone call, reading multiple drafts of this book, and talking me off the ledge all the time. (Sag Dance.) Robin Boylorn, my "bae" and CF, I am so glad for our friendship, for the ways you hold me down, for all the counsel, prayers, and encouragement.

And to all the ladies of the CFC—Rachel Raimist, Sheri Davis-Faulkner, Eesha Pandit, Chanel Craft-Tanner, and Crunkista—I love y'all. This life is so much better because we get to do this work together.

Treva B. Lindsey, I feel like we wrote these books together. Thank you for being a confidante, an ally, a mentor, a strategist, a formidable interlocutor, and one of the realest homegirls I have.

And to all of the rest of the Pleasure Ninjas—Joan Morgan, Yaba Blay, Esther Armah, Kaila Story—this work has been delightful because I have had the sublime pleasure of doing it with you.

Kristie Dotson, when I met you, I made sense to myself and my book made sense to me. Thank you for doctoring on it till it shines. Your deft hand and critical eye made all the difference. Special thanks also to Theri Pickens.

Thank you to my Up North Crew of Down South Girls—Shatema Threadcraft (my Harriet) and Melanye Price (my road dog). Thank you to my Philly Crew, Pastor Leslie Callahan, Charisse Tucker, and Bella. Thank you to my Now-Jersey girls, Theresa Thames and Candice Benbow. Thanks to Tanisha Ford and Jessica Johnson (D.O.L.s). And thank you to Raydell Gomez.

To my movement folks, nothing has been the same since August 9, 2014. To Monica Dennis, Teddy Reeves, Nakisha Lewis, Vivian Anderson, Arielle Newton and all the rest, I'd ride that terrible bus with all of you again in the cause of freedom. Joanne Smith, thank you for loving us. Akiba Solomon, thank you for putting eyes on this book in a critical moment. It made a difference.

I grew up an only child but in Mychal Denzel Smith, Darnell Moore, and Kiese Laymon, I have found brothers, cheerleaders, kindred spirits, and fam. I am eternally grateful for all of your BlackBoyMagic.

Melissa Harris-Perry, thank you for being a mentor and a model for how to do Black feminist and public scholarship with integrity. Michael Eric Dyson, thank you for looking out for a sister in tangible ways. Mark Anthony Neal, you give me hope for feminist brothers. Thank you for the quiet but insistent way that you prodded and encouraged me to "finish the book!"

Crystal Faison, clearly we've been friends for more than one lifetime. Thanks for being there since the beginning. Erica Hill, thank you and Lorenzo for letting me crash every time I have needed a place and for every pep talk and prayer.

Those who know me know I am a Southern girl, born and raised. The women I write for are the women who raised me. This book is for my Grandmother Louvenia Cooper, my Aunties Colleen, Linda, and Geraldine, my uncle Barry, my many cousins, including Brandon and Courtney, Chad and Sterling, Kasey and Brandy, for my nieces and nephews, and all the rest. It is for the Edmonds family, including my Big Mama Geneva Edmonds. It is for my step-dad, the Reverend. But more than all of them, it is for my mom, Debbie Cooper Hicks. Thank you for every bedtime story, Baby-Sitters Club book, and insistent conversation about the proper pronunciation of words in the English language. Thank you for first encouraging me to write and for typing my stories. All that I am today began with seeds you planted.

Thanks be to God almighty for keeping me.

To any one I have forgotten, please charge it to my head and not my heart.

Beyond
Respectability

PROLOGUE

Only the BLACK WOMAN can say "when and where I enter
in the quiet, undisputed dignity of my womanhood, without
violence and without suing or special patronage, then and
there the whole race enters with me."
—Anna Julia Cooper (1892)

From the moment I encountered Anna Julia Cooper's *Voice from the South* in a graduate course on race and feminist theory, I have been on a quest to understand where this nineteenth-century Southern Black woman, one with whom I coincidentally share a last name, found the courage and the audacity to challenge the thinking of Black male preachers, white male philosophers, and early white women feminists.[1] Prior to studying Cooper in the graduate course, I knew of her name only because it is embossed on a street sign in the neighborhood where she lived in Washington, D.C., a few blocks from the campus of my alma mater, Howard University. But before that graduate course, I didn't know anything about her work. Though her life and work clearly frames the backdrop for my own intellectual formation, in my time living in her neighborhood, I never read anything she wrote. When I finally came to her work, it felt like a homecoming. I was a young woman in the process of becoming an intellectual, one who, at the time, was still not quite comfortable with my own penchant for asking questions and challenging received wisdom. When I encountered her text, I came to recognize that those contrarian inclinations within me, when put to good and well-trained use, could do some serious work for Black people. Anna Julia Cooper taught me that.

Though Cooper no longer labors under the burden of intellectual obscurity, far too many Black women thinkers do. *Beyond Respectability: The Intellectual Thought of Race Women* is a book about Black women as thinkers and intellectuals. Though we know the names of women like Mary Church Terrell and Fannie Barrier Williams, Pauli Murray and Toni Cade Bambara, we still know far too little about the actual content of their thinking. Many Black women thinkers labor under the exigencies of historical triage. Their names exist almost like family photos relegated to a wall we rarely touch. We know they are important. We memorialize them with honored places on the wall of our offices and libraries and in the histories we write. We celebrate their voluminous firsts as founders of organizations, published writers, recipients of advanced degrees, and more. But then we shelve them, as though preservation is the most apt way to show respect for their critical intellectual labor. Such acts are rooted in notions of both care and carelessness. We care enough not to let these women be thrown away, but in many respects, the dearth of critical engagements with most of the women under consideration in this book suggests a lack of critical care in handling their intellectual contributions. This book is not only committed to the notion that we should "care more." It explores what a careful examination of Black women's intellectual traditions might yield for both the study of Black intellectual history and for one particular branch of Black intellectual history—Black feminist thought.

Beyond care, I would also suggest that, in order to take these Black women seriously as intellectuals, we must be willing to trust them. Dare I say, trust? By *trust*, I don't mean always agree. I mean acknowledge, appreciate, struggle with, disagree with, sit with, and question. I mean take Black women *seriously*. Most academics have been trained *to trust* that white males of all varieties are capable of "deep thoughts." *Beyond Respectability* requires that we approach Black women's long history of knowledge production with this same kind of trust. If I were aiming to show (and was successful at showing) how Black women's ideas dovetailed the ideas of Michel Foucault or Gilles Deleuze and Felix Guattari or Louis Althusser or Judith Butler, this book would be deemed sufficiently rigorous and, dare I say, "original." That I aim for a different goal, namely to show that we should take Black women, from Fannie Barrier Williams to Mary Church Terrell to Pauli Murray, as theoretically seriously as we take the work of French white males, requires a different inclination. It is perhaps counterintuitive to argue that affective considerations like care and trust are critical to the work of studying Black women's intellectual production. But Black women's knowledge production has always been motivated by a sense of care for Black communities in a world where non-Black people did not find value in the lives and livelihoods of these communities. And we are again in a moment where taking care of Black lives and livelihoods has become a matter of critical social import. The call to care here is a call for scholarly rigor, a reminder that Black women's intellectual work does still matter.

What might it mean for Black feminist scholars to say they are theorists in the tradition of Anna Julia Cooper or Fannie Barrier Williams, or Ida B. Wells or Patricia Hill Collins or Joy James, in the same way that scholars are allowed to claim that they are Marxist, or Freudian, or Foucaldian, or Kantian, or Spinozan? What might it look like to be Cooperian or Wellsian in our approach to the study of Black women's lives and Black intellectual thought?

Beyond Respectability employs an Anna Julia Cooperian approach to reading and interrogating the theoretical work and lived experiences of Black women intellectuals. To understand this methodological approach, one needs to first become acquainted with two of Cooper's cardinal commitments. They include: 1) a commitment to seeing the Black female body as a form of possibility and not a burden, and 2) a commitment to centering the Black female body as a means to cathect Black social thought. In *Voice*, Cooper places the Black female body and all that it knows squarely in the center of the text's methodology. She fundamentally believed that we cannot divorce Black women's bodies from the theory they produce.

These forms of what I term *embodied discourse* predominate in Cooper's work. *Embodied discourse* refers to a form of Black female textual activism wherein race women assertively demand the inclusion of their bodies and, in particular, working-class bodies and Black female bodies by placing them in the texts they write and speak. By pointing to all the ways Black women's bodies emerge in formal and informal autobiographical accounts, archival materials, and advocacy work, we disrupt the smooth function of the culture of dissemblance and the politics of respectability as the paradigmatic frames through which to engage Black women's ideas and their politics. Theorized by historians Darlene Clark Hine and Evelyn Brooks Higginbotham, respectively, the culture of dissemblance and the politics of respectability refer to two key strategies that Black women used to navigate a hostile public sphere and to minimize the threat of sexual assault and other forms of bodily harm routinely inflicted upon Black women. These strategies attempted to make Black women's bodies as inconspicuous and as sexually innocuous as possible. Undoubtedly, Black women did dissemble, making their interior thoughts and feelings inaccessible from public view. And they were undoubtedly obsessed with making the race "respectable."[2] But these were not the only strategies Black women used to navigate the public sphere, in part because they were acutely aware of the limitations of making themselves invisible in a world predicated in the surveillance of Black bodies. Cooper and other race women forged their understandings of Black racial identity and Black

FIGURE 1. Anna Julia Cooper. Courtesy of Moorland Spingarn Research Center, Manuscripts Division, Howard University, Washington D.C.

freedom upon the terrain of the very visible Black and female body. Thus the book asks us to consider what Black women thinkers said about Black women's lives, and Black possibility, beyond the discourse of respectability.

An iconic moment from Cooper's *Voice from the South* is instructive. In her oft-cited critical exchange with Martin Delany, she exposes the problem with masculinist conceptions of Black possibility: "Only the BLACK WOMAN can say 'when and where I enter in the quiet, undisputed dignity of my womanhood, without violence and without suing or special patronage, then and there the whole race enters with me.'"[3] A paragon of the emerging Great Race Man model of leadership that relied on a charismatic male leader as its centerpiece,[4] Delany, whom Cooper admired, represented both the potency and the danger of a masculinist approach to race progress. Delany, a staunch Black nationalist, reveled in being what Cooper called "an unadulterated black man" with no identifiable European ancestry. For him, this "pure" African bloodline meant that when he, an accomplished medical doctor, intellectual, and racial leader, "entered the council of kings the black race entered with him."[5] Delany was a quintessential race man who, by turns, attempted a race colonization scheme in Africa, and when that failed, served in the Union Army. While he was a champion of the education of women, he also thought their primary role in "the regeneration of the race" was as good mothers. But his race rhetoric was tied to his belief that his bloodline had remained unsullied by whiteness.[6] As the child of an enslaved mother and a white slave master, Cooper could make no such pronouncements about Black racial purity or an unadulterated bloodline. Histories of sexual violence and bodily trauma in Black women's lives made such accounts of racial identity untenable.

Unimpressed by Delany's definition of power, which metonymically centered formal recognition by the "council of kings," Cooper also made clear that "whatever the attainments of the individual may be . . . he can never be regarded as identical with or representative of the whole."[7] By challenging Delany's conception of power, Cooper rejected his implicit romanticization of political elitism and white male standards of power as the goal to which Black people should aspire.[8] Cooper pointed instead to the "horny handed toiling men and women of the South" as the proper measure of race progress. Focusing on the gnarled, calloused hands of working-class Black people demanded that racial accounts of progress remain connected to the material and embodied conditions of everyday Black people. Moreover, Cooper made clear that her primary social goal was not the achievement of racial respectability, but rather the achievement of "undisputed dignity." The call for dignity and the call for respectability are not the same, though they are frequently conflated. Demands for dignity are demands for a fundamental recognition of one's inherent humanity. Demands for respectability assume that unassailable social propriety will prove one's dignity. Dignity, unlike respectability, is not socially contingent. It is intrinsic and, therefore, not up for debate. And Cooper was willing to step into the ring to contest anyone who thought otherwise.

Thus, Cooper's racial conceptions remained profoundly rooted in and on the body, despite critical disagreements with Delany's requirements for African blood quantum. Racial purity and formal recognition by white bodies of power were not prerequisites for the concession and acknowledgment of Black dignity. Black women could show up, move through the world, and make profound contributions when violent and oppressive conditions ceased to inhibit their access to full bodily integrity. In this way, the Black female body became integral to how Black women theorized the politics of racial uplift.

Unlike her contemporary W. E. B. Du Bois—who famously conceptualized the black body as a site of internal striving—"two souls, two thoughts, two unreconciled strivings; two warring ideals in one dark body, whose dogged strength alone keeps it from being torn asunder"[9]—Cooper embraced racial embodiment as possibility rather than as perturbation. Where Du Bois characterized the Black body as racked with an epic internal struggle over identity, Cooper, using the Black female body as a point of reference, saw intersecting identities—primarily of race and gender, but also of class and nation—as a point of possibility. In Cooper's account of racial identity, a Black female experience of embodiment brought these competing national identities into generative tension, whereas in Du Bois's' account, competing identities threatened to dismember the Black self:

> In this last decade of our century, changes of such moment are in progress, such new and alluring vistas are opening out before us, such original and radical suggestions for the adjustment of labor and capital, of government and the governed, of the family, the church and the state, that to be a possible factor, though an infinitesimal [one] in such a movement is pregnant with hope and weighty with responsibility. To be a woman in such an age carries with it a privilege and an opportunity never implied before. But to be a woman of the Negro race in America, and to be able to grasp the deep significance of the possibilities of the crisis, is to have a heritage, it seems to me, unique in all the ages.[10]

Here, Cooper constructs Black women's intersectional position as its own kind of "crisis" of "possibility," as a space of "hope," "responsibility," and even "privilege." She inverts the logic of marginalization that one would typically assume in an argument about Black women's position at the intersection of race and gender.[11] She invokes the symbolism of a pregnant female body heavy with the weight of racial responsibility. Black women's capacity to reproduce children who would inherit the slave status of the mother had tethered their material value to their reproductive capacity, simultaneously rendering them vulnerable to endless sexual exploitation. Cooper, however, in her invocation of an expectant female body, offers new creative and procreative possibilities to Black women. At the most literal level, emancipated Black womanhood meant Black women could produce citizens rather than slaves.

All kinds of Black bodies appear in Cooper's work. In one moment, she uses embryonic imagery to describe the race as being "full of the elasticity and hopefulness of youth" and as having a "quickening of its pulses and a glowing of its self-consciousness."[12] In another moment, Cooper characterizes the race as a twenty-one-year-old Black male, "just at the age of ruddy manhood." This young man, who is eager to make his way in the world, challenges several stereotypical notions of Black males as lazy, perpetually immature, and unmotivated. She characterizes this state of maturity as a moment of profound possibility for both Black people and for America, and as a critical moment for "retrospection, introspection, and prospection."[13] This young man's youthful, healthy, sanguine complexion, exemplified in Cooper's use of the term *ruddy*, situates him as a positive addition to American life. Neither a rapist nor a potential criminal, he is a person who now has the freedom to mature to adulthood and pursue life's possibilities. Her invocation of a young male body ready to encounter the transforming American body politic intentionally concedes the value of Black manhood, in stark opposition to an ideological system bent upon alternately infantilizing or criminalizing Black men.

Cooper also daringly "writ[es] her body" onto the pages of her own book.[14] In one incident, she searched for a ladies room at a train station. When she found the bathroom, one door was marked "for ladies" and the other "for colored people." This created a moment of cognitive and experiential dissonance for Cooper, who was left "wondering under which head I come."[15] Elizabeth Alexander reads this as a moment of textual resistance for Cooper, who is faced with a choice that will necessarily "eras[e] some crucial part of her identity." The options presented to her "render her a literally impossible body in her time and space."[16] In this moment, "Cooper reminds her readers . . . that she lives and moves within a physical body with sensations and needs."[17] The discursive technologies of race that operate in the signs "for ladies" and "for colored" inherently constitute discursive and textual acts of misrecognition for Black women. The only way to achieve any recognition is to *insert a body* into the text that challenges the identities signified in the labels. The insertion of her body also demonstrates the ways in which public space was designed not only to render Black bodies as inferior, but Black female bodies as unrecognizable and unknowable in civic terms. Where Black women's bodies had been inherently publicly *knowable* under the conditions of slavery, after freedom and the conferral of citizenship, Black women did not fully fit into the categories propagated under Jim Crow. Yet, Cooper's colored *and* female body ontologically challenged the epistemological claims that those signs made. In other words, Cooper's textually present Black female body demanded to be known, in the very ways the signs attempted to foreclose. She used representations of her body in *A Voice* to challenge the race-gendered logics of those signs, hoping in the process to expose the discursive logics of racism and sexism and also to transform those discourses at the same time. "By writing her body into the texts as she does," Elizabeth Alexander reminds us, "Cooper forges textual space for the creation of the turn-of-the-century African-American female intellectual. . . . As such *A Voice* becomes a symbolic representation of the body of the African-American woman of letters newly created in the public sphere."[18]

Her intentional invocation of her own corporeality through the use of embodied discourse reminds us that intellectual work is not a disembodied project. That fact alone makes it untenable for scholars to continue to read Black women's literature solely or primarily through the corporeal frames offered to us by the culture of dissemblance or the politics of respectability. Respectability and dissemblance belong to a broader constellation of social formulations that race women theorized and enacted to protect themselves and make themselves known on their own terms. But if we fail to move beyond respectability, we will continue to miss critical parts of the story. Cooper, like other Black women thinkers of her time, recognized that muting her body, or dissembling, offered little safety and limited prospects for achieving respectability.

For instance, in what is most assuredly an allusion to Ida B. Wells's violent encounter on a train in the late 1880s, Cooper wrote, "I purposely forbear to mention instances of personal violence to colored women traveling in less civilized sections of our country, where women have been forcibly ejected from cars, thrown out of seats, their garments rudely torn, their person wantonly and cruelly injured."[19] This forthright presentation of a Black female body injured in the process of doing race work is just one of many examples of how embodied discourse shows up in Cooper's work and that of other Black women—pushing us to deal with the embodied dimensions of public Black women's lives. Cooper's use of embodied discourse as a disruptive textual practice ultimately locates Black female bodies within the project of racial knowledge production and the reorganization of place or public space. For Cooper, and for this project, Black bodies—and in particular, Black women's bodies—mark possibilities and generative tensions that are sites of inspiration and theory production. Whether the orienting Black body included a pregnant woman, a young man, an embryonic, gender neutral body, or even her own body experiencing various modes of segregation, Cooper's work can be read through tracking the varying invocations of Black bodies as a mechanism for theory production itself.

In the rest of this book, I follow Cooper's lead by looking for the variety of ways that the other Black women thinkers under examination—women like Mary Church Terrell, Fannie Barrier Williams, and Pauli Murray—invoke notions of embodiment as part of their theoretical production. By looking for the appearance of Black women's bodies, we can track the variety of ways that race women asserted their own ideas about what it means to be Black women intellectuals despite, and often in light of, the precarities of Black female embodiment. Doing so has important theoretical and methodological implications. Focusing on the ways that Black women discuss embodied experience in their social theorizing reminds us that Black women did not only seek to make Black female bodies respectable. Beyond strategic investments in dissemblance and respectability as practices that allowed for safer movement through public space, the study of race women's intellectual production suggests that, through the choice to write their bodies into texts and to use Black female embodiment as the zero point of their theorizing, they were interested in other approaches to understanding and ameliorating the precarity of Black women's lives. Though many Black women practiced a culture of dissemblance in public, in their textual work and on the lecture stage, they frequently pulled back the cloak of Black female pain and frustration, exposing the personal nature of the struggles they experienced, even as they worked to make the world safer for Black women. Ida B. Wells was mortified when she cried the first time she gave an antilynching address. The audacity to talk about how they *felt* about racism indexes an implicit belief that Black women's embodied and affective experiences of racism and patriarchy mattered in the project of Black female knowledge production. The audacity, conversely, to discuss in fleeting moments feelings of pleasure, despite daily contention with extreme racial repression, again challenges overdetermined readings of race women being obsessed in every moment with being respectable. Attending to embodiment through the tracking of embodied discourse reminds us that we cannot study Black women's theoretical production or tell Black women's intellectual history without knowing something of their lives.

At the same time, seeing Black female bodies as sites of theory production allows us to move the work of Black women's intellectual history beyond triage. One of the unfortunate methodological results of triaging Black women's histories is that when we have *recovered* a Black woman figure, that is, when we have saved her from being buried and lost to the annals of history, when we know her name and as many details as we can about her life and work, then we treat her as though it is time to move on to the next patient. That we have not yet engaged with the content of what Black women intellectuals actually *said*, even as we celebrate all that they *did*, seems to escape notice. This *recovery imperative* memorializes Black women figures like Cooper and her race women colleagues while obscuring other kinds of critical scholarly utility they have for our conversations in history, politics, literary studies, and feminist theory. Because we are familiar with Cooper, because we can call her name, because there are two books of critical scholarship about her (albeit written two decades apart), we act as though there is nothing new or groundbreaking to say about her.[20] By contrast, we never engage W. E. B. Du Bois in this way. Every year, a new scholarly text is written grappling with his work. Meanwhile, the work of Black women's intellectual history and Black feminist theory production suffers from lack of access to the rich histories of Black women's ideas. Thus, this work is not solely a work of recovery. I am deeply concerned about what these new ideas mean for making critical shifts in our intellectual genealogies, in our current Black feminist formulations, and in our telling of Black intellectual history.

Thanks to the pedagogical and scholarly work of Black feminist theorists and Black women historians, it has been many years since I thought of Anna Julia Cooper merely as a name on a Washington, D.C., street sign. In the ensuing years, I have had sense enough to return to T Street to visit the place she lived. I have had a chance to sit in the Moorland-Spingarn archives on the campus of Howard University, just a few blocks from her home, and research and read her papers. There is a way that Black women's intellectual legacies populate the backgrounds of our movements through public space and our intellectual environs, even when we are unaware of how important their thinking is to shaping the landscapes in which we move. Cooper is an origin point in an intellectual geography and genealogy of Black women's knowledge production that has led me in many unexpected and fruitful directions. But most of all, I am reminded of the inherent boldness of her demand and expectation that she be taken seriously as a thinker and theorist grappling with what she termed the "great questions of the age." And in the rest of this book she provides the theoretical and methodological blueprint that allows me to do the same for other race women.

INTRODUCTION
The Duty of the True Race Woman

> From the time that the first importation of Africans began to add comfort and wealth to the existence of the New World Community, the Negro woman has been constantly proving the intellectual character of her race in unexpected directions; indeed, her success has been significant. From the foregoing we conclude that it is the duty of the true race-woman to study and discuss all phases of the race question.
> —Pauline Hopkins (1902)

What does it mean and what has it meant to be a Black female intellectual? What does it mean to be a *race woman*? When and where are the sites of race women's becoming? In *Beyond Respectability: The Intellectual Thought of Race Women*, I argue that to arrive at an answer to the first question, we must diligently interrogate and examine the latter questions. Race women were the first Black women intellectuals. As they entered into public racial leadership roles beyond the church in the decades after Reconstruction, they explicitly fashioned for themselves a public duty to serve their people through diligent and careful intellectual work and attention to "proving the intellectual character" of the race. Pauline Hopkins declared two key tasks attached to the work of the "true race-woman."[1] They were "to study" and "to discuss" "all phases of the race question." Not only were these women institution builders and activists; they declared themselves public thinkers on race questions. Though Hopkins and her colleagues were part of a critical mass of public Black women thinkers in the 1890s, they joined a longer list of Black women who had been at the forefront of debates over "the woman question" and the role of Black women in public life throughout the 1800s.[2]

In this book, I construct both an intellectual genealogy and an intellectual geography of race women, whose work as public thinkers remains undertheorized, despite more than three decades of critical work in Black feminist theory and literary criticism and Black women's history. Thus, this book seeks to construct both an *intellectual genealogy* of the ideas that race women produce about racial identity, gender, and leadership between the 1890s and the 1970s, and an *intellectual geography* that maps the deliberate ways that Black women chose to take up and transform intellectual and physical spaces in service of their racial uplift projects.

I begin this genealogy and geography with the short epigraphic quote that Pauline Hopkins, Boston-based journalist, novelist, and clubwoman, penned for the *Colored American Magazine* in 1902 because it is the first explicit definition of the race woman in print.[3] The fact that she offered up this theorization of race womanhood, Black female leadership, and Black intellectual identity in a piece innocuously titled "Some Literary Workers," makes clear the idea that Black women did their theorizing in unexpected locations. That assumption guides much of the methodological approach I take throughout the text, combing through unexpected archives of Black women's thought to construct an intellectual genealogy and geography of this group of Black women thinkers. When I initially read Hopkins's literary profiles of Black women, I did not expect to find rich and useful social theorizations about racial politics or racial leadership embedded in what appeared to be only biographical accounts. It is my contention in *Beyond Respectability* that if we actually want to take Black women seriously as thinkers and knowledge producers, we must begin to look for their thinking in unexpected places, to expect its incursions in genres like autobiography, novels, news stories, medical records, organizational histories, public speeches, and diary entries. We must, as the editors of *Toward an Intellectual History of Black Women* charge us, "challenge common wisdom about where [Black women's] intellectual activities take place" and recognize that "the scenes of their intellectual labor have ranged from the intimate spaces of parlors, where epistolary exchanges were produced, to highly public podiums, where the oral expression of ideas often mixed with the material demands of communities."[4] Thus, I draw upon an "eclectic archive" to map and then apply Black women's theory production to questions of gender and racial identity, racial leadership, and debates about racial advancement.[5]

Hopkins's epigraphic formulation of "true race-womanhood" codified a set of practices and discussions, which Black female race leaders had been engaging since the early 1890s, about what it meant for Black women to assume the mantle of public race leadership alongside, and often in the stead of, Black men who were being actively and violently pushed out of the public sphere in the post-Reconstruction period. True race womanhood stands in stark contrast to what Barbara Welter has famously called the "cult of true womanhood."[6] The cult of true womanhood, or "domesticity," offered an explicit set of social expectations that circumscribed the lives of middle-class *white* women within the domestic sphere. The ideology of true womanhood undergirded the racial nationalism at the heart of white gender role ideology, which demanded that white women reproduce white citizens fit to propagate ideologies of white dominance in service of leading the nation. Indeed, Francesca Morgan argues that "the history of women and nationalism in the early twentieth century United States is also a history of 'race women,'" a term which applied not just to the ways Black women expressed "racial fidelity and a commitment to justice," but also to "white women's Anglo-Saxonist pride."[7]

Black women leaders actively pushed back against attempts to relegate them to the realm of domesticity. "We know," wrote Hopkins, "that it is not 'popular' for a woman to speak or write in plain terms against political brutalities, that woman should confine her efforts to woman's work in the home and church."[8] But times were changing. Black women could no longer limit speaking and writing to questions of home and church, domesticity and piety:

> The colored woman holds a unique position in the economy of the world's advancement in 1902. Beyond the common duties peculiar to woman's sphere, the colored woman must have an intimate knowledge of every question that agitates the councils of the world; she must understand the solution of problems that involve the alteration of the boundaries of countries, and which make and unmake governments.[9]

Any true race woman must be concerned not only with the moral and social character of the race, as the ideology of true womanhood dictated, but also with the "intellectual character" of the race. Whereas moral and social character traits were actively shaped by the labor of mothering that white women were asked to do in the domestic sphere, Black women did not have the luxury of confining their advocacy for the shaping of Black moral, social, or intellectual life strictly to the domestic realm.[10] For one thing, notions of public and private were not so easily demarcated for Black people without legal protection and enforcement. Second, postslavery ideas of Black womanhood were still being fiercely contested within both white and black public spheres. Third, Black female race leaders felt that such constricted ideas about gender would prevent them from doing critical advocacy work and refashioning public opinion about Black people. Hopkins argued that for "the Negro woman," "the more clearly she understands the governing principles of the government under which she lives and rears her children, the surer will be an honorable future for the whole race."[11] Hopkins's race women colleagues had been carefully and intentionally fashioning a more public leadership role for themselves as thinkers at the nexus of the race problem and the woman question since the early 1890s.

Explicitly throwing off the parochial dictates of the cult of true womanhood, Hopkins argued for a more expansive intellectual vision for the true race woman. An explicitly Black woman–centered formulation of race womanhood became necessary because existing ideas about public and private did not accurately demarcate the social terms of Black womanhood. Unsurprisingly, the public was historically considered a male domain, in stark contrast to the private, domestic "woman's sphere." And even these ideas about a woman's or domestic sphere were deeply racialized, so that "private and domestic" was a stand-in for "white womanhood." Jean Bethke Elshtain defines the public as "the opposite of private," and as that which "pertains to the people as a whole, to community, or nation-wide concerns, to the common good, to things open in sight, and to those things that may be used or shared by all members of the community."[12] Political theorist Mary Hawkesworth concludes that "because only some men—men of a specific race, class, education, and ancestry—are positioned to represent the public, the 'public' is a raced, classed, and gendered concept.[13] Thus, when Black women advocated for opportunities to engage their thought leadership "beyond woman's sphere," they were arguing explicitly for the right to do intellectual work in public space.

Lucy Craft Laney, a Georgia school educator and founder of the Haines Institute in Augusta, argued a similar position for an expanded public role for Black women in an 1899 speech:

> The educated Negro woman, the woman of character and culture, is needed in the schoolroom not only in the kindergarten, and in the primary and the secondary school; but she is needed in high school, the academy, and the college. Only those of character and culture can do successful lifting, for she who would mould character must herself possess it. Not alone in the schoolroom can the intelligent woman lend a lifting hand, but as a public lecturer she may give advice, helpful suggestions, and important knowledge that will change a whole community and start its people on the upward way. To be convinced of the good that can be done for humanity by this means one need only recall the names of Lucy Stone, Mary Livermore, Frances

Harper, Frances Willard and Julie Ward Howe. The refined and noble Negro woman may lift much with this lever.[14]

Now certainly, Lucy Laney's call for intellectual Black women to be people of "nobility," "refinement," and "culture" betray troubling elements of an emerging respectability politic that shaped the entrance of all Black women onto the public platform. It goes without saying that to talk about early Black women public intellectuals is to talk about a class of elite women with unprecedented educational access. But in our contemporary feminist critiques of respectability and elitist class politics, often we do not acknowledge the sexual vulnerability that animated these women's calls for "refinement." In a historical moment wherein Black women were forced to adjudicate their moral rectitude in public, the sexual and gender policing at the center of their calls for respectability, conservative as they are, emerge as a reasonable, though not particularly laudable, approach to protecting the sanctity of Black women's bodies. Moreover, these calls for respectability were meant to serve as a guard against white male sexual objectification. Part of the work of cultivating the public platform as a site for Black women to stand was making the space as safe as possible for Black women's physical bodies, which would be publicly on display. Black female leaders theorized the public platform as a site for community transformation via the dispensation of useful knowledge that they themselves helped to produce. That required them to put their bodies on the line and to confront the very kinds of troubling discourses about their sexual promiscuity that shaped how public audiences would perceive them.

Though the term is contemporary, I choose to understand race women intellectuals as *public intellectuals* because it is my contention that the models of racial leadership and public lecturing, in which these Black women historically engaged, created the paradigm for contemporary modes of Black public intellectual engagement. Black women thinkers have always been public intellectuals, both because they cared about producing accessible forms of knowledge for and with communities involved in the Black freedom struggle, and because the confluence of racism and patriarchy exempted them from access to academic institutions and from the protections of the private sphere. Black women have never had the luxury of being private thinkers. Thus, though the term *public intellectual* is fairly contemporary, the origins of practices that connote public intellectual work are much longer. In fact, according to historian Lucindy Willis, the appearance of the term *intellectual* in nineteenth-century discourse "connotes a distinct shift in perspective, making the concept less theoretical and more pragmatic."

Related to, but distinct from, thinker/philosophers like Socrates or Virgil, the term, in the nineteenth century, referred to individuals who "generated, applied and dispensed culture. Like great thinkers, [public intellectuals] were philosophers of sorts, but they seemed to possess a more developed sense of audience. As did their predecessors, they viewed life in its broadest contexts—socially, politically, and economically—yet often took active roles in challenging contemporary social conditions."[15] In this book, I intentionally and unapologetically foreground the *intellectual* work of race women because they themselves spent a great deal of time making arguments about their importance as intellectuals. Moreover, I make this move in line with historians and biographers of Black women thinkers who in the last decade have sought to foreground the critical intellectual labor that public Black women did in addition to their work as activists, organizers, educators, and churchwomen. Additionally, I understand Black women's knowledge production to encompass the range of places and spaces, thoughts, speech, and writings that Black women engaged to both know and understand themselves and the world around them more fully. In this book, I focus on the kinds of knowledge Black women produced about racial identity, gender identity, and gender politics in their books, speeches, and organizational work. Because I focus on women who had access to public platforms, this limits the scope of the Black women knowledge producers under consideration here—for example, poor and working-class Black women who produced knowledge in other forms. It is not my contention that middle-class race women were the only or the most important producers of racial knowledge. Rather I argue, that the intellectual contributions of race women thinkers still remain greatly understudied, often because this work is included under the guise of autobiographical writing or writing about organizational work. Shifting focus to these genres of race women's work offers new avenues for thinking about how they have enriched existing bodies of political and social thought on issues of race, gender, and sexuality.

A New School of Thought

One of the key questions that animates my thinking about race women intellectuals is, "Where and how did they become intellectuals?" Most of the late-nineteenth-century Black women public intellectuals helped both to start and to shape critically the Black Clubwomen's movement. Thus, in *Beyond Respectability*, I turn to the National Association of Colored Women (NACW) as a space integral to fashioning race women into intellectuals. This organization constitutes a critical site in the intellectual geography that shaped the knowledge production of race women at the turn of the twentieth century. Founded in 1896, the NACW acted as the training ground for the first generation of Black women public intellectuals. Though much historical scholarship has focused on the NACW as an activist and social welfare organization, I make a critical pivot in this book to consider the NACW as its own school of racial thought. I do so because that is how Fannie Barrier Williams, one of the most visible clubwomen of the early twentieth century and the theorist whose work I interrogate in chapter one, understood the organization. "The first thing to be noted," Williams argued in her 1901 organizational history about the function and activities of the clubs, "is that these club women are students of their own social condition."[16] Moreover,

> the clubs themselves are schools in which are taught and learned, more or less thoroughly, the near lessons of life and living. All these clubs have a program for study. In some of the more ambitious clubs, literature, music and art are studied more or less seriously, but in all of them race problems and sociological questions directly related to the condition of the Negro race in America are the principal subjects for study and discussion.[17]

Here, Williams argues that the NACW functioned as a school of social thought that empowered local organizations to create their own curricula of study relative to their specific needs. Tommy Curry argues that "it is of the utmost import to see Black organizations as schools of thought that dedicated their research, inquiry, and scholarship towards specific methods for investigating and resolving the race question."[18] These assertions require a scholarly pivot that acknowledges forthrightly the intellectual import of the NACW as the training school for the first generation of Black female public intellectuals.

Williams further argued that there had been three major preparatory schools for Black women's leadership. "Churches have been and still are the great preparatory schools in which the primary lessons of social order, mutual trustfulness, and united effort have been taught," she wrote.[19] She recognized even in 1900 that "the churches have been sustained, enlarged and beautified principally through the organized efforts of their women members."[20] Moreover, women's work in the church had taught them "unity of effort of the common good" and "broad social sympathies." Next, secret or mutual aid societies, which "demanded a higher order of intelligence" than church membership, had helped Black women to do a range of care work "for the indigent," the orphaned, and others in need.[21] These two groups—the church and secret societies—had made "colored women acquainted with the general social condition of the race and the possibilities of social improvement."[22]

It should also be noted that these two groups were critical nodes in the creation of what Martha S. Jones refers to as Black "public culture" as well, lending further credence to Williams's attempt to place the NACW on a continuum with these institutions.[23] However, because she made a clear distinction between the moral work of churches and the care work of secret societies, it would be impertinent to continue to read the NACW merely as an amalgam of these two. Instead, the NACW, in Williams's estimation, added another dimension to the work of these institutions by creating a systematic ideological approach to the social regeneration of the race. Not only had the NACW excerpted the church's program of moral instruction, but it also took the local approach to care and social service work that had been pioneered by numerous women's fraternal and mutual aid societies from the 1870s forward. Combining these approaches provided a systematic way to both meet local needs and to generate a body of shared knowledge that created a national picture of the state of African Americans. The NACW women actively embraced their role as creators of public knowledge about African Americans in general and African American women in particular. The organization desired a broad role in the intellectual reformation of public opinion regarding Black people.

Williams argued that the NACW woman was

> the real new woman in American life. . . . She is needed to change the old idea of things implanted in the minds of the white race and there sustained and hardened into a national habit by the debasing influence of slavery estimates. This woman is needed as an educator of public opinion. She is a happy refutation of the idle insinuations and common skepticism as to the womanly worth and promise of the whole race of women.[24]

Williams unapologetically insinuated Black women into the discourse of the *new woman*, a term that sought to characterize white women who were involved in the progressive movements at the turn of the century.[25] Not only were Black women new women, but they were the *real* new women, even more so than their white counterparts! The role that Williams ascribed to Black new women is even more telling. In language reminiscent of both Lucy Laney and Pauline Hopkins's true race woman, Williams described the African American new woman as "an educator of public opinion." Their job was to shift public perception and ideas about African American women through their work on the public stage. This call for Black women to shift public opinion, through both their pristine embodiment of respectable Black womanhood and their choice to make visible the particular struggles and precarity that attended to Black women's lives, exemplifies Cooper's ideas of using embodied discourse as a textual and discursive strategy to combat negative and damaging ideas about Black women.

Undoubtedly, these ideas were steeped in moral condescension toward Black women of lower-class status. Williams balked at the treatment of nonelite colored women who had "been left to grope their way unassisted toward a realization of those domestic virtues, moral impulses and standards of family and social life that are the badges of race respectability."[26] Though her views were steeped explicitly in respectability politics, she also critiqued middle-class Black people for their neglect of the Black poor. Moreover, she continued:

> There has been no fixed public opinion to which they could appeal; no protection against the libelous attacks upon their characters, and no chivalry generous enough to guarantee their safety against man's inhumanity to woman. Certain it is that colored women have been the least known, and the most ill-favored class of women in the country.[27]

Here, Williams turns to the notion of changing public opinion as the animating force of race women's "intellectual activism."[28] Reshaping the public discourse about Black women topped the list of racial priorities of race women and of the NACW's intellectual agenda. Black women's strategic deployment of respectability, on the one hand, and embodied discourse that pointed to the extreme racial and sexual vulnerability Black women experienced, on the other, was critical to shifting public perception and opinion about the value of Black women's lives.

Thus, Laney, Williams, and others imposed a respectability requirement on those women who would become educators of public opinion, in part because the work required an intrinsic placing of the Black female body on display for white public consumption. Certainly, the class policing that anchors respectability discourse remains persistent and troubling; and I suspect it is the reason that many of these women have been given short shrift in existing conversations about Black intellectual thought. Most work has focused on respectability as a marker of problematic class hierarchies among turn-of-the-twentieth-century African Americans. Many middle-class Black women expressed acute anxiety about how the practices of poor Black women would make them look bad. But I want to suggest that we move beyond focusing only on the ways that respectability discourses attempted to instantiate class hierarchies.[29] I am not offering social conditions as an apologetic for elite Black women's problematic class politics. Rather, I argue throughout this book that respectability discourse also constituted one of the earliest theorizations of gender within newly emancipated Black communities.

The post-Reconstruction push to style Black people as respectable men and women indexes a community's attempt to understand and articulate what it meant to be a man or a woman. As Hortense Spillers has suggested, the Middle Passage and chattel slavery stripped all but the most crude gender identifications from the Black body. To the extent, Spillers reminds us, that the "New-world, diasporic plight [of Black people] marked a theft of the body. . . . [W]e lose at least gender difference in the outcome, and the female body and the male body become a territory of cultural and political maneuver, not at all gender-related, gender-specific."[30] "The materialized scene of unprotected female flesh—of female flesh 'ungendered'" created an indeterminate social terrain for the articulation of Black gender identity.[31] Although I think much of the violation and violence that shaped Black life during enslavement was predicated on a denial of access to gender norms— which is to say that much of the treatment was gender-specific (e.g., denying Black women the protections of womanhood) or, at the very least, specific to the biological sex of the person—Spillers's larger observation is instructive, namely that enslavement was predicated on a dialectical doing and undoing of gender that frequently rendered the Black body a space of indeterminate gender terrain.

The Black female body, because it was the conduit through which enslavement passed to her descendants, was historically deemed the ground-zero site for the propagation of Black inferiority. Katherine McKittrick argues that the ownership and exploitation of Black women during slavery has geographic implications, for such practices "territorialized the body," making it "publicly and financially claimed, owned, and controlled by an outsider. Territorialization marks and names the scale of the body, turning ideas that justify bondage into corporeal evidence of racial difference."[32] McKittrick continues, clarifying that "once the racial-sexual body is territorialized, it is marked as decipherable and knowable—as subordinate, inhuman, rape-able, deviant, procreative, placeless."[33] But the terms upon which Black bodies came to be gendered (and ungendered) were imprecise, capricious, and contingent, such that much of the political project of Reconstruction among Black people became preoccupied with creating legible categories of manhood, womanhood, and childhood that would make clear the "undisputed dignity" of Black people.

So race women, engaging in the project of what Hazel Carby called "reconstructing womanhood," confronted a social terrain of gender for the Black body that was wholly indeterminate and discursively illegible. Thus, many of the intellectual concerns of the NACW School focused on making Black women epistemologically significant by addressing the problematic ways that Black women were (un)known and publicly conceived in social discourse. Race women took it as their political and intellectual work to give shape and meaning to the Black body in social and political terms, to make it legible as an entity with infinite value and social worth. In doing so, they hoped to create livable terms upon which Black women could be both known epistemologically, and upon which Black women could live and engage socially. So when race women like Cooper talked about the race as being only twenty-one years old, she and others made the literal claim that the Black person (and forms of Black personhood), which emerged after Emancipation, constituted an entirely new conception of Black life, Black gender, and the human. Moreover, when she and her NACW counterparts insisted on using embodied discourse to make the Black female body legible, such acts attempted to counteract an obtrusive history of "ungendered," or "de-gendered," Black female flesh shaped by experiences of trauma and violence.

Beyond Respectability makes the critical intellectual pivot toward viewing the NACW as its own school of thought because such a move makes the NACW visible as a key intellectual site in which race women theorized notions of both gender and sexuality. Much of the scholarship on race women has focused so much on the unsavory nature of the class politics that elite and aspiring Blacks sought to impose on their counterparts without fully examining how respectability ideology provided a foundation for articulating what a Black woman or Black man actually was.[34] For instance, E. Frances White's groundbreaking book *Dark Continent of Our Bodies: Black Feminism and the Politics of Respectability* first turned our attention to what she termed the "double-edged" nature of the politics of respectability. She noted that while Black club and churchwomen used respectability as a "discourse of resistance," their investment in social propriety often unwittingly authorized negative stereotypes about Black people.[35] Scholars of Black women's history have read the NACW as the primary location for the creation and dispensation of the ideologies of respectability and dissemblance.[36] However, *Beyond Respectability* joins a growing body of critical work in Black women's history and literary studies that seeks to complicate the narrative of the politics of respectability among Black women. Susana Morris has pointed to what she calls the "paradox of respectability," a desire to achieve respectability in the face of racist denigrations of Black humanity while being confronted over and over again not only with the way that structures of power hold respectability out of reach for many Black people in the United States, but also its limits as a strategy for achieving freedom.[37] Danielle McGuire has written about the ways that rape compelled Black women to overcome the dictates of dissemblance and respectability during the Civil Rights Movement and to testify publicly to the violence they experienced. But these public testimonials have a much longer history, as Black women can be found attesting to violent treatment publicly and in print throughout the nineteenth century.[38]

Much of the contemporary foothold that respectability discourses have in Black communities has everything to do with the fact that ridding ourselves of respectability entirely would mean completely upending the gender system that Black people, particularly Black women, theorized and created after Reconstruction. We have failed to think through the implications of respectability and dissemblance as part of a gender system theorized by Black intellectuals because, politically, this gender system is rooted not only in a conservative form of class politics, but also in a conservative form of sexual politics. Darlene Clark Hine argues that "at the core of essentially every activity of the NACW's individual members was a concern with creating positive images of Black women's sexuality."[39] Redeeming images of Black women's sexuality was inarguably a core concern of the NACW School of Thought. However, because early scholarship in Black women's history collapsed ideas of gender and sexuality, rather than decoupling them as later feminist scholarship has done, our strident critique of the NACW's attempt to restyle Black women's sexuality has missed the ways that respectability and dissemblance were also part of a broader system of attempting to create legible gender categories for Black men and women.

That gender system made Black women's and men's lives legible as humans rather than as chattel and has subsequently created deep affective investments in Black communities over the last 150 years. Thus, we cannot only see respectability politics as a problematic mode of articulating class identity, though it certainly is that. It is also a complicated, contingent, and (rightfully) contested mode of articulating Black gender identity vis-à-vis the social resuscitation of Black women's sexual morality. In fact, all of the NACW intellectuals did not subscribe to respectability as a wholesale ideology for racial progress. In one moment, Mary Church Terrell, Fannie Barrier Williams, Lucy Craft Laney, and others evinced the most conservative kinds of ideas about the value of respectability in Black women's lives. In other moments, however, clubwomen followed in the footsteps of Anna Julia Cooper, deploying forms of embodied discourse that offered up the Black female body for social consideration on their own terms. In chapters one and two of this book, my examinations of the political theorizing of two of the NACW leaders—Fannie Barrier Williams and Mary Church Terrell—reveal a far more complex picture of the gender and sexual ideologies that emerge from the NACW School than a singularly focused set of investments in respectability politics and the culture of dissemblance.

Turning to the places where Black women made Black female–embodied experience visible complicates a respectability narrative that casts them as wholly parochial and gives Black women thinkers credit for the complexity of their theorizations of both race and gender identity. Moreover, since these complex adjudications of Black gender identity happened in the context of Black women's formal organizational and intellectual work, we must approach the NACW in a manner befitting of its intellectual function in Black communities—which is to say, as a school of thought. Under the valence of the NACW, race women acted as theoreticians of Black gender identity. In the first two chapters of the book, I delineate the range of concerns about gender and sexuality that emerge from the NACW School. In the last two chapters, of the book, I consider the ways that mid- to late-twentieth-century Black women intellectuals respond to, revise, or reject these ideas. The ideas about gender and racial identity put forward by the NACW School have had an inordinately long shelf life, having laid the foundation for debates well into the twenty-first century about what it means to properly perform and inhabit the categories of Black manhood and Black womanhood.

Moving beyond the Great Race Man Narrative

Race women were not the only people invested in theorizing a robust and clear definition of racial leadership. Local Black communities also had strong opinions on the matter and joined in naming their expectations for race leaders. In an extensive footnote in their 1945 book, *Black Metropolis*, St. Clair Drake and Horace Cayton included a discussion of race men and race women. The race man, they argued, "is one type of Race Hero," a person who "'fights for the race,' and is 'all for The Race.'"[40] Drake and Cayton found it noteworthy, however, that race men and race women were perceived very differently within the community: "It is interesting to note that Bronzeville is somewhat suspicious generally of its Race Men, but tends to be more trustful of the Race Woman."[41] Deemed more "sincere," community members alternately described the race woman figure as "'forceful, outspoken, and fearless, a great advocate of race pride,' 'devoted to the race,' and as one who 'studies the conditions of the people.'" "The Race is uppermost in her activities," they continued, she is "known by the speeches she makes," and finally, "she champions the rights of Negroes." Cayton and Drake observed that the Race Woman had been "idealized as a fighter" and that "her role as 'uplifter' seem[ed] to be accepted with less antagonism than in the case of the Race Man." These rich locally based, community descriptions of Black female leaders confirm that many Black communities in the twentieth century placed great value on the work of race women. They indicate that fifty years after race women first came to theorize and embody the race woman archetype, race women as leadership figures remained critically important to the ways local Black communities understood themselves and their prospects for racial advancement. Though these fleeting moments of celebration did not exclude race women from encountering sexism and attempts at silencing, communities vested race women with a tall and public order to fill when it came to the project of racial uplift.

Yet when scholars tell the stories that comprise Black intellectual history, they persist in using a Great Race Man framework to guide the narrative. This study, *Beyond Respectability*, is driven in part by the desire to challenge the study of Great Race Men as the primary paradigmatic frame through which scholars understand African American intellectual history and African American knowledge production.[42] Such an approach obscures the ways in which the term and category of the intellectual is both historically contingent and deeply contested ideological terrain among African American women and men. Moreover, intellectual work and the material conditions that affect knowledge production were, and are deeply contoured by, the politics of racial manhood and the attendant masculinist gender regimes that have persisted across time, although to varying degrees, within Black communities.

Although Black women have professed and proclaimed intricate, compelling, and important ideas about the state of Black people in the public—since Phillis Wheatley began writing poetry—when the term *Black public intellectual* is used, only a limited number of people come immediately to mind. In the nineteenth and twentieth centuries, there is Frederick Douglass (but not his mentees, Mary Church Terrell and Ida B. Wells); Booker T. Washington (but not his wife, Margaret Murray Washington); W. E. B. Du Bois (but not his contemporaries, Anna Julia Cooper or Fannie Barrier Williams); E. Franklin Frazier, Martin Luther King (but not their contemporaries, Anna Arnold Hedgeman and Pauli Murray); and Harold Cruse (but not his contemporary, Toni Cade Bambara). The history of Black public intellectualism is a history of race men.

I think here of a spate of Black intellectual history texts written over the last decade, which continue to narrate the major ideas that have undergirded the Black freedom struggle through two dominant frames. First, W. E. B. Du Bois predominates as the central intellectual figure of the late nineteenth and early twentieth centuries. Second, his supporting cast is always men. Representative texts include Jonathan Holloway's *Confronting the Veil: Abram Harris, Jr., E. Franklin Frazier, and Ralph Bunche, 1919–1941*, Eben Miller's *Born along the Color Line: The 1933 Amenia Conference and the Rise of a National Civil Rights Movement*, and Zachery Williams's *In Search of the Talented Tenth: Howard University Public Intellectuals and the Dilemmas of Race, 1926–1970*. Despite laudable attempts by both Miller and Williams to substantively include and make clear that Black women shaped the social environs of Black intellectual production in the early twentieth century, these texts simply do not go far enough in disrupting an intellectual history narratively enamored of race men. For instance, while Williams mentions many women that were a part of what he terms the "Howard Public Intellectuals," he says little about their intellectual contributions, and more about their work challenging sexism and recruiting more women to train at Howard.[43] Pauli Murray, a student at Howard during the heyday of Howard's public intellectual dominance and a key figure under consideration in this book, created the term *Jane Crow* specifically to respond to the sexist and homophobic forms of intellectual exclusion that she experienced as a law student there.

More recently, Martin Kilson's *Transformation of the African American Intelligentsia* reveals how deeply entrenched the Du Boisian narrative is to our framing of Black knowledge production. Based on Kilson's 2012 Du Bois lectures at Harvard, *Transformation* returns to the Du Bois–Washington debates as the paradigm through which to understand key issues in Black political thought in the twentieth century. Recycling the well-worn framework of Washington, the accommodationist, and Du Bois, the civil rights strategist, Kilson argues that Washington and Du Bois were responsible for "producing two competing leadership methodologies to guide the transformation of twentieth-century African American society."[44]

Many scholars have already problematized the drawing of strict lines of ideological demarcation between Washington and Du Bois. Yet, this narrative persists. But what is more troubling than the mischaracterization of Du Bois is the way that this narrative perpetuates the wholesale erasure of these men's female colleagues. Race women like Fannie Barrier Williams and Mary Church Terrell disrupt the neat ideological boundaries that Kilson draws between Washington and Du Bois. Williams, for instance, was an ardent Bookerite, but also a strong defender of training Black women in communities to be intellectuals and social theorists. Williams believed that Black women could be trained to be thinkers and theorists about their own social condition, a critical dissension from the kinds of training that Washington thought Black communities should have in the move "up from slavery." In the case of Terrell, she moved with aplomb across the social and political circles of both Washington and Du Bois, managing to gain the respect of both. She wrote and thought across the breadth of her career about effective strategies of activism, forging a unique path, as I will argue in chapter two, between respectability and agitation. Neither woman fits neatly into the overdrawn Washington–Du Bois binary. In fact, interrogation of Williams's and Terrell's intellectual contributions disrupts our desire to continue to read the early twentieth century on Washington's and Du Bois's terms at all.

One of the key ways that Black women thinkers have actively combated the Great Race Man narrative across time is to compile their own lists–their own genealogies of Black women thinkers. I do not think of these lists as mere *lists*. Instead, this intentional calling of names created an intellectual genealogy for race women's work and was a practice of resistance against intellectual erasure. The way Hopkins used her biographical profiles of Black women literary workers to do the work of Black women's intellectual history points us to important methodological approaches among Black women thinkers well into the twentieth century. Hopkins's profiles of Black women literary workers participate in a long practice of what I term *listing*, in which African American women created lists of prominent, qualified Black women for public consumption. These lists situate Black women within a long lineage of prior women who have done similar kinds of work, and naming those women grants intellectual, political, and/or cultural legitimacy to the Black woman speaking their names. *Listing* also refers in the fashion industry to an edge produced on a piece of fabric and applied to a seam to prevent it from unraveling. In similar fashion, Black women's long traditions of intellectual production constitute a critical edge, without which the broader history of African American knowledge production would unravel and come apart at the seams.

Hopkins's list began with Phillis Wheatley. Through Wheatley, Hopkins mapped the course of Black women's literary and intellectual production since the era of the American Revolution, pointing to a long and prominent lineage in her intellectual genealogy of race women thinkers. She demonstrated through Wheatley that Black women's intellectual development was coterminous with the development of the American nation-state. Her other profiles included Gertrude Fortune Grimke, Ida B. Wells, Mary Church Terrell, and Frances Harper. In her own list, Hopkins, like Laney, made sure to speak to the intellectual character of these women. Wheatley was characterized as an "intellectual prodigy." Gertrude Grimke had an "intellectual countenance" and a "gifted mind." Wells, she noted, was "an acknowledged power upon the public platform." In part two of the series, she heaped effusive praise on Frances Harper whose "seventeen years of public speaking" had "moved mountains of prejudice." She also celebrated the rising star of Mary Church Terrell, who, having stepped down from her post as the first president of the National Association of Colored Women just one year prior, had become "highly . . . thought of as a public speaker on race questions and women's work." Finally she profiled Mary Ann Shadd Cary, a teacher, newspaper publisher, and attorney, as "a brilliant speaker, ready and witty in debate."[45] In this regard, Hopkins followed more than a decade of work by race women who had been constructing lists of their best, most qualified women. Anna Julia Cooper's "list of chieftans in the service" included Frances Harper, Sojourner Truth, Amanda Smith, Sarah Woodson Early, Martha Briggs, Charlotte Fortin [sic] Grimke, Hallie Quinn Brown, and Fannie Jackson Coppin.[46] Gertrude Mossell's 1894 book, *Work of the Afro-American Woman*, included profiles of Black women journalists, poets, novelists, and "our representatives at the World's Fair" alongside her own short essays and poems.

Given the important political function of Black women's lists, we cannot dismiss this practice as mere racial self-congratulation. It is clear from a close reading of any of these biographical profiles that race women used listing not only as a practice to combat their historical exclusion but also to resist sexism, theorize about racial politics, and even gesture toward the kinds of political priorities that mattered based on the fields of work of the Black women they highlighted. More pointedly, these lists challenged the Great Race Man leadership model (and the liberal white leadership model) by offering profiles of qualified, talented race women who could lead.[47]

In *Want to Start a Revolution? Radical Women in the Black Freedom Struggle* (2009), the editors Dayo F. Gore, Jeanne Theoharis, and Komozi Woodard address the broad historiographical tendency to treat women as "subsidiary or symbolic figures." "Rather than examining women as pivotal historical actors," they note, "far too many of these studies simply mention various women as key participants and note the damage of sexism and the relevance of gender politics."[48] The scholarly tendency to be preoccupied with mentioning gender and sexual politics over and above a substantive engagement with the intellectual contributions of many Black female leaders is mirrored in analyses of the women themselves. Black women's intellectual contributions are frequently reduced to the terrain of the gender intervention, wherein the primary thrust of Black women's intellectual work is calling out sexism. Certainly, Black women did spend time challenging Black male sexism because they had to. But these women went far beyond merely pointing out that gender matters.

Kristin Waters and Carol Conaway's *Black Women's Intellectual Traditions* (2007) asks us to revisit the significance of the intellectual thought of women like Maria Stewart, Frances Harper, Anna Julia Cooper, and Ida B. Wells.[49] Waters and Conaway's work "serves as a corrective to the prevailing view that no long-standing Black women's intellectual traditions exists."[50] The editors of *Toward An Intellectual History of Black Women* (2015) note that "most scholarship on black women [has] focused on their work as activists, or discussed them as the objects of intellectual activity, but they rarely receive attention as producers of knowledge."[51] Although groundbreaking works of Black feminist scholarship like Paula Giddings's *When and Where I Enter* (1984), Hazel Carby's *Reconstructing Womanhood* (1986), together with Patricia Hill Collins's *Black Feminist Thought* (1990) laid the groundwork for taking Black women seriously as thinkers and theorists, Black feminist theorizing has reached a state of critical inertia in its engagement with the intellectual work of early Black women theorists. White argued that this inertia was somewhat visible more than a decade ago when she called for black feminists to "engage each other's ideas more seriously," and to stop worrying about whether "racists were looking to reveal our failures."[52] Still much of the inertia has persisted. For instance, Vivian May's *Anna Julia Cooper, Visionary Black Feminist* (2007) is the only book-length scholarly work on Cooper to critically engage her entire body of intellectual work, including her book of essays *Voice from the South*, alongside two doctoral dissertations, and a host of other short essays. May, together with Karen Baker-Fletcher, whose book contextualized Cooper's contributions to womanist theology, have rescued her from the problem of what May calls "bodily hypervisibility" but intellectual obscurity.[53] Because May's work resists a biographical imperative and focuses in each chapter on the body of Cooper's thought, it exists as a singular type of in-depth intellectual engagement of a Black woman intellectual. Additionally, much of the critical work on Black women thinkers like Claudia Jones, Ella Baker, Ida B. Wells, Fannie Barrier Williams, Eslanda Robeson, Rosa Parks, and Anna Arnold Hedgeman are critical biographies.[54] Although this book is indebted to the intellectual foundations laid by many of these works, which do take great care to engage the intellectual contributions of the women under study, these biographies are bound in many respects by the limits of biography as a genre. Rarely among male thinkers is the presence of a critical biography the precursor to engaging the male thinker as theorist. But in Black feminist theory, frequently Black women have to be established as "somebody" before the theoretical import of their contributions enters the scholarly narrative in a significant way.

Considering the ways in which otherwise respectable, educated, middle-class, liberal Black women refigure the terrain of Black gender, Black militancy, and Black queerness, this work augments a growing body of scholarship that locates Black radicalism in the work of Black women labor activists.[55] The story of serious Black women's intellectual thought is not solely the province of Black women on the radical left. While elevating the stories of radical left Black women demonstrates the pitfalls of focusing on respectable racial elites like many of the women under consideration in this book, again, our contemporary commitment to rejecting the ideology of middle-class respectability should not foreclose our engagement with significant sites of Black women's knowledge production in the nineteenth and twentieth centuries.

A Procession of Chapters

In chapter one, I expand the intellectual geography I am mapping in *Beyond Respectability* by examining the National Association of Colored Women (NACW) as a site of Black female knowledge production. In particular, I use the work of Fannie Barrier Williams, a Chicago-based clubwoman, to map many of the key intellectual interventions of the NACW as a school of social thought. Drawing on Williams's theorization of what she calls *organized anxiety*, I take up and critically examine her claim that the NACW was responsible for creating "race public opinion" and, by extension, giving shape and form to an emergent Black public sphere. As a concept, organized anxiety politicizes the emotional lives of Black women and constitutes one more iteration of the ways that race women invoked embodied discourse in their public intellectual work. I also examine her invocation of a discourse that I term *American peculiarity*, a kind of oppositional discourse challenging claims of American exceptionalism. Finally, I interrogate her concept of racial sociality, a sophisticated way to think about ideas of racial unity and social connections between African Americans of different geographic and class backgrounds. Williams was a formidable political theorist, who, through her work in the NACW, introduced a rich conceptual milieu through which to think about Black politics, Black organizations, and gender politics in the late nineteenth century.

In chapter two, I seek to recuperate Mary Church Terrell as a critical theorist of Black racial uplift. The first President of the NACW, Terrell went on to have a sixty-year career in Civil Rights activism. This chapter moves across the span of her career, mapping her development of a concept called "dignified agitation," which she introduces in a 1913 speech. She returns to this formulation throughout her career, and I argue that this idea of dignified agitation is one that she both learned and propagated as part of the NACW school of thought. But it also acts as a bridge concept, and she, as a bridge figure to Civil Rights–era Black women intellectuals, who both respected the NACW school of thought and sought to move beyond it in critical ways. Because of the deliberate ways that Terrell wrote about her love of dancing in her autobiography, I also consider in this chapter the ways in which she is part of a genealogy of Black women's pleasure politics, even though the current Black feminist discourse on pleasure typically focuses on blues women in this time period. Because Terrell is considered one of the foremost proselytizers of respectability, a turn toward her articulation of pleasure politics richly complicates the manner in which we read her as a theorist of racial resistance and gender progressivism.

In chapter three, I turn to the work of Pauli Murray, one of the young activists that Terrell mentored. In the 1940s, Murray enrolled at Howard University Law School and went on to graduate as the only woman and top student in her class. In the 1930s, the convergence of several important Black male intellectuals at Howard University, including Abram Harris, E. Franklin Frazier, and Ralph Bunche, had cemented a new formal model of the academically trained Black male public intellectual. When Murray enrolled in the 1940s, she experienced great sexism from these Black male intellectuals. She termed their treatment of her *Jane Crow*. While she went on to have a storied career as a legal expert, Episcopal priest, poet, and writer, all of which place her firmly in the tradition of the race woman, her identity as both a woman and queer person in the 1940s and 1950s collided with the Howard model of public intellectual work. This chapter brings together Murray's time and training at Howard, her archives, and an examination of her two autobiographies to suggest that her concept of Jane Crow grew out of the collision of race-based sexual politics and limited ideas among Black men about who could provide intellectual leadership for Black people. Moreover, Jane Crow exposed the heterosexist proclivities of Black public leadership traditions, and offers a framework for thinking about how Black women negotiated gender and sexual politics even as they devoted their lives to theorizing new strategies for racial uplift.

Chapter four returns to the question of what it means to be a Black woman intellectual by interrogating the claims in an article in *Ebony Magazine* in 1966 called "Problems of the Negro Woman Intellectual." Given the ferment of racial crises in the 1960s, this chapter argues that much like the transitional period of the 1890s, the transition from Civil Rights to Black Power was marked by a tension over the roles that Black women would play, not only as political activists, but as intellectual leaders. Thus Harold Cruse's *Crisis of the Negro Intellectual* erased a long and significant history of Black women's intellectual labor in order to sustain his narrative of racial crisis. What really seems to be in crisis are the terms of Black masculinity. I read Toni Cade Bambara's book of essays *Black Woman* as a critical corrective to Cruse's assertions because *Black Woman* presses the case for Black women's centrality as thought leaders and public intellectuals in racial justice struggles, and Bambara and her comrades approach the same political moment as an opportunity for creativity around the articulation of new modes of what she terms *Blackhood* rather than embracing the narrative of crisis. In many ways, her anthology and the feminist anthologies that come after it expand on Black women's intellectual practice of *listing* from the nineteenth century. In every period where Black communities struggled to find their thought leaders, Black women always named the women doing the work, but usually receive little credit for it. By the late twentieth century, these lists became full anthologies of Black women's thinking about race, gender, and politics. This chapter makes clear that the struggle to be known and to have the range of Black women's experiences properly articulated in the public sphere is a recurring struggle for Black women thinkers. At the same time, these women engage in a range of creative practices to make Black women's lives legible in public discourse.

Like the works of late-nineteenth- and early-twentieth-century Black women intellectuals, *Beyond Respectability* proffers its own kind of list of Black women public intellectuals. But it is just one list out of many that have yet to be constructed. I chose these women not only because of their overlooked or understudied intellectual contributions, but because they are linked together through their work. Anna Julia Cooper, Fannie Barrier Williams, Mary Church Terrell, and other nineteenth-century Black women who make cameos in this book were colleagues, who in many cases knew each other. Mary Church Terrell is offered here as an ideological bridge between the early race women and later ones like Pauli Murray and Toni Cade Bambara. Terrell and Murray met while doing desegregation campaigning in Washington, D.C., in the 1940s, and Terrell was always among Murray's own lists of influential Black leaders. Murray herself was connected with the advent of the Black feminist movement of the 1970s and was a key legal and social theorist, alongside colleagues like Toni Cade Bambara. There are many maps and linkages that could be drawn when telling the stories of Black women intellectuals. This is one intellectual map, offering one set of geographic and genealogical routes that can be taken to more clearly understand the long and rich history of African American women's knowledge production. My hope is that this map, this genealogy, leads us all, as Hopkins foresaw, in luminous and unexpected directions.

Organized Anxiety

*The National Association of Colored Women
and the Creation of the Black Public Sphere*

> The club movement . . . is nothing less than the organized
> anxiety of women who have become intelligent enough
> to recognize their own low social condition and strong
> enough to initiate the forces of reform.
>
> —Fannie Barrier Williams (1900)

In 1899, the NACW held a storied second biennial meeting in Chicago, one that cemented the presence of the Association as a formidable racial advocacy organization.[1] By custom, racial organizations often held multiple organizational meetings in one city to cut down on travel costs. That year, the meeting occurred around the same time as the meeting of the National Afro-American Council, one of the forerunners of the National Association for the Advancement of Colored People (NAACP). After the conventions, W. E. B. Du Bois wrote a short newspaper article comparing the "Two Negro Conventions." Du Bois heaped praise upon the female convention-goers for their physical beauty, noting the "varying hues of female costumes contrasting with the infinite variety in color and tint of skin [and] the predominance of the soft Southern accent." He was especially appreciative of papers given at the women's meeting on "equal moral standards for men and women," "the convict lease system," and "practical club work." Of particular importance in all papers was the primary theme of "the necessity of work among children."[2]

Then, he turned his attention to the first meeting of the Afro-American Council. He noted that "the Council was a far different body from the Association; its members were mostly male, its scope and aims were wider, and in its attendance it was more faithfully representative of the rank and file of

American negroes. . . . [I]ts candid earnestness and faithful striving made it a far more reliable reflex of the mental attitude of the millions it represented."[3] In Du Bois's estimation, the Afro-American Council, in its vigorous conversations about confronting lynching, debates over the Great Migration, and battles over leadership, seemed to be more relevant to the concerns of the race as a whole, with the Council representing, as he noted, millions. And yet, his own crude characterization and inappropriate eroticization of his female peers indicate that his judgments were rooted in a politics of racial manhood that worked to confine Black women's participation to work traditionally understood as feminine and therefore intellectually unserious. Moreover, he understood that work as being of less importance to the "broader" vision being created by race men.

Though she never used his name, Fannie Barrier Williams took Du Bois's characterization of the NACW to task in her article, "The Club Movement among Colored Women in America." Published originally in an ambitious compendium entitled *A New Negro for a New Century: An Accurate and Up-to-Date Record of the Upward Struggles of the Negro Race* (1900), the essay, unlike a traditional organizational history, attempted to make sociological and intellectual sense of the work of the NACW. In it, she argued first that the NACW had made great progress in creating "public faith in the sustained virtue and social standards" of colored women.[4] As this chapter's epigraph attests, Williams characterized the Club Movement as an outgrowth of the "organized anxiety of women," a result of their recognition of their "low social condition" and their desire to reform it. The Club Movement had also helped Black women build racial self-esteem: "to feel that you are something better than a slave, or a descendant of an ex-slave, to feel that you are a unit in the womanhood of a great nation and a great civilization, is the beginning of self-respect and the respect of your race."[5]

Looking outward, however, the NACW's work impacted far more than just Black women. "The National Association," Williams averred, "has also been useful to an important extent in creating what may be called a *race public opinion* [emphasis added]. When the local clubs of the many States became nationalized, it became possible to reach the whole people with questions and interests that concerned the whole race."[6] Du Bois had attempted to localize the impact of the NACW, arguing that its primary impact would be on its work with children. Meanwhile, he claimed that the Council had a better handle on national racial concerns. Williams argued exactly the opposite. The NACW was the first major national organization to effectively coordinate local Black social and political concerns on a national scale. "For example," Williams pressed her case, "when the National Association interested itself in studying such problems as the Convict Lease System of the Southern States or the necessity of kindergartens . . . it was possible to unite and interest the intelligent forces of the entire race." Moreover, clubwomen railed against the sexual and labor exploitations of the convict lease system from the time of their earliest meetings. They created committees to study the problem, drafted reports, which always made sure to mention the especial difficulty Black women faced in labor camps, and made abolition of the convict lease system a hallmark of their advocacy.[7] This spirit of racial cooperation across locales "is new," Williams argued, "and belongs to the new order of things brought about by nationalized efforts."[8]

Well known as a member of the late-nineteenth-century Chicago Black elite, Fannie Barrier Williams gained wide acclaim when she secured the only position offered to a colored woman on the 1892 Chicago World's Fair's Board of Lady Managers. A staunch Bookerite, Williams and her husband, attorney S. Laing Williams, rose through the ranks of the Chicago elite from the 1890s through the early 1900s, as her writings in a range of Booker T. Washington–owned publications secured her position as one of the most formidable thinkers of her generation. Wanda Hendricks notes that "because of her intellectual analysis of how industrialization and urbanization were transforming the Midwest and reshaping the lives of women, she was often a principal speaker at local and national conferences about the intersectionality of gender and labor."[9] World's Fair organizers invited her to give two speeches at the event, one to the World's Congress of Representative Women at which Anna Julia Cooper and Frances Watkins Harper also spoke, and the other to the World's Congress of Religions. While there has been an increasing and deserved focus on the work of Anna Julia Cooper,[10] it bears noting that Cooper's comment at the World's Fair was in response to the longer speech given by Williams on "The Intellectual Progress of Colored Women." Though Cooper had published *Voice from the South* to critical acclaim among the African American intelligentsia just a few months earlier, Williams, in her Fair speech, laid out the most intellectually sophisticated and compelling narrative about race women's progress and racial aspirations. The prolific body of social theorizing that Williams produced at the turn of the twentieth century remains understudied.

Critical attention to the social and political theorizing of Williams, "one of the leading intellectuals of the turn of the [twentieth] century," calls forth a "new order of things," in our understanding of existing traditions of Black intellectual production.[11] In particular, I turn in this chapter to a series of speeches and articles she produced between 1893 and 1905, in which she forthrightly theorized the relationship of the club movement to the building

FIGURE 2. Fannie Barrier Williams. Courtesy of Moorland Spingarn Research Center, Manuscripts Division, Howard University, Washington D.C.

of Black civil society. She introduces a series of terms and formulations, among them, *organized anxiety, American peculiarity, race public opinion*, and *racial sociality*, that are central to her broad political vision for African American people and that anchor her strident critique of the American democratic project. Like her clubwomen counterparts, Black women existed at the center of her narrative of Black and American nation-building.[12] Her desire to take seriously the plight of Black women meant that she routinely critiqued Black men in her public work, especially W. E. B. Du Bois. Although some of her enmity toward Du Bois might be attributed to her and her husband's devotion to Washington, a closer examination of her writings reveals legitimate ideological differences in her understandings of how to address Black social problems, particularly those of Black women. Making Black women's problems visible within post-Reconstruction, turn-of-the-twentieth-century social discourses on the race problem necessitated clear and dedicated attention to studying Black women and their organizations.

The goal of this chapter, then, is twofold. First, it offers an intellectual history of the NACW School of Thought vis-à-vis the pioneering work of Fannie Barrier Williams, one of its key architects. Focusing on the intellectual history of the NACW builds on a voluminous body of literature on the Clubwomen's Movement, which approaches it primarily as a social welfare organization. The germinal text among these histories is Deborah Gray White's *Too Heavy a Load: Black Women in Defense of Themselves, 1894–1994*. White and other historians have demonstrated the ways in which the NACW became the training ground for a Black female elite leadership class in the late nineteenth and early twentieth centuries.[13] Moreover, such work has also documented the sophisticated social welfare, educational, and political initiatives undertaken by the NACW both locally and nationally, particularly in the form of building schools, social settlement houses, and convalescent homes and offering parental training to Black communities that did not have access to these services. Williams has a formidable history of organizing and club work in her own right.[14] However, her work as a theoretician of racial identity, public space, and what I term the *civic unknowability* of Black women offers a critical picture of the first two decades of the intellectual work of the NACW School.[15]

Second, in this chapter, I use a Black feminist analytic framework to evaluate the salience and usefulness of many of the key ideas that Williams created as part of the NACW School. One of the goals of excavating Black women's intellectual history in this book is to consider the ways that this rich body of ideas might vivify the intellectual environs of Black feminist thought by offering up to us a treasure chest of ideas that place Black female embodiment at the center. Using a Black feminist analytic lens does not require that all the women under study use the term *feminist*, a term that would have been anachronistic in its usage in Williams's case. Instead, a Black feminist analytic framework invites us to consider the ways that Black women have thought through the particularities of race and gender as identity positions—and racism, sexism, and classism as interlocking structures of power. And because Williams and other race women cared so deeply about combatting civic unknowability, or what Kristie Dotson calls "epistemic erasure," their concerns about the terms and conditions under which Black women come to be known place their theorizing squarely in the center of the intellectual concerns that have animated the development of Black feminist theory.

The Call for Systematic Study of Black Women's Lives

The first call for the systematic study of Black women as a separate and distinct category among African Americans came from Fannie Barrier Williams during her 1893 Chicago World's Fair address. "Less is known of our women than of any other class of Americans," she told her audience.[16] There were "no organizations of far-reaching influence for their special advancement, no conventions of women to take note of their progress, and no special literature reciting the incidents, the events, and all things interesting and instructive concerning them are to be found among the agencies directing their career." "There has been," she concluded, "no special interest in their peculiar condition as native-born American women."[17] The difficulty in indexing Black women's intellectual progress, she explained, reflected the fact that "separate facts and figures relative to colored women are not easily obtainable," while also revealing a still more fundamental problem, namely that the "peculiar condition" of Black women rendered them invisible within the intellectual dictates of traditional knowledge production. Moreover, Williams maintained, the lack of information on black women underscored that the thrust of American knowledge production was not a race- or gender-neutral endeavor. In the case of white women, "nearly every fact and item illustrative of their progress and status is classified and easily accessible." By contrast, Black women "had no advantage of interests peculiar and distinct and separable from those of men that have yet excited public attention and kindly recognition."[18] Williams used an intersectional analysis to demonstrate the ways in which movements to emancipate both women and Black people often worked to obscure Black women as both unique producers of knowledge and subjects worthy of knowledge production.

Williams did not merely advocate for black women to have access to the "same opportunity for the acquisition of all kinds of knowledge that may be accorded to other women." Rather, she suggested more specifically that Black women were eager to produce knowledge, and that if given the chance to educate themselves, in one generation Black women "will be found successfully occupying every field where the highest intelligence alone is admissible. . . . [T]he exceptional career of our women will yet stamp itself indelibly upon the thought of this country."[19] "In short," she told them, "our women are ambitious to be contributors to all the great moral and intellectual forces that make for the greater weal of our common country."[20] Like Cooper had done in the publication of *Voice from the South*, Williams informed audiences that Black women wanted a stake in the intellectual leadership, not only of their race but also their country.

The second call for the systematic study of the race came from Victoria Earle Matthews in 1895. After a Missouri journalist issued a vicious assault on the character of African American women, precipitated by the rising prominence of Ida B. Wells, a bevy of "about one hundred" "public spirited Afro-American women" convened in Boston for the First Congress of Colored Women.[21] "The convention afforded a fine exhibition of capable women," Williams wrote. "There was nothing amateurish, uncertain or timid in the proceedings. Every subject of peculiar interest to colored women was discussed and acted upon as if by women disciplined in thinking out large and serious problems."[22] Though the women roundly condemned John Jacks, the Missouri journalist, for his vitriolic attacks on Black womanhood, the women "soon felt that a National Convention of responsible women would be a misplacement of moral force, if it merely exhausted itself in replying to a slanderous publication."[23] Thus, they began to set an agenda to confront, study, and address the myriad problems facing Black local communities.

It was to this specific moment that Williams referred as "the organized anxiety of women." As the women met together and shared information about the terribly troubling conditions Black women were facing, an anxiety emerged, borne of a deep and growing consciousness of their "low social condition" and their "desire to initiate the forces of reform."[24] They were both outraged at and anxious about the public assaults on Black women's character because they knew that this public discourse of vilification subjected Black women not only to discrimination but also to rape and violence. Thus, they organized themselves to change it, not only by offering social services but also through the mechanism of intellectual activism. Williams's term *organized anxiety* roots the intellectual content of racial change within Black women's bodies, identifying collective racial discontent and collective racial anxiety as forces that propelled institutional and social change through the work of organized Black women. This discussion about the affective nature of the work returns us to Anna Julia Cooper's ably demonstrated narrative of embodied discourse as a characteristic feature of Black women's knowledge production. In particular, Williams's choice to place Black women's emotions and feelings about the impacts of racism and white supremacy at the fore of her political theorization marks a critical shift from Darlene Clark Hine's theory of dissemblance, which suggests that Black women never made their private emotions the province of public fodder. Hine writes that

> Black women as a rule, developed and adhered to a cult of secrecy, a culture of dissemblance to protect the sanctity of inner aspects of their lives. The dynamics of dissemblance involved creating the appearance of disclosure, or openness about themselves and their feelings, while actually remaining an enigma. Only with secrecy, thus achieving a self-imposed invisibility, could ordinary Black women accrue the psychic space and harness the resources needed to hold their own in the often one-sided and mismatched resistance struggle.[25]

Moreover, Hine locates the origin for this "cult of secrecy" in the institutional work of the NACW. She argues that "at the core of essentially every activity of the NACW's individual members was a concern with creating positive images of Black women's sexuality."[26] Thus, she concludes that "the culture of dissemblance found its most institutionalized form in the founding" of the NACW.[27] Hine formulates the culture of dissemblance as one of the anchoring political projects of what I understand to be the NACW School of Thought, which disseminated the ideology of dissemblance as a mechanism to help Black women achieve social and political respectability.

The problem is that such theorizations overdetermine and oversimplify the complex ways that Black women both theorized and engaged the politics of Black female embodiment. Certainly, race women worked hard to keep their private lives out of public view, but the readiness with which they spoke about their feelings and about their experiences of bodily violation suggests that dissemblance as a theoretical framework can cause us to misrecognize the powerful ways that Black women *did* choose to make their bodies and their feelings visible to the public. Mary Church Terrell, the first president of the NACW and one of the key architects of the ideology of Black women's respectability, spoke in her autobiography not only to intergenerational issues with depression but also of her own bodily commitment to pleasure through dance (see chapter two). Perhaps Black women's expressions of feeling in public were part of a larger enigmatic dissemblance project, as Hine suggests. But if we view the public expressions of feeling and public invocations of embodied discourse as forms of dissimulation, then we also mire Black women's theorizing and public work in a kind of mistrust that makes them always unknowable. But Williams and Matthews's explicit investment in removing Black women from the veil of obscurity and in making Black women knowable entities suggests that to read them primarily according to the terms of dissemblance is to miss the powerful ways that they attempted to both frame and politicize their interior lives and feelings. Melissa Harris-Perry argues that Black women's "emotions affect how we engage in politics" and that "to understand black women as political actors we must explore how intersecting disadvantages based on race, gender, class, and sexuality influence how these women feel and think."[28] Williams argued that Black women's feelings, particularly their anxiety, influenced and shaped their political agenda.

Her naming of Black women's anxiety and her theorization of it as an emotion integral to race women's politics is rooted in an intrinsic bodily awareness about Black women's corporeal vulnerability. Social discourses about Black women's sexuality made oblique the ways that Black female bodies were affected by the systemic violences of Jim Crow. Yes, reclaiming and renaming the terms upon which Black women's sexuality was made legible in the broader American public shaped a great deal of the social and political work of the NACW. However, the intellectual project of situating Black women as knowledge producers and human entities worthy of political consideration cannot be reduced to a conversation about Black women's obsession with systems of sexual representation. Race women had to comb through a morass of sexual misrepresentations in order to make Black women visible on more socially sustainable terms. They sought to construct the race woman intellectual as a foil to the sexually deviant Black female specter that haunted the American political imagination. For these women, the fictive social narratives of Black women's sexuality intruded upon the facticity of Black women's intellectual ability and interests. But the fact that race women deployed a combination of strategies of respectability, dissemblance, *and* embodied discourse suggests that they were less interested in evacuating all modes of sexual expression from the social terrain of the Black female body and more interested in making sure that ideas of sexuality did not overdetermine and limit the scope of Black women's social possibilities. Thus, they concerned themselves with creating a body of thought and a series of social strategies that would shift the public discourse about Black women's bodies.

Matthews, one of the featured speakers at the Congress, felt that this shift could occur through the creation of what she called "Race Literature." Thematically, her speech on "The Value of Race Literature" took up where Williams had left off, systematically laying out a call for the intellectual development of the race. She anchored her talk conceptually by framing what she meant by the terms *race* and *literature*. "By race literature we mean ordinarily all the writings emanating from a distinct class—not necessarily race matter, but a general collection of what has been written by the men and women of the race."[29] This collection of literature could include every conceivable genre from "history, biographies, scientific treatises, sermons, addresses, novels, poems, books of travel, miscellaneous essays and the contributions to magazines and newspapers."[30] She addressed critics who might find a notion of distinct "race literature" separate from American literature objectionable. The "conditions, which govern the people of African Descent in the United States" created a "marked difference in the limitations, characteristics, aspirations and ambitions of this class of people."[31] In other words, Matthews believed "all this impious wrong has made a Race Literature a possibility, even a necessity."[32] Thus, in her view there existed both the potential and the necessity for a distinctive African American literary tradition.[33]

Race women by and large agreed with this claim. Mary Church Terrell wrote that she regretted her inability to become a formidable fiction writer because she had "thought for years that the Race Problem could be solved more swiftly and more surely through the instrumentality of the short story or novel than in any other way."[34] For race women, race literature instantiated both a literary tradition and constituted the creation of an "intellectual history" for the race, by which the intellectual possibilities of African Americans would be judged. As Gertrude Bustill Mossell had been so keen to note just one year earlier in her book, *Work of the Afro-American Woman*, "the intellectual history of a race is always of value in determining the past and future of it."[35] Race women made "African American literary culture fundamental to the racial uplift agenda of social reform."[36] "When the literature of our race is developed, it will of necessity be different in all essential points of greatness, true heroism and real Christianity from what we may at the present time, for convenience, call American Literature," Matthews made clear.[37]

This Race Literature, Matthews further argued, would also serve as "a counter-irritant against all such writing" that deliberately misrepresented Black women and Black people. It would have "as an aim the supplying of influential and accurate information, on all subjects relating to the Negro and his environments, to inform the American mind at least, for literary purposes."[38] Race literature did not merely have a political function, but rather an intellectual one to transform and reshape "the American mind," and what Williams called "public opinion" regarding the Negro.

Matthews's speech was given at the first national gathering of African American women in 1895, and many of the themes it delineated further refined and clarified the intellectual concerns that drove the NACW's intellectual agenda. In fact, she made sure to specifically address the role women would play in the creation of race literature. "Woman's part in Race literature, as in Race building," she proclaimed, "is to . . . receive impressions and transmit them."[39] Matthews invoked the sentimental discourse of *impressibility* to connect women's role in race building to the production of race literature. Feminist theorist Kyla Schuller has recently excavated the significance of the discourse and theory of impressibility to nineteenth-century formulations of evolution. According to the "impression theory of sensation," "the more refined and delicate the tissue, and by association the individual, the greater the organism's capacity for impressibility. Heightened impressibility leads to growth and the acquisition of knowledge. Those of the higher classes, especially women, were thought to have highly responsive natures and a correlated delicacy that frequently threatened weakness."[40]

Anna Julia Cooper sounded a similar note when she argued that because Black people were in a rapid state of advancement as a race, "a race in such a stage of growth is peculiarly sensitive to impressions." These "high strung people," needed a strong presence from Black women who "must stamp weal or woe on the coming history of this people."[41] As mobilized by white women, the discourse of impressibility served to suggest that their race was civilized and therefore responded well to impressions. Among black women, the discourse of impressibility was invoked to contend that their race was impressible and therefore capable of civilization.[42]

Such ideas about the relationship between discourse and the body emerged from Lockean ideas about the body as a tabula rasa, upon which ideas and experiences could be inscribed. Williams's language of organized anxiety, coupled with Cooper's characterization of Black people as a "high strung people" "sensitive to impressions," makes clear that Black women perceived an integral relationship between discourse and embodiment. Matthews argued that Black women's intellectual work—their writing—could transmit impressions. Her assertion that Black women's intellectual work was akin to transmitting an impression directly to the body is an example of the ways Black women used embodied discourse to suture the material to the discursive, linking the fleshy precarity of Black life to the forward-looking possibilities of progressive social discourse. They aimed to use their knowledge production to reshape the Black body (the language and thinking behind impressibility) in social discourse and to create new ideological and social terrain in which Black bodies (and the Black people inhabiting them) could safely exist.

From the Exceptional to the Peculiar: Black Women as Citizen-Women

Shifting white American public opinion regarding the plight of Black women required fervent advocacy from race women, not only in race literature, but also in public exchanges. During her World's Fair speech, Williams took great care to explicate for her mostly white female audience "the bitterness of our experience as citizen-women."[43] A figurative compound expression known as a *kenning*, the term *citizen-women* refracted Black women's experience of womanhood through the lens of citizenship. Black women's experience as women relied upon their civic construction in the public sphere. By placing the word *citizen* first in the kenning, Williams gave priority to Black women's status in the American body politic, attempting yet again to make Black women legible as civically knowable persons. Simultaneously, the term pointed to the ways that gender acted upon public identity categories, like that of "citizen," where it was often invoked to signal both exclusion and the limits of democracy, rather than more noble realities. Black women's civic experience of womanhood had been "bitter," after all. Thus their civic experiences exposed deep fissures in the narrative of American exceptionalism, a narrative that the ceremony and fanfare of the exhibition attempted to quell.

One of the examples that Williams gave of Black women's peculiar experience as citizen-women was their continual struggle to secure employment. The difficulty of finding work was a direct result of Americans' poor opinion of Black women's moral stature: "[T]aught everywhere in ethics and social economy that merit always wins, colored women carefully prepare themselves for all kinds of occupations only to meet with stern refusal, rebuff, and disappointment."[44] Understanding themselves to be disadvantaged both by the labor dictates of the Peculiar Institution and the meritocratic myth of American exceptionalism, Black women frequently invoked what I term a *discourse of American peculiarity*. This discourse is exemplified in Williams's question, "[A]re we not justified in a feeling of desperation against that peculiar form of Americanism that shows respect for our women as servants and contempt for them when they become women of culture?"[45] By highlighting Black female desperation, Williams continued to place Black women's emotions front and center in her political discourse, a move that humanized them and that demonstrates the variety of anxiety-producing encounters Black women had with racist and sexist discrimination.

In another case, during her struggle with the Lady Managers for Black female representation on the board and at the fair, elocutionist and Wilberforce Professor Hallie Quinn Brown wrote in a letter to one of the members, "[C]onsidering the peculiar relation that the Negro sustains in this county [*sic*], is it less than fair to request for him a special representation?"[46] Through reference to America's peculiarity, Black women highlighted the fact that the American nation-state is defined not by its stated ideals of liberty, equality, or freedom, but rather by its racist practices toward its African American citizenry. Like most race women of her day, Williams firmly believed that colored women were "as thoroughly American in all the circumstances of citizenship as the best citizens of our country."[47] They were thus entitled to the rights and protections of American identity.

To invoke the language of peculiarity was to challenge the presupposed benevolence of slavery, by interrogating the euphemism most often used to describe it: "The Peculiar Institution." White racial claims about the inferior morality of the Black race were deeply gendered and typically characterized Black women as sexually lascivious, cunning, devious, and therefore incapable of victimization. Although Williams could "appreciate the offensiveness of all references to American slavery," she believed that calling attention to slavery's actual impact on African American women mattered more than preserving white racial mythologies of benevolence.[48] Her use of the term *peculiarity* referred not only to the particularity of Black and female experience, but also to a kind of studied bewilderment at the utter illogic of American racism, the refusal to come to terms with the level of devastation that it had heaped upon Black people, and the deep investments of white people in maintaining white supremacy despite the progress of African Americans.

Moreover, according to Williams, the Peculiar Institution and the peculiar forms of Americanism that it spawned had created a peculiar experience for Black women. "Though there is much that is sorrowful," she maintained, "and much that is wonderfully heroic, and much that is romantic in a peculiar way in their history, none of it has as yet been told as evidence of what is possible for these women."[49] Black women's peculiarity within the American body politic, coupled with a blind allegiance on the part of the white public to the gospel of American exceptionalism, had rendered Black female experience and personhood illegible within the American public: "The American people have always been impatient of ignorance and poverty. They believe with Emerson that 'America is another word for opportunity,' and for that reason success is a virtue and poverty and ignorance are inexcusable. This may account for the fact that our women have excited no general sympathy in the struggle to emancipate themselves from the demoralization of slavery."[50]

Williams's words point out that the great irony of the American system was that Americans' deeply held disdain for inequality was outmatched only by their deep disdain for those who were unequal. Consequently, American exceptionalism had to be contested, not only in terms of its political implications, but also in terms of its epistemological implications. Failure to do so meant that Black female progress, and thus Black women's lives, would continue to go intellectually unrecognized within the larger American body politic.

Race and Public Opinion

Reshaping the public discourse about Black women topped the NACW's list of racial priorities. Challenging recalcitrant public opinion was necessary for Black women to move from being the "least known" group of women to a group of *civically knowable* persons. Figuring out how to name the proper terms upon which Black women know the world, and to create the proper terms upon which Black women can be known, constitutes a perennial and enduring epistemological crisis among Black women intellectuals and Black feminist theorists. Kristie Dotson argues that Williams's theorization of Black women's "unknowability" refers to "the negative, socio-epistemic space Black women exist in within US social imaginaries."[51] Williams returned to this idea of Black women being "not known" in a 1905 essay called "The Colored Girl": "That the term 'colored girl' is almost a term of reproach in the social life of America is all too true; she is not known and hence *not believed* in, she belongs to a race that is best designated by the term 'problem' and she lives beneath the shadow of that problem which envelops and obscures her."[52] Here, Williams points to the myriad negative impacts of the epistemic subjugation of Black women and girls. Because she is not known, she is not "believed in," which is to say both that Black women and girls are not *believed*, and their claims about their lives are found lacking in credibility; and that they are not believed *in*, which means there is limited communal investment in Black women's and girls' lives as a site of *possibility*. Like Cooper, Williams tries to rewrite Black women's and girls' lives as a space of possibility, rather than as a space of *impossibility* beckoned by having one's existence confined, "enveloped," and "obscured" by existence in a negative socio-epistemic space.

Since Frances Watkins Harper's publication of *Iola Leroy, or Shadows Uplifted* in 1892, race women had argued that Black women occupied an umbral position with regard to broader public discourses on race. They existed in the shadowy contours of discussions of the race problem, their problems remaining obscure to the "light" of broader discourses. Thus, here Williams makes clear that there are other facets to Du Bois's 1903 formulation about the problematization of race. To the extent that Black men labored under the construction of the race as a social *problem*, Black women existed, as Williams noted above, "beneath the shadow of that problem, which envelops and obscures her." Williams and other race women sought to remedy this epistemic subjugation by transforming the public discourse about Black womanhood and by creating viable models of respectable womanhood for Black women.

After evaluating the social impact of America's peculiar relations of power on Black women, Williams came to the same conclusion as many of her contemporaries: Black women had a unique and *public* role to play in reshaping America's public discourse on Black women. In fact, questions about the operation of public opinion and about the power of organized women to reshape public opinion emerged over and over again in Williams's thought. She was convinced that the intellectual talents of an organized African American womanhood could be used to shift the weight off of Black women who suffered under "the vile imputations of a diseased public opinion."[53] Though this was not a wholly original conclusion, as Black women had been fighting for a place in public life throughout the century, this active assertion of Black women's ability to mold public opinion and reshape the American mind, *was* new and was an outgrowth of shifting late-nineteenth-century conversations in political theory.

After 1893, the concept of "public opinion" recurs repeatedly in Williams's theorizing. Not only does she invoke it in the World's Fair speech, but she also claims, as I will discuss shortly, that the NACW created the first "race public opinion." The title of an article she penned in 1904 is "The Negro and Public Opinion." Theoretical work on the concept of public opinion first appeared in Alexis De Tocqueville's *Democracy in America*. But there was a resurgence of conversation about the concept in the work of political theorist Viscount James Bryce, whose classic political tome, *American Commonwealth* (1888), devoted twelve chapters of the book to delineating the operations of public opinion, its forms, functions, and effects in the American body politic. It is not clear whether Williams read Bryce's work, but his work received much popular coverage in the national press, making it conceivable that her deliberate engagements with the concept of public opinion do attempt at some level to engage his work.

In a chapter of *American Commonwealth* called "The Nature of Public Opinion," Bryce delineated the differences between passive and active public opinion. *Passive opinion* referred to "the opinion of those who have no special interest in politics, or concern with them beyond that of voting, of those who receive or propagate, but do not originate, views on public matters."[54] However, taking into account that "opinion does not merely grow; it is also made," Bryce observed that "[t]here is not merely the passive class of persons; there is the active class, who occupy themselves primarily with public affairs, who aspire to create and lead opinion."[55] Disturbed "that public opinion concerning the Negro in this country is largely based on ignorance of nearly everything that is good and prophetic in the life of the race,"[56] Williams was interested in the ways that race women and the organizations they created could function as an active class of opinion shapers.

Williams argued, "[T]he National Association has also been useful to an important extent in creating what may be called a race public opinion."[57] To be clear, this assertion from Williams constitutes political theorizing. She studies, then offers a name, for a social phenomenon. I am making this elementary observation because we spend a great deal of time acknowledging this kind of intellectual labor when men like Du Bois name "double-consciousness" or "twoness" but pay little attention when women like Williams name other social phenomena critical to the existence of Black communities. The explicit link that she makes between the work of the Association and the work of shaping "race public opinion" again suggests a direct engagement with Bryce who argued that "associations have great importance in the development of opinion, for they rouse attention, excite discussion, formulate principles, submit plans, embolden and stimulate their members, produce that impression of a spreading movement which goes so far towards success with a sympathetic and sensitive people."[58] Written thirty-five years after Emancipation, Williams's theorization demonstrates that the NACW was critical to shaping the function of a still-emergent Black public sphere by helping to facilitate collective and measurable Black public opinion.[59] Although free Black people in the North had created literary societies, churches, and mutual aid societies throughout the whole of the nineteenth century, the period after Emancipation created a national free Black populace working across regions and class statuses to figure out a proper path for racial advancement. Because the club movement spread nationwide, it was the first major organization besides denomination-based church organizations and fraternal organizations to have a broad level of reach and a specific set of racially driven concerns.

Black women's associations approached the work of changing public opinion quite differently than Black men's associations did. A brief historical account of the American Negro Academy (ANA) makes clear these differences. When Alexander Crummell founded the all-male ANA in 1897, this organization, comprised exclusively of race men, took as their primary goal a systematic study of "the Negro." A formal academic organization with explicit intellectual goals, the ANA should be understood at the convergence of two prior Black intellectual traditions. It incorporated both the numerous literary societies and lyceums that had been a part of Black public life in major cities from the 1830s forward and the more recent professionalization of various disciplines including History and Sociology through the creation of professional academic associations throughout the 1880s and 1890s. Literary societies and lyceums, such as the famed Bethel Historical and Literary Association in Washington, D.C. (1881), brought together various members of the community, often weekly, to present, discuss, and debate papers on everything from literature, to politics, to travel, to economics. These literary societies were more democratic in nature than the professional associations that formed later, largely because churches or community groups facilitated them. Of course, their presenters had to be literate and, to some extent educated, so these groups were not by any means fully inclusive, but the memberships were not, by nature, restrictive. By contrast, the ANA sought an exclusive membership of highly educated, well-known Black men only. In its nearly thirty-one-year history, the ANA invited only two women to address the group—Anna Julia Cooper and Maritcha Lyons.

While the ANA understood its restrictive membership in terms of professionalization, its choice to be a gender-exclusive organization aptly illustrates the ways in which cultural and political anxieties about Black gender politics—and in this specific case, Black men's anxiety over being pushed out of Black public life—informed the production of African American intellectual history and the operations of Black public spaces. That Black men would again actively seek to circumscribe Black women's participation in Black public culture, which, according to Martha Jones, "encompassed a realm of ideas, a community of interpretation, and a collective understanding of the issues of the day," demonstrates the extent to which Black women's ascent to public life, even in the Woman's Era, remained hotly contested terrain.[60] And these continued battles demonstrate why Williams and other race women remained deeply invested in making explicit arguments about the role of Black women's public and organizational work in creating and sustaining Black public life. The ANA's membership choices implied that intellectual work was a male domain open only to a select few women vetted and rubber-stamped by the male membership. The organization's choice to commandeer intellectual work as a male-exclusive practice came after a decade of legal and cultural shifts that had fully destabilized the shaky ground of post-Reconstruction racial manhood; the exclusion of women was a choice designed to delineate clear boundaries for the performance of Black intellectualism via performances of racial manhood. Despite Gertrude Mossell's optimistic assertion in 1894 that "our men are too much hampered by their contentions with their white brothers to stop and fight their black sisters,"[61] it is quite clear that Black men actively regulated Black women's access to the Black public sphere. Black men's own sense of personhood seemed to be bound up with the ability to stake territorial claim to the project of racial uplift. But Black women simply were not having it.

Unlike the ANA, which dedicated itself to producing scholarly papers that informed racial thought, the NACW and its local clubs used their insights and research findings to create social programs to benefit local communities. This dearth of published scholarly work should not be read as an indicator of Black women's lack of intellectual production, but rather as a reflection of their wholly different understanding of the proper aims, ends, and uses of their intellectual work. The immediate social challenges facing Black communities, compounded by the gendered expectation that Black women should do various forms of "care" work for the race, created an environment in which Black women could not prioritize the publication of intellectual tomes in the same way that their male counterparts did. Yet Black female leaders insisted that "the lessons learned in these women's organizations of the country all have a direct bearing on the social conditions of the negro race."[62] Black men's race work did not have to fulfill these gendered notions of service, and black men were also far less bound by gendered notions about who counted as intellectual.

Because of their proximity to local communities, black women's clubs created an important feedback loop for Black intellectuals that allowed them to disrupt top-down hierarchies of knowledge production. Many of the clubs invited "prominent men and women to address them on questions of vital interest," which helped club members to be more informed "in questions of importance to themselves and their community."[63] These encounters also gave "men and women who help to make and shape public opinion . . . an opportunity to see and know the better side of the colored race."[64] Notwithstanding the elitism in Williams's reference to the "better side" of Black people, her theorizing about the public intellectual work of the NACW clarifies its function as a school of social thought committed to equipping Black people in local communities to address a range of social problems. Rather than relying solely on the Du Boisian Talented Tenth top-down leadership model, the NACW trained local Blacks to be students of their social condition and critical interlocutors with national race leaders. Simultaneously, the NACW trained race women to be educators of public opinion. Williams's careful delineation of the public and intellectual functions of the NACW suggest that Black women created theoretical frameworks around these terms that allowed for the inclusion of Black women in them.

Du Bois, on the other hand, was still groping for an effective leadership model, and it would take another decade before he successfully helped spearhead the founding of the NAACP. Through its mastery of the local-national organizing model and its extension of the work of churches and fraternal groups in new directions, the NACW had helped to crystallize the operations of a nascent Black public sphere that could identify major problems, create local solutions, and collate information into a national picture of racial conditions. Unlike preexisting organs of the Black public sphere—the press, the church, mutual aid societies, and literary societies, Williams argued that "race public opinion," or an identifiable set of popularly agreed-upon racial ideas and priorities, did not fully exist until the NACW created an organizational structure that tied national leaders to local bodies addressing concerns. The sheer reach of the NACW, which at its height boasted 50,000 members, coupled with its explicitly stated intellectual goals and its solid organizational structure, gave that body ready access to sociological information in a way that groups like the ANA and the precursors to the NAACP could not handle. In the following section, I want to use Williams's theorizing about the nature of the Black public sphere to demonstrate the ways in which her thinking should inform our contemporary conceptions of Black publics and the gendered operation of those spaces.

Racial Sociality and the Forging of a Black Public Sphere

In an 1897 article for the *AME Church Review*, Williams addressed deep class divisions among African Americans. These debates among the Black elite over class divisions between race leaders and the masses were part of an ongoing debate about uplift ideology and politics. Kevin Gaines notes that after the rise of Jim Crow, "uplift increasingly bore the stamp of evolutionary racial theories positing the civilization of elites against the moral degradation of the masses."[65] The NACW's motto, "Lifting as We Climb," only reinforced these divisive class politics. As Mary Church Terrell said of the motto in one of her NACW keynote addresses, "Even though we wish to shun them, and hold ourselves entirely aloof from them, we cannot escape the consequences of their acts. So that, if the call of duty were disregarded altogether, policy and self-preservation would demand that we do go among the lowly, the illiterate, and even the vicious to whom we are bound by the ties of race and sex, and put forth every possible effort to uplift and reclaim them."[66] Despite his concession that "Black women denounce[d] those who exploited the ideas of uplift for personal power or gain," Gaines notes that "black elites' claims of class differentiation were self-serving in accepting oppressive constructions . . . placing a moral stigma on poverty."[67] Williams's thinking on class represents the kind of contradictory positions to which Gaines points. On the one hand, she did believe that "what the lower half of our social life wants is not money or institutions, but a sense of relationship and fellowship with the upper half."[68] On the other hand, despite her ill-conceived and bombastic assumptions about the aspirations of the working class, she focused her critique on the machinations of the elite, charging them with a responsibility to help those less fortunate.

First and foremost, the elite must "establish some sort of relationship between those who need help and those who can render help." Not only did she not take this relationship as given, but she insisted, "[A]pparent differences must not be emphasized."[69] This proclamation was not a facile attempt to gloss over class differences or relations of power. Rather, she called for a total shift in racial thinking around charitable work: "Many of us must unlearn many things that we have already learned as to social questions." For instance, "[I]t is important that we should learn that sociality is a very different thing from 'society' as we ordinarily understand the term." Whereas society "differentiates the world of humanity into infinite groups or companies for social intercourse . . . as the essence of high living," *sociality* denoted "a means of sisterhood and brotherhood based on something deeper than selfish preferences."[70] She did not reject notions of "society," which she used synonymously with class, but she did call for a racial focus on sociality. Sociality was "divine" and grew out of a "larger element of love," which consequently gave "peculiar value to woman's work."[71] By making this shift from a notion of society to sociality, women would be able to ascertain needs and "apply the remedies" to the causes of misfortune. "Thus," she concludes, "do we begin to feel the difference between the old and new philosophy of social relationships."[72] This "new philosophy of social relationships" should emerge, not from class-driven sentiment, but rather from a sense of love, kinship ("brotherhood and sisterhood"), and connectedness to one's fellow human beings. Women would bear the primary responsibility to cultivate this new sociality.

Williams rejected a notion of "natural" and essentialist racial unity as the basis for Black racial affinity. Rather, she believed in what I refer to as a cultivated and intentional *racial sociality* born out of love for one's fellow wo/man and radical empathy for members of one's race. In multiple places, she argued that race unity was not an automatic byproduct of the experiences of slavery and racism. Racial identity was not "natural" but rather contingent, and conceived through an active process of community organizing and knowledge making. It was a product not of shared essence, but rather an increasing commitment to a kind of social relationship based on acknowledgement of a shared set of social conditions, namely "race prejudice." Her ideas about "racial sociality" add an important dimension to critical theories of race at the turn of the century by both rejecting notions of biological essentialism or automatic affinity and yet retaining a deeply embodied sense of racial connectivity, which I will turn to momentarily. The focus on *racial sociality* upends the narrative of the uncritical elitism of the clubwomen and suggests that they both acknowledged class differences and thought in complex—though critically insufficient—ways about how to ameliorate the effects of those differences through their race work.

To facilitate this new sociality, Williams charged her audience—readers of the *AME Church Review*—with cultivating a broad and deep sense of "untrammeled sympathy" for the suffering and misfortune of others. "By sympathy is not meant that far-away, kid-gloved and formal something that enables women merely to know of those who need them, but that deeper and more spiritual impulse to helpfulness that will help them find delight in working with, rather than for, the unfortunate of their sex."[73] Her use of "with rather than for" bespeaks a deep respect for the agency of poor Black women, despite her desire to make them respectable. This new sociality, rooted in "untrammeled sympathy," encoded a deeply affective and embodied sense of the ways in which Black women's (and Black people's) lives were interconnected. In fact, the recourse to affective notions of sympathy, love, and delight point to a long history of affective politics among Black women. Consequently, these early Black feminist theories of race should inform the contemporary "turn to affect." The invocation of affect in Black women's theorizing and activism is fundamentally tied up, as Melissa Harris-Perry has argued, with a desire for social recognition as both fully human on the one hand and as fully capable citizens on the other. Drawing on the work of Hannah Arendt, Harris-Perry argues that "the public sphere makes a unique contribution to human self-actualization by offering opportunities for recognition."[74]

Though Williams misunderstands this desire for recognition in terms of a working-class desire for recognition from the upper class, she rightly realizes that there is a fundamental need for mutual recognition in the work of racial uplift. Her work appreciated the fact that, as Megan Watkins has argued, "the corporeal instantiation of recognition, the sensations one may feel in being recognized" . . . accumulate "over time, fostering a sense of self-worth. Moments of recognition, therefore, function as affective force."[75] This notion of corporeal instantiation—that is, embodied awareness—coupled with nineteenth-century Black women's deep insistence on the notion of impressibility as a mechanism for the social regeneration of the race, suggest that affective ideas informed their notions of kinship, intellectual labor, and political activism.[76] Moreover, the NACW, as an organ of race public opinion and a social service organization that *recognized* both the intensity of Black suffering and the limitlessness of Black possibility, marshaled a certain level of "affective force" in order to do its intellectual and political work.

That shared sense of care and sympathy for the suffering of Black women that animated the work of the NACW arcs back to the affective term used to frame this chapter: *organized anxiety*. Williams demonstrated the ways that the work of the NACW helped to inculcate a notion of racial unity through the cultivation of broad racial sympathy and the ways that the NACW helped to codify race public opinion.[77] Racial sociality and race public opinion are two critical components in the creation of a Black public sphere. So Williams's work offers a fundamental insight about the operation of Black public life, namely that Black publics are forged—organized—on anxious terms. *Anxiety* is used in her work not only in the negative but also in the positive sense; that is, not only in terms of what Black people are *anxious about* but also what they are *anxious for*. It is simultaneously an anxiety of adversity and an anxiety of aspiration. There was a collective anxiety of aversion to the oppressive social conditions Black people endured and also a kind of aspirational anxiety to achieve something different. Williams uses anxiety in both senses in "The Club Woman" essay. She registers her aversion to the social repression of Black women in her proclamation about organized anxiety. Later, in celebrating the work of a group of Midwestern clubwomen who had started a kindergarten, she wrote that their success "is a happy justification of the wisdom and anxiety of the colored club woman to extend these schools wherever it is possible to do so."[78] In this latter case, her use of the term *anxiety* referred to Black women's aspirations to create better schools for Black children.

Certainly, much of the anxiety at the heart of the club movement came from an investment in respectability politics, middle-class aspiration, and the demand that all true race women conform to such dictates. Indeed, racial respectability emerges again and again as a critical pillar of the NACW School of thought. However, racial respectability had both class-based and gender-based investments. Much of the anxiety that race women experienced issued from their concern over the stultifying and damaging definitions of Black women's sexuality and gender identity. Thus, racial respectability acted not only as a tool of class and gender disciplining (see chapter three) but also as a tool of gender *definition* and theorization. This fact, together with the other pillars of the NACW school—the combatting of Black women's civic unknowability and epistemic subjugation, the training of a Black female leadership class, the forging of a new racial sociality that respected the agency of *all* Black women regardless of class, the reshaping of public opinion through embodied discourse, and the systematic study and dispensation of practical forms of knowledge within local Black communities—militates against an uncritical dismissal of these women on the grounds of elitism.

The organized anxiety of women placed Black women's own racial struggles and aspirations at the center of Black public life. These women became not only builders of Black social and brick-and-mortar institutions, but also knowledge creators and shapers of public opinion. Their organized anxiety was rooted in the recognition that Black women's lived realities are deeply tied to the set of ideas circulating about them in the social world. At the same time, however, Williams's notion of racial sociality suggests the need for a less superficial form of racial recognition, one less concerned with shifting race public opinion and more concerned with allowing Black women to both see and be seen by each other as subjects worthy of social protections and possibilities.

Fannie Barrier Williams and Mary Church Terrell combined intellectual and political resources (and class access) to shape the NACW into a formidable intellectual and political force driving Black politics in the early twentieth century. Mary Church Terrell managed to steer the critical terrain of her life beyond her initial involvement with NACW into a larger and more prominent leadership role that lasted through several decades. In the next chapter, I consider the creative ways that Terrell carried the influence of the NACW School of Thought into a whole new generation of Black politics.

"Proper, Dignified Agitation"

The Evolution of Mary Church Terrell

Because there are blatant, rattle-brained people who tear passion to tatters about wrongs, both real and fancied, in season and out, it is unreasonable to condemn the proper, dignified agitation which is the only way to arouse the conscience of the public against evils and injustice.

—Mary Church Terrell, ca. 1913

In early November 1950, the Coordinating Committee for the Enforcement of D.C. Anti-Discrimination Laws (CCEDADL), under the chairship of eighty-seven-year-old Mary Church Terrell, launched an eight-week campaign to stop discrimination at the Kresge's Five and Dime Store at the corner of 7th Avenue and E Street in the Nation's Capital.[1] Over the course of two months, they picketed and boycotted Kresge's because store policy would not allow Black patrons to sit down to eat at the store's lunch counters; instead Black customers were forced to stand and wait in long lines. After forcing the store to change its policy, the Coordinating Committee sent a letter on January 15, 1951, to supporters declaring victory. The Committee asked African Americans to begin patronizing Kresge's again "so that the victory won will not be lost through lack of exercise of a new-won right." The letter urged patrons and their friends: "SIT DOWN, DON'T STAND UP!"[2] This particular victory fit within an effort begun in 1944 by Howard University students to desegregate the restaurants on U Street that flanked the Howard campus. Terrell lived in the center of the social upheaval on T Street in LeDroit Park, located between U Street and Howard University.

Even as an octogenarian, Mary Church Terrell often showed up to participate in protests and on picket lines. In one photo of the Kresge's protest, she dons what appears to be a long Black fur coat, a pocketbook, a decorative hat, and a cane, while holding a sign that says "Don't Buy at Kresge's, the only Jim Crow Dime Store on 7th Street." In another, she stands proud and resolute, peering fiercely at the camera, as she and a group of comrades protest segregation at Murphy's Restaurant on U Street. Vitality and verve, and what might today be called "swagger," animate what Terrell herself called "dignified agitation." Though she helped to construct the framework for the politics of respectability and racial uplift as the first President of the NACW, reading her impressive life of intellectual and political accomplishments through a respectable frame emerges as both a limiting and reductive approach. In this chapter, I seek to do three things: first, I hope to recuperate Mary Church Terrell as a critical theorist of twentieth-century racial resistance efforts. Her formulation of "dignified agitation," which she worked out over the course of fifty years of public speaking and writing, conceptually bridges the uplift politics that characterized the work of the NACW School and other nineteenth-century Black organizations with the twentieth-century nonviolent, direct-action civil rights strategies that came to characterize Terrell's activism during the early 1950s at the advent of the Civil Rights Movement. As an architect of uplift politics and the uplift infrastructure for most of her life, Terrell's life fully inhabits the paradigm of respectable race womanhood. At the same time, she also mischievously and defiantly exceeds the frame of respectability politics. Second, I excavate her importance as a theorist to the intellectual history of Black feminist thought. She offers one of the earliest and most forthright formulations of what we now term *intersectionality* in the opening pages of her memoir, in addition to offering humorously progressive takes on dating in the midst of retrograde gender politics about women's roles in the home.[3] Thus, I consider what her discussions of dance and creative maneuvers in the face of racism might have to teach us about Black women's pleasure politics and about the pleasures of resistance. Third, I undertake key close readings of moments from her autobiography, which offer us a sense of the social forces that shaped her life and the public and private lives of race women.

Colored Woman in a White World (1940) is simultaneously theoretical tome, political manifesto, and memoir. As the first book-length public leadership memoir published by a Black woman, it fits within the genre of what Margo V. Perkins calls "political autobiography," which many prominent African American women such as Angela Davis, Assata Shakur, and Elaine Brown will turn to in the latter half of the twentieth century.[4] It therefore constitutes a critical site in the intellectual geography of race women being mapped in this book. More importantly, it offers a rare look into the interior life of one of the most prominent race women of the twentieth century. In it,

FIGURE 3. Mary Church Terrell at a Protest. Courtesy of Moorland Spingarn Research Center, Manuscripts Division, Howard University, Washington D.C.

she shares her thoughts on the politics of dating and marriage as a race leader, her struggles with depression, and her love of dancing. The information in the text, coupled with materials from her archives, also offer a complex picture of her social and intellectual relationships with other race leaders like her mentor Frederick Douglass and her sometimes-rival Ida B. Wells. Terrell gives us a picture of some of the humorous, mischievous, and often complicated ways that she resisted both the politics of racism and the politics of racial respectability throughout her life. The ephemeral and affective aspects of outwitting constricting social forces around the operations of race and gender—that is, the joys and pleasures—are frequently harder to capture, particularly if we look at race women solely through frames of dissemblance and respectability. But Terrell emerges in this book as deft negotiator of the competing private and public demands of her life.

Race Women's Leadership after
Frederick Douglass

As the story frequently goes, the death of Frederick Douglass in February of 1895 left a gap in public Black racial leadership, and Booker T. Washington stepped in to fill that gap. However, the autobiographies of Mary Church Terrell (1940) and Ida B. Wells (1970) intentionally contest this Great Race Man account of turn-of-the-century racial leadership. Both women pointedly situate themselves as protégés of Douglass and, consequently, as heirs-apparent to his trajectory of racial leadership.

Terrell happened to see Douglass on the day he died at a meeting of the National Council of Women in Washington, D.C. The two initially met in Washington in the early 1890s. During the 1893 World's Fair, they toured some of the exhibits together, and he introduced her to the poetry of Paul Laurence Dunbar. A celebrity among Black and women's audiences, the National Council of Women received Douglass with great fanfare and a "Chatauqua salute," Terrell recalled in her autobiography.[5] Terrell described her encounter with Douglass after the meeting:

> He and I left what is now called the Columbia Theatre and walked together to the corner. There he stopped and asked me to have lunch with him. But I was not feeling very well and declined the invitation, alas! Lifting the large, light sombrero, which he often wore, he bade me good-bye. About seven o'clock that evening a friend came by our house to tell us that Frederick Douglass had just died suddenly, while he was at the table describing to his wife the ovation tendered him in the forenoon by the members and officers of the National Council of Women.[6]

Colored Woman in a White World copiously (and tediously) recounts all the famous people that Mary Church Terrell met over the course of her life. But her choice to mention this encounter with Douglass serves the dual function of confirming her status as a member of the Black elite, while also narratively positioning herself as his intellectual and political progeny. By speaking of his advocacy on behalf of women, Terrell framed Douglass's life not solely in terms of his advocacy for racial freedom, but also in terms of his fervent and unyielding commitment to women's equality, a move that symbolically made space for her and other young women race leaders like Ida B. Wells.

Ida B. Wells also gave extensive mention of her relationship with Douglass in her autobiography, *Crusade for Justice*. Douglass and Wells became acquainted after Douglass read her 1892 editorial in the *New York Age* about the lynching of her friends in Memphis. He invited her "to give an address before his home church, Metropolitan AME, in Washington, D.C." in late October.[7] Douglass also helped Wells raise money to produce her World's Fair Pamphlet "Why the Colored American Is Not at the World's Fair," and wrote a foreword for it. Wells called him "the greatest man our race has produced."[8]

Even so, Douglass's relationship to Black women intellectuals was not uncomplicated. Despite his relationships, he acted as a racial gatekeeper for women seeking racial leadership. In August 1892, in response to a query from Monroe Majors for Douglass's recommendations on women to be included in a book entitled *Noted Negro Women*, Douglass wrote:

> [W]e have many estimable women of our variety but not many famous ones. It is not well to claim too much for ourselves before the public. . . . I have thus far seen no book of importance written by a Negro woman and none among us who can appropriately be called famous. . . . Many of the names you have are those of admirable persons, cultivated, refined and ladylike. But it does not follow that they are famous. Let us be true and use language faithfully.[9]

To be fair, these words were written a few weeks before Anna Julia Cooper's book was published and before Wells published her first antilynching pamphlet. However, Cooper had been lecturing to wide public acclaim from the mid 1880s forward, and Frances Harper was certainly famous by 1892. On the one hand, Douglass confronted the same problem that Fannie Barrier Williams confronted and addressed in her World's Fair Speech. There was not yet a public Black women's leadership class. On the other hand, his choice to parse the word *famous* in such conservative terms made it impossible for women to meet his strict criteria. In many ways, this foreshadows the meticulous parsing of the term *intellectual* in the 1960s, which I discuss in chapter four, that was designed to exclude Black women from that designation. Douglass lived in Washington, D.C., with the prominent women who had founded the Colored Women's League in the spring of that year. He most assuredly knew or knew of Cooper, Terrell, Ella D. Barrier, Hallie Quinn Brown, and others. Yet he deliberately chose not to mention any of them.

Laying claim to Douglass as a kind of mentor did, however, create room for Terrell and Wells to share in his leadership inheritance after his death. By placing this discussion in their autobiographies written in the 1930s, these women sought to revise the racial leadership genealogies that favored the Du Bois–Washington dyad at their expense. The discussion of his death in both their memoirs offers an important racial leadership counter-narrative to the race man leadership model that seemed to take firm root after 1895.[10]

Meddling: A Theory of Agitation

In 1904, a group of Black editors, headed by J. W. E. Bowen, created a Black literary and political magazine called *Voice of the Negro*. Terrell regularly contributed biographical sketches of prominent race figures and, occasionally, a political essay. She published one of those essays, "The Mission of Meddler," in August 1905. "Everybody who has tried to advance the interests of the human race by redressing wrongs or by inaugurating reforms has first been called a meddler," she wrote.[11] Yet, she laid out a systematic case for the political necessity of meddling. As both public intellectual work and political theorizing, Terrell's essay marks an important moment in mapping her own intellectual terrain and her increasing interest in racial agitation as a form of political engagement. The essay—a defense of meddling as a political act—also contains the seeds of comic whimsy and political mischief that sometimes emerge in Terrell's work. For instance, to those who took issue with meddling on the principle that it would unduly involve them in the affairs of someone else, she wrote, "[T]his definition tickles the selfish old crustaceans to death; for they consider that it absolves them completely from all responsibility for their neighbor's welfare."[12]

Nevertheless, The United States had an "imperative need" for "active, insistent and fearless meddlers who will spend their time investigating institutions, customs, and laws whose effect on any color or class is depressing or bad."[13] For instance, in the U.S. context, unlike Russia or Great Britain, which also needed their own meddlers, "the meddler should take it upon himself to ask disagreeable questions about the political corruption which makes a single white man in one section equal to seven in another." The American meddler should further

> inquire why intelligent, worthy, and well-to-do citizens are denied the rights guaranteed them by the constitutions, because their complexion happens not to be fashionable in the particular section which treats them as peons and slaves, while men who are inferior to them in both intelligence and respectability are granted all their rights, privileges, and immunities simply because their faces are white, although it is through no effort, or merit, or prowess on their part that this desirable complexion has been secured.[14]

Like her counterpart Fannie Williams had done a decade earlier, she exposed the myth of American meritocracy and the unfairness of white-skin privilege.

Yet, she noticed that Black people with class privilege were known for not meddling: "[T]hose who have had the advantages of education and culture do not, as a rule, make sufficient inquiries about the habits and conditions of the unwashed, unlettered, and the unkempt."[15] Despite her important critique of class privilege, she undercut the power of her own observation in the next line by suggesting that "the literate do not interfere sufficiently with the illiterate, whose conduct and whose crimes bring shame to the race and disgrace to themselves."[16] On the one hand, Terrell seemed disgusted at the apathy of the Black middle class and framed agitation, interference, and meddling as work in service of racial justice. On the other hand, she often shamed and demonized the Black poor. At best, Terrell's formulation of meddling is understood as a double-edged sword. Her condescension reeked of the worst kind of racial respectability politics that unwittingly upheld the logics of white supremacy, even as she and her counterparts tried to ameliorate the terrible social conditions faced by the Black poor.[17]

Despite these critical blind spots in regards to the Black working class, Terrell had begun under the guise of "the meddler" to lay out an explicit theory of racial agitation. She continued to develop her theory of agitation in an unidentified speech written around 1913. "Some time ago it became the fashion to hoot and jeer at agitators in every conceivable way," she told her audience.[18] Those colored people who insisted

> that it was our duty to let the world know, for instance, how we felt about having our rights as citizens violently snatched away, how alarmed we were at the result of wholesale disfranchisement of colored men in a whole section, how we were misrepresented when lynching was discussed, how cruel and terrible is the Convict Lease System, that new form of slavery in some respects more cruel and more crushing than the old & If a Colored Person insisted that it was our duty as a race to call attention to all this, I say, he was told that he was just stirring up trouble, that he had better be quiet, agitation never did any good.[19]

Not much had changed in the way of Black elite apathy by 1913. Not only had these people not become meddlers, but they also had become the group, who in Terrell's estimation, most stridently discouraged agitation: "Intelligent men and women who hold doplomas [sic] from college, whose brains had been trained to think were as loud and bitter in their denunciation of agitators as was the humble toiler who did not know his a-b-cs. And yet these people had read history."[20] That reading of history, she argued, should have exposed them to men such as abolitionist William Lloyd Garrison. In her 1905 essay, she had invoked Garrison as an exemplary meddler whose willingness to interfere with the Peculiar Institution had been instrumental in ending slavery. By 1913, she argued that Garrison's history in the abolition movement demonstrated that "if it had not been agitation, continuous, earnest almost fierce agitation against the iniquitous institution of slavery, we might have all been slaves today."[21] Meddling, then, had merely been a euphemism for agitation, and by 1913, she clearly determined to throw off the use of euphemisms and drive right to the point. Surely "college educated men and women knew that no race which allowed its rights violently to be snatched away without a loud and earnest protest against it, could maintain its own self-respect." Yet, much to her chagrin, racial elites continued to suggest that "agitation would do us no good."[22]

To these critics, she riposted, "it is quite true that the wrong kind of agitation would do us no good. The wrong kind of church-going or the wrong kind of any good thing will do us no good."[23] In language that she would return to in her 1951 speech, she set about making clear exactly what the *right* kind of agitation should look like. Deriding the "blatant, rattle-brained people who tear passion to tatters about wrongs, both real and fancied, in season and out," Terrell insisted that it was nonetheless "unreasonable to condemn the proper, dignified agitation which is the only way to arouse the conscience of the public against evils and injustices of a certain kind."[24] *Dignified* agitation was *proper* agitation; and the *dignified* class should be in the vanguard of dignified agitators. Dignified agitation took as its goal the shifting of public opinion by unapologetically calling attention to the violation of rights and the preponderance of wrongs. Her invocation of dignity also recalls Cooper's calls for Black women to secure the "undisputed dignity of [their] womanhood." On the one hand, Terrell, as I will demonstrate momentarily, invoked "dignified" synonymously with respectable. But her use of that word also suggests that she concedes the inherent dignity and personhood of Black people, and that it is from that space of "undisputed dignity" that she advocates for the importance of agitation as a means to secure the dignity of Black life.

Her commitments to racial agitation both revise and augment existing genealogies of racial agitation theory within Black intellectual thought, especially among African American women. Ida B. Wells is usually the race woman most associated with the work of racial agitation. She developed her philosophy of racial agitation under the mentorship of newspaper editor T. Thomas Fortune, one of the most radical race theorists of the nineteenth century.[25] Under Fortune's tutelage, Wells rejected saccharine aspirations toward racial integration and embraced armed self-defense as a response to lynching and white racist violence. Terrell is rarely understood to be a part of this same intellectual genealogy, usually because of her class politics, but like Wells, she rejected uplift politics as the sole or primary path to Black freedom. Both women believed in insistent and sustained agitation to bring about social change.

Wells and Terrell had a contentious relationship, because Wells blamed Terrell for disinviting her as a speaker at the 1899 NACW Convention in Chicago. In fact, Fannie Barrier Williams and the Chicago Clubwomen initiated the snub, undoubtedly put off by Wells's growing and vocal disdain for the philosophies of Booker T. Washington.[26] Unaware, Wells directed her vitriol toward Terrell, a figure whom she had deeply admired up until that moment. The difference in leadership styles between the two women also did not help their relationship. Terrell was a political power broker who had the ability to bring coalitions of people together because of her judicious parliamentary skills. Wells's abrasive approach tended to alienate her colleagues, though they usually had deep respect for her. Terrell weighed political allegiances carefully, and often acted as mediator between competing interests. Her membership in the NAACP provides a case in point.

Though she was an ardent admirer of the Tuskegee model, and her husband a Bookerite political appointee, Terrell believed in liberal democratic ideas and thought that Black people should agitate for political rights. She, therefore, chose to join the NAACP even though her "husband was warned that this action on his wife's part would alienate Dr. Washington from him and would finally lead to political ruin."[27] In response, the Terrells attempted a rhetorical sleight of hand in their reply to Washington supporters: "[T]he people who took it for granted that Dr. Washington was antagonistic to the principles enunciated by the National Association for the Advancement of Colored People . . . evidently believed he was in favor of having the rights, privileges, and opportunities which other citizens enjoy withheld from his own heavily-handicapped group."[28] Such a view of Washington was "reprehensible." When the attempt at inversion failed, and Washington voiced his displeasure, Robert Terrell ostensibly decided that it was worth the risk. In actuality, however, Mary Terrell managed to stay in Washington's good graces by giving him insider information, particularly around racial dissension within the NAACP. She also convinced him that she and Du Bois "[had] absolutely nothing to do with each other."[29] Washington, consequently, came to view Terrell as an invaluable ally that would keep him informed of the inner workings of the organization. That Terrell both participated in the founding of the NAACP and butted heads with Du Bois, yet managed to remain in the good graces of Washington, is a testament to her skill as a negotiator.[30]

However, the differences between Wells and Terrell were not only in style but in substance. In 1891, Wells wrote an editorial for the *New York Age* justifying her defense of the "retaliatory measures" taken by Black citizens in Georgetown, Kentucky, in response to a lynching. She wrote, "[F]undamentally men have an inherent right to defend themselves when lawful authority refuses to do it for them."[31] Terrell, however, insisted on never "tearing passion to tatters." As a peace activist in both World Wars, Terrell would not have supported Wells's calls for armed self-defense, though she was sympathetic to Black people who were being attacked in race riots. Terrell also had a far more optimistic view of white people than did Wells. Terrell made sure, in the introduction to her book, to acknowledge the "many genuine friends in the dominant race as I have had." Wells, on the other hand, always remained skeptical of white people's capacity for change, despite her friendship with prominent whites like Susan B. Anthony. For instance, in an editorial she wrote in 1885 attempting to dissuade African Americans from aligning with either political party, she considered whether "if appealed to in honesty the white people of the South could not and would not refuse us justice." In answer to this query, she replied: "I don't believe it, because they have been notably deaf to calls for justice heretofore, as well as to the persuasions in our behalf, of their own people."[32]

Despite these critical differences, they both believed that those who perpetrated injustices toward Black people should be exposed, shamed, and compelled to change, often through the power of the pen. Terrell challenged those in her audience during her "Dignified Agitation" speech "to learn to express their thoughts as forcibly and clearly as possible." But lest they misunderstand her admonition, she told them:

> [D]o not understand me to advise you to learn to do pretty writing. In this day and time, when everybody is too busy to read even the books and articles bearing directly upon their business, pretty writing will do no good. It is as much out of fashion as knee-breeches and hoop skirts. But there is an imperative of strong, clear-headed writers who know how to present facts in a forceful, tactful, attractive manner, so that sentiment may be created in behalf of the race."[33]

Deeply influenced by the calls of their clubwomen comrades and colleagues back in the 1890s for women's participation in the production of a robust race literature, Terrell would return repeatedly to the importance of writing as a political act. And it is this belief that inspired her to begin writing her own autobiography sometime during the late 1920s.

The Double Handicap of Race and Sex: Toward Intersectionality

Terrell began her narrative with a declaration: "This is the story of a colored woman living in a white world. It cannot possibly be like a story written by a white woman. A white woman has only one handicap to overcome—that of sex. I have two—both sex and race. I belong to the only group in this country, which has two such huge obstacles to surmount. Colored men have only one—that of race."[34] The clear framing of her life in terms of dual and interlocking operations of racism and sexism is very important to mapping the genealogical development of intersectional thought within Black feminism. Although a range of both academic and political thinkers would emerge in the latter quarter of the twentieth century to articulate the political implications of Black women's interlocking and simultaneous oppressions, Terrell very clearly articulates what is at stake by 1940. What Frances Beale will call "double jeopardy" in 1970, Terrell called a "double-handicap" thirty years earlier.

Though a cursory nod is always granted to Terrell in conversations on Black feminism, her assertion of the ways that race and gender politics work to make the stories and experiences of Black women invisible is one of the earliest articulations of the political stakes of intersectionality. Not only did she want to distinguish her narrative from that of white women, but she also wanted "to show what a colored woman can achieve in spite of the difficulties by which race prejudice blocks her path."[35] Race women experienced sexism differently from white women, and racism differently from Black men. By framing her life narrative in intersectional identity terms, she made the case that womanhood in particular is a significant category of experience in shaping Black female race leaders. Through her narration of the personal experiences of marriage and motherhood, and her more public experiences of intellectual and political development, she demonstrates the manner in which her social location as a Black woman uniquely shaped each of these experiences.

Terrell's autobiography should be understood within the context of her broader political framework of "proper, dignified agitation." For instance, invoking language identical to that found in the epigraph to this chapter, she writes, "I have not tried to arouse the sympathy of my readers by tearing passion to tatters, so as to show how wretched I have been."[36] By reminding her audience that she refused to use unnecessarily incendiary and divisive speech, she invoked her own notion of dignified agitation: "I do not want to wage a holy war or any other kind of war upon a group which is strong and powerful enough to circumscribe my activities and prevent me from entering fields in which I should like to work. . . . No colored woman in her right mind who has had as many genuine friends in the dominant race as I have had . . . could be bitter toward the whole group."[37] Becoming conciliatory and racially respectable in tone, Terrell undoubtedly wanted to win the trust and confidence of her audience, whom she clearly understood to be multiracial.

She also returns to this sentiment at the end of the book:

> In writing the story of my life I might have related many more incidents than I have, showing my discouragement and despair at the obstacles and limitations placed upon me because I am a colored woman. Several times I have been desperate and wondered which way I should turn. I have purposely refrained from entering too deeply into particulars and emphasizing this phase of my life. I have given the bitter with the sweet, the sweet predominating, I think.[38]

In speaking of what is not spoken about in her narrative, of her inability "to tell the whole truth," Terrell points us to an absence that is at the heart of this project. Carla Peterson, drawing on the work of postcolonial theorists, argues that these kinds of elisions in African American women's literature signal a challenge to the boundaries of dominant discourse by "inscribing both presence and absence in [these] texts."[39] Terrell, then, resists narrating a story of discouragement, despair, and desperation but fully acknowledges the ways that her encounters with racism and sexism have produced this full range of emotion. Instead, she focuses on a more public story of triumph, one that is perhaps more politically palatable. In this regard, the public nature of her story fits with Williams's conception of organized anxiety as the kind of animating emotional ethos of Black public life. Terrell does not deny the range of anxiety-producing experiences, but she frames these experiences in terms of how they influence and inform her career as an organizer and thought leader.

Black women's leadership memoirs have been a critical site for the articulation of their intellectual and political goals. Less concerned with the interiority of their subjects, this genre afforded Black women, particularly those who emerged during the 1890s, the opportunity to theorize about race and gender politics in ways that their lack of access to producing more formal academic texts did not. In fact, the leadership memoir is the most common kind of book-length work produced by early Black women public intellectuals, a fact that stands in marked distinction to the range of texts produced by public Black men. For Black women "the personal narrative became a historical site on which aesthetics, self-confirmation of humanity, citizenship, and the significance of racial politics shaped African American literary expression."[40] But these narratives also served as a site of theorizing about racial and gender identity, in addition to providing space in which race women could set forth their public agenda for racial advancement, citizenship, the defense of Black humanity and personhood, and a historical knowledge of Black achievement. Of this theoretical impulse undertaken in Black autobiography, Kenneth Mostern avers that "*nearly all* African

American political leaders (regardless of politics; self-designated or appointed by one's community) have chosen to write personal stories as a means of theorizing their political positions."[41] Terrell understood her position as "a colored woman in a white world" to be a politicized position, which made her life of activism unique. Thus, her autobiography provided space for her to articulate how her race and gender identity had shaped her life and her politics. Though intersectional accounts of identity are the current order of the day in contemporary feminist scholarship, Terrell's explicit intersectional framing of her life story, her invocation of a Black woman's standpoint through which to tell her narrative, is the first of its kind.

Black Marriage Politics and Race Work

The first chapter begins with an unexpected revelation: Mary's mother attempted suicide while pregnant with her. She attributes Louisa Church's actions only to an unexplained "fit of despondency" and then moves swiftly on to fonder memories and descriptions of herself as an infant.[42] Though beginning with one's origin story is standard for these types of narratives, certainly Terrell narrates an uncommon set of circumstances in framing her own life. She, curiously, never elaborates. Yet, the fact of her mother's suicide attempt, and her pointed mention of it, points to a history of Black women's pain and despair that remains largely unimagined and unnarrated or examined in the work of public Black women. Even within public narratives that are largely not meant to give voice to Black women's interior lives, moments like this point us to a kind of affective archive that emerges in public Black women's works, and to which we should pay attention to counteract the obscurantism borne of dissemblance. That archive at least gestures toward the debilitating emotional effects of racism and sexism on Black women's lives, even though these accounts are not fully developed. It is beyond the scope of this book to excavate all the truths Black women's affective archives might have to tell, but their presence in Black women's public narratives should be acknowledged and interrogated more fully.

Though both her father and mother were formerly enslaved, they were individually and collectively economically prosperous. Her mother was a successful owner of one of Memphis's most exclusive hair salons and an artist in her spare time. She divorced Mary's father when Mary was a young girl. Terrell noted that it "pained and embarrassed [her] very much," since "in those days divorces were not so common as they are now."[43] The gender relationships that Terrell encountered as a child were very much unconventional. Because the family fared well economically, it is conceivable that Lou Church did not have to work. But her mother was a formidable businesswoman, eventually moving her hair shop to New York after Mary left for school in Ohio. That her mother was willing to divorce her father suggests a woman very much willing to defy the politics of respectability in pursuit of her own goals.

Terrell's account of her upbringing, then, suggests that her own notions of womanhood were deeply informed by a mother insistent on making her own way in the world, uninhibited by the demands of motherhood and marriage or the social dictates of respectability. Mary admired her mother's business acumen and spent several pages bragging about her many talents and gifts. The care with which Terrell narrates her mother's despair, the pleasure her mother took from painting, and her mother's defiance of social conventions creates a frame for understanding Black women's interior lives. Her mother's unconventional post-Emancipation life granted Terrell permission to narrate, in the midst of her documentation of her public life, her own interior life of pleasure and pain, one in which she enters into marriage on her own terms, battles with depression and maternal despair, and humorously and creatively negotiates race politics in the District of Columbia.

In the fall of 1891, she married Robert Terrell, a Harvard law graduate and future D.C. court judge. At age twenty-eight, she was a late bride by the standards of her day, and her decision to marry Robert had not been easy. She worried as a student at Oberlin that her choice to pursue the "gentleman's course" would decrease her prospects for marriage: "Some of my friends and schoolmates urged me not to select the 'gentlemen's course,' because it would take much longer to complete than the 'ladies course.'" More to the point, her peers thought that learning Greek, a requirement in the gentlemen's course, "was unnecessary, if not positively unwomanly."[44] "It might," she wrote, "ruin my chances of getting a husband." According to her classmates, she wrote, "I wouldn't be happy if I knew more than my husband, and they warned that trying to find a man in our group who knew Greek would be like hunting for a needle in a haystack." Despite their protestations and her worry, she "decided to take a long chance."[45] This discussion about her gender socialization and its connection to intellectual training is remarkable, because it is the first published Black woman's memoir to tell a story about a Black woman being personally and publicly discouraged from pursuing intellectual training because it would unsex her and make her unsuitable for marriage.

Anna Julia Cooper took a more sardonic approach—one we would see in today's parlance as "snarky": "Now, as to the result to women, this is the most serious argument ever used against the higher education. If it interferes with marriage, classical training has a grave objection to weigh and answer."[46] But she shared her derision for such arguments in a political essay, rather than as a personal reflection on her own life. Not only is Terrell's frank discussion about courtship rituals and stresses over marriage uncommon within Black women's autobiography, but this also constitutes one of the first accounts of a Black woman's choice to pursue intellectual work despite its potential ramifications for romantic relationships.

Terrell's choices around marriage are very important to understanding the kinds of negotiations public Black women made in order to position themselves for lives of racial service. In addition to her parent's unconventional trajectory, the brouhaha over Frederick Douglass's marriage to his second wife (a white woman named Helen Pitts Douglass) played a significant role in Terrell's thinking about what she wanted in a partner. Frankly, both she and Wells had a lot to say about Douglass's marriage and the reactions to it. Terrell wrote:

> I was greatly surprised and pained at the attitude assumed by many colored people, who criticized Mr. Douglass savagely because he had married a white woman. And these very people were continuously clamoring for equality—absolute equality along all lines. . . . And yet, when a representative of their race practices equality by choosing as his mate an individual classified as white, these very advocates of equality pound down upon him hard and condemn him for practicing what they themselves have preached long and loud, more insistently than anybody else.[47]

"While I have not patience with people who assume such an attitude as that," she continued:

> I decided that under no circumstances would I marry a white man in the United States. I have always felt very keenly the indignities heaped upon my race, ever since I realized how many and how big they are. And I knew I would be unhappy if I were the wife of a man belonging to the group, which sanctioned or condoned these injustices or perpetrated these wrongs. At an early age I reached the conclusion that under existing conditions in this country marriage between the races here could bring very little happiness to either one of the parties to the contract.[48]

On the one hand, Terrell vigorously defended Douglass's right to marry the partner of his choosing. But her sweeping statement that "marriage between the races here could bring very little happiness to either one of the parties," suggests that she was more than a little skeptical about the prospect of success for interracial marriages. Moreover, she signified on Douglass's choices by making it abundantly and humorously clear that, though she had had the option, she would never marry a white man: "[N]ot including the blind musician, three white men have proposed marriage to me."[49] One of these men, an American whom she met abroad, outrageously suggested that they could simply move to Mexico, because "you look like a Mexican." Terrell made clear that she spent so much time addressing marriage politics in her book because, she states, "I am persuaded the average Caucasian in this country believes that there is nothing which colored people desire so much as to marry into their group. It seems to me it is my duty to inform those who entertain this opinion that at least one colored woman voluntarily rejected such a proposition three times."[50]

Wells argued that she approved of Douglass's marriage because "he, a colored man, and she, a white woman, had loved each other and married so that they might live together in the holy bonds of matrimony rather than in the illicit relationship that was the cause of so many lynchings I had noted and protested against." However, Black women who visited Douglass apparently routinely snubbed his wife. Douglass mentioned to Wells that she was the "only colored woman save Mrs. Grimke who has come into my home as a guest and has treated Helen as a hostess has a right to be treated by her guest."[51] Attuned to Black women's disappointment that the Great Race Man, Frederick Douglass, had chosen to marry a white woman, Ida wrote: "I, too, would have preferred that Mr. Douglass had chosen one of the beautiful, charming colored women of my race for his second wife. But . . . he loved Helen Pitts and married her and it was outrageous that they should be crucified by both white and black people for doing so."[52]

That both women devoted several pages to Douglass's second marriage, decades after the fact, suggests that his choice was significant in informing their own ideas about marriage and racial leadership. Terrell considered the hue and cry against his marriage to be a contradiction against larger arguments for racial equality that Black people could not really afford to make. Yet, she also stridently insisted that not only was interracial marriage personally undesirable, but she was not especially optimistic about its broad prospects either. She made an exception for Douglass, perhaps like Wells did, because Helen Douglass had good racial politics. Both women, however, affirmed a desire to see Black men marry Black women, and expressed their own commitment as Black women to marry Black men. These debates demonstrate the extent to which the politics of marriage are deeply bound up with racial leadership, at least for race women. It is clear that Black women race leaders felt both an explicit personal and political commitment to marrying within the race, in a way that Douglass, the consummate nineteenth-century race man, did not share.

Both women married men who were remarkably progressive on gender issues. "Some of my husband's friends," Terrell wrote, "warned him gravely against allowing his wife to wade too deeply into public affairs. . . . When a woman became deeply interested in civic affairs and started on a public career, they said, that was the beginning of a disastrous end. Under such circumstances a happy home is impossible."[53] To his credit, Robert Terrell supported his wife's career and had been an early supporter of women's suffrage. In fact, Terrell noted that she had little confidence in her ability to speak and was reluctant to take on speaking engagements that were offered to her. "This irritated my husband considerably," who thought that "when so few colored women had been fortunate enough to complete a college course . . . it was a shame for any of them to refuse to render service which it was in their power to give."[54] Both Ferdinand Barnett (husband of Wells) and Robert Terrell had the kind of liberal views on marriage and gender roles that enabled their wives to pursue public careers without causing tension at home.

After resigning her position as teacher in the M Street School because married women were not allowed to teach, Mary threw herself fully into both club work and motherhood. Despite the Terrells' attempt to start a family immediately, the couple lost three pregnancies in five years, one of which was a son who died shortly after birth. Middle-class privilege notwithstanding, Terrell could not escape the racist exigencies of late-nineteenth-century medical care. Tormented by the loss of her infant son, she wrote, "I could not help feeling that some of the methods used in caring for my baby had caused its untimely end," including the use of a makeshift incubator. She sank into a deep depression after the loss of her son that only intensified because of the lynching of her childhood friend from Memphis, Tom Moss.[55] He and two business partners were lynched for defending themselves against a group of white men in town who were jealous of his grocery business. It was this same lynching that launched Ida B. Wells's antilynching crusade.

Perhaps it was best, Terrell morbidly concluded, that her son had not survived. Invoking a belief in impressibility, she wondered if "[t]he horror and resentment . . . coupled with the bitterness that filled my soul might have seriously affected the unborn child. Who can tell how many desperadoes and murderers have been born to colored mothers who had been shocked and distracted before the birth of their babies by the news that some relative or friend had been burned alive or shot to death by a mob?"[56]

Her use of intersectional framing makes visible the uniquely volatile and unsafe conditions under which colored women gave birth to children. The idea that racial traumas could create heritable traits related to social deviance reflected the deeply embodied sense through which Black women understood themselves and their experiences as racial beings. She did not elaborate on her beliefs, but her beliefs do illustrate the stakes of embodied discourse for Black women. It was important for their lives to reflect the highest forms of racial and social values because they literally carried those values within their bodies and believed they could physically transmit them to their children. Moreover, Terrell's discussion of Black women's particular embodiment of racial trauma and its attendant pain and despair suggests that she thought and cared deeply about the social and material impacts of racial violence on Black women's bodies.

To Trip the Light Fantastic: The Pursuit of Pleasure

Terrell's invocation of embodied discourse in *Colored Woman* did not only index Black women's pain and trauma. She also deliberately inserted a body in search of pleasure into her text. Her account of sneaking out at night, while at Oberlin, to dance in the gymnasium provides an example. "It was against the rules for girls to dance at any of the college functions, and decidedly against the rules for young men and women to dance together anywhere." Undeterred, the mischievous young Terrell found "a girl in Ladies Hall who loved to dance as well as [she] did," and the two would go "to the gymnasium every evening after supper and trip the light fantastic to our heart's content, priding ourselves especially on the fact that we knew all the latest steps."[57] The pleasure she derived from dancing and knowing the latest dance steps might seem like the frivolous and normal pursuits of college-aged women. But detailed accounts about engaging in physically pleasurable activities, especially those like dancing, that were socially forbidden because of social anxieties around sex and women's sexuality, are virtually nonexistent in any autobiographies written by Black women until the publication of Terrell's book.

Dancing was "frowned upon by everybody who wanted to be considered intellectual or who sighed to be classified as highbrow."[58] Her choice to dance, to flout the conventions of respectability and to do so deliberately and in full knowledge of many in the community, including "several of the teachers who boarded in the Ladies Hall and some very serious-minded young women," indicates that Black women had a range of strategies for resisting the kind of respectable gender socialization that would deny them access to pleasure. Moreover, it indicates that Terrell had reckoned on multiple levels with her body both as a site of pleasure and as a site of political potentiality. She chose to own all parts of herself.

Certainly, Terrell's privileged class background and the very place of her micro-rebellion—Oberlin College—undercut the broad historical impact of a quotidian form of resistance like dance. But her insistence on including something so potentially trivial within an already expansive tome suggests that, in fact, Terrell pushed, both during her young womanhood and in her latter years, to insist on the importance of creating a space of pleasure in the midst of doing race work. Well into her late seventies, she discussed her love of dancing. In fact, it became a kind of framing narrative for her autobiography because she returns to it in the final chapter of her book, "Carrying On":

> I can dance as long and as well as I ever did, although I get very few chances to do so. There seems to be a sort of tradition that after a woman reaches a certain age she should not want to trip the light fantastic and that even if she is anachronistic enough to wish to do such an unseemly thing, she should not be allowed to indulge in this healthful and fascinating exercise. I believe if a woman could dance or swim a half hour everyday, her span of life would be greatly lengthened, her health materially improved, and the joy of living decidedly increased.[59]

Terrell argues here that Black women have the right to joy. Moreover, she locates that joy in an active notion of unapologetic embodiment and bodily movement, whether through dance or swimming. She rejects the idea that Black women's pursuit of pleasure and joy is "unseemly." Her ownership of her body as a site of creativity, pleasure, and joy challenges existing Black feminist attempts to locate genealogies of Black female pleasure solely within the blues tradition. Apparently, even respectable race ladies liked to dance, too! Terrell's rebellious use of embodied discourse in her political autobiography created a context for her—and us—to think more expansively about how Black women used their bodies in mischievous, subversive, and pleasurable ways to achieve both personal and political ends.

A Sense of Duty to My Race

By 1898, Terrell gave birth to a daughter Phillis, named for Phillis Wheatley, and a few years later, she adopted her brother Thomas's daughter, Mary. In the meanwhile, she threw herself fully into club work. In 1892, she became founding member of the Colored Women's League (CWL) in D.C. The CWL pledged as its first goal "to collect all facts obtainable to show the moral, intellectual, industrial and social growth and attainments of our people."[60]

A clear intellectual impulse undergirded race women's organizing in the District. One of the first initiatives of the League was the establishment of a small night school. Terrell chaired the Education Committee and taught courses in English Literature and German.[61] Terrell believed that club work could take the model pioneered by "colored women who have been binding themselves together in the interest of the church" and apply it to more secular social goals. From her perch as the first president of the NACW, Terrell and her colleagues became the architects of an expansive racial uplift infrastructure that included fund-raising for and establishment of kindergartens, schools of domestic science, settlement houses, and sanatoriums. And they also became fierce advocates against lynching, convict leasing, and Jim Crow.[62]

After five years of extremely successful club work, Terrell had created a powerful public platform for herself as a public intellectual and racial thought leader. She enjoyed the work despite the physical toll it took on her body. In a letter dated August 18, 1900, written from Danville, Illinois, Terrell wrote to Robert:

> I enjoy very much doing this kind of work because I really feel that I am putting the colored woman in a favorable light at least every time I address an audience of white people, and every little bit helps. . . . But it is a great sacrifice for me to leave my home, I tell you. It grows harder and harder every time I leave—I traveled around so much during my childhood and youth that journeys have not the charm for me that they possess for some people—Only a sense of duty to my race and thrift for myself could induce me to sally forth as a lecturer—I have already begun to count the minutes which must run off the clock before I can get home.[63]

Terrell was initially paid fifteen dollars per talk, but she became so popular that she eventually made twenty-five dollars per talk. While she initially did speaking tours in three-week increments, she eventually gave a tour that was seven weeks long and included twenty-five cities, primarily in the Southern states of Alabama, Texas, Louisiana, and Mississippi.[64]

Committed to the idea that Black public intellectuals could transform the racist opinions of white people through sound argumentation, Terrell had very particular standards for speech-making. She "decided never to crack a joke at the group's expense [because] nobody could be more fed up on the chicken and watermelon stealing jokes than I am."[65] She was uncompromising, however, about "showing the injustice and brutality to which colored people are sometimes subjected," even though her friends had warned her that this "would militate against [her] success as a speaker."[66] One commentator noted that in Terrell's lecture "The Bright Side of a Dark Subject," "[s]he fired no pyrotechnics. She touched lightly on southern bonfires lit with living, human flesh. She only incidentally hinted at the flaying alive of negroes and other holiday sports whereby the 'superior race' whiles away the festive hour. The whole discourse was lacking in all efforts at blood-curdling and blood-boiling effects."[67] Terrell told difficult truths in her speeches, but she maintained a poised, elegant speaking style that impressed audiences, even as she challenged them to address the racial concerns. Moreover, her refusal to tell jokes at the expense of other Black people indicated a deep respect for the inherent dignity and personhood of members of her race. Her speeches were a study in the practice of proper, dignified agitation.

Negressions: In Search of Free Black Womanhood

Terrell's personal reckoning with what it meant to be the descendant of slaves began in childhood. Offering a picture of her internal reckoning with a social discourse of Black inferiority, she helped us to understand how Black people came to understand their fundamental human dignity. During a school history lesson as a young girl, she realized her own descent from enslaved parents. She identified this moment as a moment of rupture, which led to a critical redefinition of self: "When I recovered my composure, I resolved that so far as this descendant of slaves was concerned, she would show those white girls and boys whose forefathers had been free that she was their equal in every respect. At that time, I was the only colored girl in the class, and I felt I must hold high the banner of my race."[68] She used her personal ties to the history of enslavement to signify her racial identity and to inform her subjectivity as a *free woman*. Both of Terrell's articulations here about the ways that racial liberation becomes implicated in her life as a gendered subject reflect an emergent critical consciousness about the intersecting nature of race and gender as salient categories of analysis. Her inner dialogue about her racial positionality and its stigma is publicly expressed through the outward claim to being "free" and through an embrace of a social disposition as a "free woman," whose social interactions are characterized by confidence or holding one's head high—being in a word: dignified. Mae Henderson argues that reading the text according to these simultaneous, competing discourses allows us to address not only the "subject en-gendered in the experience of race" but also "a subject 'racialized' in the experience of gender."[69]

Becoming a free woman, able to move unencumbered in the public sphere, was critical to doing the work of the race; similarly, freeing herself from the stigma of racist ideology had direct ramifications for Terrell's experience of womanhood. By presenting a notion of freedom embodied in the confident performance of womanhood, Terrell subverts the very terms that attempt to circumscribe her experience; "race" is not allowed to operate with its characteristic opacity vis-à-vis other forms of difference, nor is womanhood an identity left restricted to white women. And the visual imagery of her freedom is that of a woman with her head held high, which points us toward, rather than away from, Terrell's experience as an embodied, Black female subject.

Terrell not only offered a glimpse into her narrative of personal reckoning with destructive effects of racism. She also offered an account of her public battle with white women to occupy the space of "free womanhood." In 1904, she was invited to deliver an address at the International Congress of Women in Berlin. Because of her very light skin, many of the German conference attendees mistook her for a white woman. When two German women discovered that she spoke German but was American, they began to ask Terrell about "'die Negerin' (the Negress) from the United States whom they were expecting."[70] Initially, Terrell did not understand that they thought she was white, but she discovered "that they had no idea they were talking to this very unusually anthropological specimen whom they were seeking."[71] The ever-mischievous Terrell had a laugh at their expense and kept up the comedy of errors for several days as people inquired of her repeatedly about "die Negerin." Terrell's choice not to identify herself as Black effectively, if not intentionally, rendered her a white woman.

Because Terrell was fluent in both German and French (not to mention Latin and Greek), she decided to give her address in German. Even when she finally stood to give her speech, no one realized she was Black. Thus, she had to intentionally mark herself as nonwhite with a "discourse that would impress that fact upon [her] audience."[72] As she said, "I wanted to be sure that they knew I was of African descent." Thus, she began her address, "If it had not been for the War of the Rebellion which resulted in victory for the Union Army in 1865, instead of addressing you as a free woman tonight, in all human possibility I should be on some plantation in one of the southern states of my country manacled body and soul in the fetters of a slave."[73] This act of public self-naming as a Black woman constituted an act of embodied discourse in which Terrell literally sought to reframe her audience's misunderstanding of her body through a pointed invocation of racial discourse. Terrell further informed her audience that she was the "only woman speaking from the platform whose parents were actually held as chattels," and thus, "as you fasten your eyes upon me, therefore, you are truly beholding a rare bird." Don't miss the *shade* that Terrell threw at this

FIGURE 4. Mary Church Terrell. Courtesy of Moorland Spingarn
Research Center, Manuscripts Division, Howard University,
Washington D.C.

group of white women who had been referring to her as "the Negress" for
days on end.[74] She was a "rare bird," a marvel, not a common Negress, she
let them know. Terrell's heteroglossia, or literal ability to speak in tongues,
not only allowed her to communicate across lines of difference but also to
refract the audience's gaze.[75] She recognized that she could not fully invert
the gaze once her audience knew she was a Black subject, so she made her

body into a racial spectacle on her own terms, characterizing herself as rare and valuable rather than common.

Interestingly enough though, those terms upon which her body became legible to her audience were explicitly gendered. Concluding the first part of her speech, Terrell told the audience that, given these historical contingencies, she was "rejoicing . . . not only in the emancipation of my race, but in the almost universal elevation of my sex."[76] Her gendered invocation of Black racial history and her racial experience of womanhood at this international conference of predominantly European women point again to the importance of Terrell's autobiography as a site of intersectional theorizing. Black women chose to make their embodied experiences of both Blackness and womanhood visible through strategic invocations of embodied discourse rendered in clear intersectional terms. Repeated recourse to theories of dissemblance and respectability would cause a misrecognition of the ways that Terrell's body is very much on public display and under intense scrutiny in a room full of white women shocked to learn that she is a woman of color. Clearly, Black women could not fully and effectively mute the corporeal in their public work. Thus, they drew on common assumptions about who they must be and refigured those assumptions in ways that allowed their message to be heard more effectively.

In Terrell's case, she knew that her audience did not believe Black women were capable of being dignified, elegant, or articulate. They certainly would not expect a Black woman to speak multiple languages. Thus, by disrupting their attempts to read her as a white woman, by forcing them to see her as a Black woman *after* they had come to respect her intelligence and education, she was able, through the use of embodied discourse, to reframe the ways they thought about Black womanhood. But it only worked because her body was a spectacle. The logic of dissemblance theory and the respectability paradigm suggest that Black women thought they could achieve respect only by muting the body. Terrell demonstrates that they sometimes achieved respect by drawing attention to the body on their own terms.

In the spirit of Terrell's wry and subversive humor in the face of having endured her white women colleagues referring to her as a "negress" for days on end, I'd like to think that her big reveal at the podium was a *negression*, an act of social transgression designed to bring visibility to Black women on their own terms, and to resituate, even if briefly, the power of the gaze— of looking—in the eyes and at the hands and body of the Black woman. Terrell's subversive performance of race womanhood constitutes, then, a broader "negressive politics" that indexes an unapologetic occupying of space, a claiming of visibility, a repositioning of the gaze, and a determination of how one's body gets to be made spectacle. To the extent that negressive politics are rooted in the particular experiences of how Black women navigate and resist in the public sphere, these politics call to mind acts of embodied transgression against a discourse of racial regression. This means that Black women transgress the limits of existing social discourse and resist regressive attempts to tether their bodies to a "negative socio-epistemic space."[77] A negressive politic is an embrace of transgression as a legitimate strategy for making clear one's politics and a simultaneous refusal of regression. It is transgressive body politics rendered on Black women's terms.

The Politics of Passing

Terrell's choice in Berlin to leave her identity unstated for several days gave her the freedom and privilege to pass for white. She often passed on trains as she traveled to give race lectures or in order to secure safe hotel accommodations. On multiple occasions as a young woman, she was sexually harassed, and her ability to pass often provided her safety. It would be inappropriate then to read her racial passing as a form of self-hatred, or as an attempt to secure white privilege, even though her very light skin certainly afforded her privileges unavailable to other Black women doing similar work. She wrote of her deep sense of sexual vulnerability during her many travels: "There are few experiences more embarrassing and painful than those through which a colored woman passes while traveling in the South." While coming home from college, she was forced to ride in the Jim Crow car, a relatively new experience for Black people in Memphis at the time. As the night wore on, Terrell grew increasingly fearful, having "heard about the awful tragedies which had overtaken colored girls who had been obliged to travel along on these cars at night." When she asked the conductor to let her move into another car which had more people, she wrote, "[H]e assured me with a significant look that he himself would keep me company and remain in there with me."[78] She narrowly escaped harm by "calling the conductor's bluff" and telling him she would leave the train. Afraid that he might lose his job since Jim Crow had not yet been legalized, the conductor relented.

On another trip, Terrell was forced to get off a train and secure arrangements in Texas. Knowing no one, she asked the conductor for help. Again, she was mistaken for a white woman, and he urged her to go to the hotel. Terrell chose to pass and was able to do so without incident. But she remembered feeling great "apprehension and fear" at being caught. Terrell's unintentional passing on the train had acted as a form of protection for her, entitling her to the best treatment. In future travels, she often made the choice to pass—not on short trips, but certainly on long journeys. She remarks, "I felt it was my duty to my family, to myself, and to the audience I had been invited to address to keep as fit as possible by taking the proper rest, so that I could give the people the very best I had to offer."[79]

As ironic as her choice was to pass while traveling to do race work, Terrell thought it had a worthy justification:

> I taught my daughters they were doing their Heavenly Father a service when they prevented anybody from treating His children with injustice, scorn, or contempt solely on account of color or race. I taught them also they were justified in using any scheme, not actually criminal or illegal, to secure for themselves what representatives of other racial groups enjoyed, but of which they would be deprived on account of their African descent. I impressed upon them that they would perpetrate a great injustice upon themselves if they failed to take advantage of any good thing which they had the right to enjoy, simply because certain people had the power to deprive them of it by making arbitrary and unjust laws.[80]

Passing and using light-skinned privilege to help others get access to segregated spaces constituted a form of proper, dignified agitation against "arbitrary and unjust laws." It is, thus, with humor that she recounted several instances of her daughter passing at a local theater while using the privilege to get her other, often darker-skinned friends admitted along with her. Terrell clearly distinguishes passing as a form of protest from passing done by those who "cross the color line," never to return. She viewed her moments of passing not as deliberate attempts to misrepresent herself, but rather as opportunities to capitalize upon the prejudices of others who were "obsessed with race prejudice."[81]

It was, therefore, with supreme irony and disappointment that Terrell realized in 1951 that Black access to public space had not improved much since her daughters were children. In a 1951 speech, she told a mass audience: "When I came here sixty years ago I did not dream that sixty years from that date colored people would still be subjected to practically the same discrimination and segregation as they were at that time. But colored people are still excluded from the Movies on F Street and are still refused service in many hotels and eating places, just as they were sixty years ago. In fact, conditions are worse today."[82] With the benefit of long historical context at her back, Terrell tacked hard to the left, urging her audience to take the exact opposite of the approach she took in *Colored Woman*: "Let us continue to wage a Holy War against discrimination and segregation and all the other manifold evils and ills which race prejudice forces us to endure."[83]

To Make This Country a Democracy

In 1950, Mary Church Terrell and some of her friends in the Coordinating Committee began a campaign of sitting in at Thompson's Cafeteria.[84] This was the second attempt to desegregate Thompson's. A group of Howard Law students, under the guidance of law librarian A. Mercer Daniel, had unearthed the text of what were called the Lost Laws in 1944. These Reconstruction era laws had desegregated all public places in the District; though they had been forgotten and remained unenforced, they had never been repealed. Confident that these laws were still in force, a group of undergraduate students from the Howard campus chapter of the NAACP began their own sit-in and picket campaigns. In that first effort, Pauli Murray, a student at Howard Law School, served as the "student 'legal adviser'" for the desegregation efforts.[85] Though the student groups were marginally successful, their larger effort was quashed by the conservative administration of Howard University president Mordecai Johnson, who worried that the students' radical actions would put Howard's federal funding in jeopardy.[86]

A few years later, Terrell took up this local lost cause, with an interracial group of comrades who joined her in regular sit-ins at Thompson's.[87] When Terrell's entourage was refused service, she and her party filed suit on behalf of the Coordinating Committee, with joint support from the City's District Commissioners. In July of 1950, the D.C. Municipal Court held in favor of Thompson's Restaurant, a decision that Terrell's group immediately appealed. In June of 1951, the group scored its first legal victory when the Municipal Court of Appeals in D.C. declared that in fact the "Lost Law" of 1873 was valid and that restaurant owners in D.C. were subject to a fine and loss of license for racial discrimination. In complete defiance of the Municipal Court's ruling, a local official pledged not to enforce the ruling. His defiance put a bit of a damper on the mass celebratory meeting that boycott organizers had pulled together for June 15. After nearly six decades of strategizing the most effective ways to "make democracy" for Black people in the U.S., Terrell sensed a deep urgency in her battle to desegregate the District. On discovering that local officials would not enforce the Appeals Court's ruling to desegregate, she told her audience, "I am no longer 'Sweet Sixteen,' and I would like to live long enough to see this law enforced."[88] Moreover, she told them, "it pains me greatly to think that the Capital of my own country, the Capital of the United States of America—is the only Capital in the whole wide world in which restaurants refuse to serve colored people solely on account of their race."[89]

Ever the poised and eloquent speaker, Terrell began by thanking her audience for their commitment "to try to improve the conditions under which we live in the Capital of the United States of America, called the Greatest Democracy on Earth." "We are trying," she reminded them, "to devise ways and means of making this country a Democracy in fact as well as in name by injecting a little bit of Democracy here in Washington, D.C." The recent ruling was a "indeed a great victory for a group to celebrate which has been humiliated, handicapped, and harassed [*sic*] by segregation and discrimination in the Capital of the United States for nearly 100 years!"[90] She then turned her attention to the defiance of local officials. "Let us rejoice with an exceeding great joy in spite of the determined, diabolical efforts which have been made to snatch from us the fruits of that blessed victory which the law gives us the right to enjoy."[91] Invoking both Christian religious rhetoric and the rhetoric of liberal democracy, Terrell held forth their victory as both divine and legal right. Delivered in a local D.C. church, her liberal use of biblical phrases had the effect of letting her audience know that God was in fact on the side of the protesters, not on the side of the "diabolical" local officials. Even so, she reminded her audience about the kind of agitation that would be most effective: "We are not going to tear passion to tatters here tonight. We are not going to fuss and fume. But in a dignified, disgusted way we are going to say we are shocked beyond expression that Corporation Counsel West has used his power as a law-enforcement officer to encourage proprietors of hotels, restaurants, and other eating places deliberately, openly to violate the law by telling them he will not prosecute them if they do."[92] Terrell insisted on dignified, if disgusted, methods of registering collective racial protest. Despite her fiery rhetoric, her calls for dignified protest could be read as subdued. However, she had honed and articulated her theory of agitation over the course of nearly forty years. Where she had generally always insisted on a certain level of propriety with her agitation, by 1951 she had moved from proper and dignified, to dignified, disgusted, and defiant.

Moreover, her speech, given just as McCarthyism and the Red Scare were set to reach a fevered pitch, connected African American struggles in the U.S. to the struggles of "four-fifths of the world's population [who] are colored people."[93] "Russia," she told the audience, "is assiduously cultivating the friendship of colored people all over the world." Fanning the flames of anticommunist, anti-Russian sentiment and attempting to use that sentiment for her argument, she insinuated that communism would become an increasingly attractive option to "these colored people," who "are dominated by the great white countries through the medium of Colonialism which the colored people of the world hate and are determined to throw off just as fast as they can." "And," she warned with even more foreboding, "I believe they will succeed."[94] These colonized peoples, including Black people in the

U.S., whom she implicitly connected to those struggles, were paying close attention to the racial politics of the U.S. The blatant and unrepentant racial discrimination at the hands of a "Law Enforcement Officer of the Capital of the United States" had great symbolic import around the world. "It was hard to understand," Terrell argued, "how anybody who loves his country can deliberately do something which will cause four-fifths of the world's population to hate it."[95] Terrell offered a sophisticated analysis of the ways that radical left social movements would come to appeal to people of color in global anticolonial struggles over the next decade. She believed that "making democracy" more inclusive would halt the forward march of communism. She thus attempted to co-opt the rhetoric of the Cold War to advocate for racial freedom in the U.S.

In light of these consistent failures regarding racism, she reminded the audience that it was their "duty to try to save our country from ridicule and from the disgrace of having the world call the United States of America an Hypocrisy instead of a Democracy."[96] Returning then to religious rhetoric, she urged them to "wage a Holy War against discrimination and segregation." Resolute, she declared, invoking a Bible verse from the Book of Romans, "Let us decide right here and now, decide tonight to allow neither death nor life, nor angels nor principalities nor powers nor things present nor things to come nor height nor depth nor any other creature to separate nor stop us in our efforts to secure all the rights, privileges, immunities and opportunities to which the Constitution of the United States entitles us and which Justice demands we should be allowed to enjoy."[97] She had taught her daughters "that they would perpetrate a great injustice upon themselves if they failed to take advantage of any good thing which they had the right to enjoy," when she supported their choice to pass at the movie theater. Several decades later she turned her attention outward, seeking to change the conditions that would deny them access in the first place. Rather than speaking of "injustices one could perpetrate on oneself" she acknowledged that these were rights that "Justice demands we should be allowed to enjoy."

Mary Church Terrell did live to see the desegregation of the nation's capital. The Supreme Court ruled in her favor against Thompson's Restaurant in 1953. Terrell also lived to see the passage of the *Brown v. Board* decision, just two months before she died. Eleanor Holmes (Norton), a student activist in the 1960s, who sought to understand the context of that decade's activism, argued that out of the "early forties" "came the search for a new, dignified, and more direct way to protest."[98] Holmes's comments make clear that the "dignified agitation" in which Terrell and others engaged participated in laying the groundwork for the next decade of nonviolent direct action. Terrell's Supreme

Court victory, the culmination of more than sixty years of dignified agitation, also created the context for the *Brown* decision. Her shifting ideas about what constituted proper agitation paralleled a broader racial shift from uplift politics to direct action and institutional agitation. Moreover, Terrell, along with the young colleagues she mentored, challenged the charismatic male leadership model that continues to frame not only Black politics but also Black scholarship. From her earliest leadership days as a protégé of Frederick Douglass, to her latter days as a civil rights activist, Terrell created a new genealogical branch for Black politics and Black leadership, one that proceeds through a range of Black women directly into the Civil Rights struggle. Her life demonstrates very concretely the ways that notions of racial respectability came to inform not only uplift politics in the nineteenth century but also civil rights politics in the twentieth. And she did all that while also offering a clearly liberal Black feminist vision rooted in intersectional politics, a commitment to democracy, and a belief in institutional transformation that would "make democracy" real for Black women.

One of the Black women inspired concretely by Terrell's long history of Civil Rights was Pauli Murray. In her own autobiography, Murray remembered Terrell as "a militant civil rights activist and longtime feminist who had fought for woman suffrage," and as "the Essence of Victorian respectability."[99] It was Terrell who had "completed the struggle" begun by those precocious Howard students in the 1940s. In doing so, she concretely connected past battles for racial freedom to contemporary ones, making space for the dignified forms of protest that would be undertaken by a new generation of feminists fighting for civil rights and women's rights. In the next chapter, I turn specifically to Pauli Murray's story; for her path creates a unique thread of Black female leadership directly from this moment of the 1950s into the tumultuous 1970s.

Queering Jane Crow

*Pauli Murray's Quest for an
Unhyphenated Identity*

"The Inverted Sex Instinct
and Other Questions"

While a patient at the Long Island Rest Home, on December 14, 1937, Pauli Murray struggled to understand what might be the cause of her recurring bouts of severe mental distress. She wondered if her self-described "psychosis" was a result of wanting to have her own way in a distressing mental and emotional battle about the nature of her sexual and gender identity.[1] Frustrated by the lack of definitive answers from her doctors about why she, a biological female, experienced sexual attraction to women and preferred a masculine gender identity, Murray responded in her relentlessly inquisitive fashion, peppering her caretakers with questions, requests, and demands. Two days into her stay, she was finally ready, after some hesitancy, to name the cause of her "mental and emotional conflict." In her questionnaire written on December 16, Murray wrote out a series of questions. She wondered about the kind of women she seemed to like—hyperfeminine and maternal. She asked about her own counter-narrative of her gender identity—her belief that she was male—even though it ran counter to existing medical understandings of sexuality and gender.[2] She inquired both earnestly and humorously about her preference for masculine clothing and her desire to be a man among men. Perhaps, she concluded, her "problem" was hormonal.[3]

A civil rights activist, feminist, attorney, Episcopal priest, poet, and writer, Murray's work on behalf of antiracist and feminist struggles places her within the most active traditions of Black women's leadership. At the same time, her struggles with queer and nonnormative sex and gender identities no easy identification with either Blackness or womanhood. In this chapter, I juxtapose her early and fervent belief that she was physiologically an intersex person with her later refusal to classify herself in terms of a binary Black-White racial classification system, in order to suggest that her later racial theorizing reflected her desire to expand the universe of racial leadership possibilities for queer-identified Black women. As a young woman who was, in many ways, mentored by Mary Church Terrell and other early-twentieth-century racial leaders, Murray's life and writing provides an opportunity to consider the intellectual and political legacy of the NACW School of Thought for succeeding generations of Black women race leaders. In particular, because much of the work of the NACW focused on giving form and shape to social conceptions of Black womanhood, Murray's own struggles to both inhabit the bounds of middle-class racial respectability and to embrace her gender nonconformity to accepted ideals of Black femininity, challenge the terms upon which the conception of the race woman proceeds into the latter half of the century. More precisely, her failure, indeed her refusal, to inhabit the category of respectable racial womanhood in socially accepted terms exposed her to a mode of institutionalized gender disciplining and discrimination that she came to name "Jane Crow."

Within the context of the intellectual geography and genealogy of the book, I turn to Murray's time in the early 1940s as a student at Howard University Law School. I consider Howard Law and the stultifying gender politics that Murray encountered there as a significant site in her intellectual formation as a race leader and feminist. It was at Howard, as she encountered the sexism of the all-male Howard Law faculty and student body, that she created the term *Jane Crow*. I want to suggest that in addition to being an early formulation of intersectional theory, Jane Crow also sought to name a powerful system of gender disciplining within Black intellectual communities. This system, propped up by deep investments in the heteronorms of respectability politics, demanded proper sexual and gender performances from Black women if they desired to be race leaders, and attempted to silence, humiliate, and isolate them when they chose not to comply. Commensurate with the cultural and gender disciplining that she experienced at Howard, it was there, I argue, that Pauli Murray became a race woman.

Armed by the end of her tenure at Howard with both medical confirmation of her biological femaleness and intricate knowledge of rampant sexism among race men, Murray turned her attention to seeking legal remedies for segregation and sexism. Her fervent advocacy for women's equality within the law redirected some of Murray's internal conflicts over her gender identity to a righteous cause—the cause of women. However, Murray was still sexually attracted to women, and she found little support for openly pursuing her sexual desires within the confines of her work as a race leader. Thus, I argue that at the height of her legal career, unable to resolve her identity conflicts fully through science, she used her legal training and broad historical knowledge to craft a fluid racial identification scheme that supported her liberal vision of a racially integrated society and resolved through sublimation her continued conflicts over what it meant to be a queer Black female race leader. My examination of Pauli Murray's archival materials, coupled with a close reading of her 1956 autobiography, *Proud Shoes: The Story of an American Family*, and her posthumously published second autobiography, *Song in a Weary Throat*, reveal an emerging framework of resistance to both institutional and cultural definitions of race, gender, and sexuality.[4] Like many of her race women forebears, she enacted this resistance by using her two autobiographies as sites for racial theorization, while also employing embodied discourse as a textual strategy that allowed her, both publicly and privately, to contest received discourses within science, history, and the law about the nature of Black female identity and Black female sexuality.

Historian Doreen Drury's groundbreaking dissertation on Pauli Murray, and a subsequent article that she published based on that work, deeply inform my thinking here about the "ways that Murray's approach to gender and sexuality were shaped by powerful discourses of respectability in the Black community."[5] Like Drury, I, too, argue that Murray's politics "as expressed in her 1956 family history *Proud Shoes* cannot be separated from the way she viewed her gender and sexuality." While the goal of Drury's work on Murray is to have us "rethink certain understandings of African American history, the history of sexuality, the history of leftist political thought and activism, and U.S. women's history, more generally," I make some specific and focused interventions in this chapter.[6] First, I situate Murray's contributions to the intellectual history of Black feminist thought. I use both her archives and her two autobiographies in this chapter to map both the personal and political dimensions of her feminism, with an ultimate view of putting her forth as a feminist legal theorist and a Black feminist theorist more broadly. Like so many of the other Black women under examination in this book, many claim Pauli Murray as an important feminist figure, but far fewer people actually explicate, as I seek to do here, the content of the *ideas* that she contributed to the intellectual project of Black feminism. Second, I move beyond Drury's examination of how respectability shaped Murray's engagement of gender, to posit that respectability politics actually *produced* African American racial conceptions of gender in the several decades following the end of Reconstruction. Because of Murray's complicated relationship to existing conceptions of gender, within both an American context and an African American one, her story aptly demonstrates the ways that respectability operated both as a system of gender disciplining and as a system of gender production within Black communities still working out their notions of manhood and womanhood. Finally, where Drury seeks to show how the racial politics of *Proud Shoes* is connected to Murray's gender and sexual politics, my work places Murray's theorization of race in *Proud Shoes* within a broader intellectual genealogy of the ways that Black feminist thinkers have written and conceptualized notions of race and of blackness within the history of Black women's intellectual thought.

———

Throughout the 1930s and 1940s, Murray, then in her twenties and thirties, was repeatedly hospitalized with bouts of depression. She wondered about her lifelong struggles with anxiety, which for her seemed connected to a series of romances and romantic attractions to young women.[7] The deceptively simple answer would have been for Murray to accept her identity as a lesbian. However, in her questionnaire she indicated that other homosexuals irritated her. She acknowledged a clear attraction to straight, feminine women, but simply could not accept that "homosexuality" was the proper label for her feelings. She insisted and resolved that her ultimate romantic goal was a heterosexual, monogamous partnership.[8] Today, we would understand Murray's rejection of the conflation of her sexual attraction and her gender identity in terms of transgender identity. Because Murray identified as a male, who was attracted to women, she understood herself to be heterosexual, not homosexual. But she was born in a female body, during a time where there was not yet language to articulate the distinctions between sexuality and gender, and to name the possibility of being transgender. Murray's struggle was made more difficult by her acceptance of deeply entrenched and societally imposed heteronormative assumptions that made it nearly impossible for her to consider expressions of sexuality and gender that we would today call queer or gender nonconforming.

Hospitalized again on March 8, 1940, she noted that she had been having severe bouts of emotional crisis since the age of nineteen. They usually emerged, she wrote, after she had fallen in love with a woman without having any acceptable social outlet to express her romantic attractions to women. She lamented that she could not publicly fall in love, or date, or share expressions of affection with members of the same sex.[9] Because the explanations doctors offered were unsatisfactory, Murray proposed—in her characteristic take-charge fashion and often to the great aggravation of her doctors—her own set of theories regarding her sexuality. She believed that she would have to turn to experimental treatments rather than to psychiatry for answers to her questions. But even then, she questioned her own investment in a scientific solution, because she considered herself a deeply religious person.[10]

After concluding that science was still, indeed, her best bet, she asked doctors whether or not she might have intersex characteristics, such as undescended testicles.[11] Murray was so convinced of the possibility that she was an intersex person that for the next three years she asked doctors to administer hormone treatments, possibly injections of testosterone, that would allow her to become a normally functioning male. Despite her doctors' attempts to steer her away from male hormone treatments, she insisted that she would like to experiment with a hormone regimen that could affirm her masculine gender identity.[12]

Murray fundamentally rejected the idea that a "scientific" diagnosis was intrinsically accurate and, though she could not precisely articulate why, seemed to intuitively understand some form of disconnect between how her sexuality was being described (i.e., diagnosed) and what it actually was. As Michel Foucault has so carefully documented, homosexuality was a discursive invention, "a category . . . constituted to codify normal and abnormal sexualities from the moment it was characterized" in 1870.[13] Murray tried at different turns to resist each of these discourses: first, rejecting science in favor of a belief in herself; next embracing science rather than psychiatry, which would have labeled her as deviant; and finally, turning to religious explanations coupled with experimental science. Though Murray evinced a tension at the labels that religion, science, and psychoanalysis all sought to impose upon her, she was also mired in the discursive in a way that absolutely exasperated her.

The questionnaires in her archive, coupled with the copious amounts of research she did about available scientific treatments, demonstrate both legibly and tangibly that race women's use of embodied discourse as a textual strategy was deeply informed by struggle and contestation. Although prior race women used embodied discourse to contest assertions of Black inferiority, the justifications for lynching, and the attempt to malign Black women's morals, Murray literally struggled to make her masculine gender identity and her female sexual physiology adhere to accepted scientific categories. As Foucault has made clear, scientific categories of sexuality are discursive constructions that shape how we live and experience these identities. Whereas nineteenth-century race women used their autobiographies, speeches, and other writings to challenge derogatory social discourses about Black womanhood, Murray—in her private correspondence to doctors, campaign for hormone therapy, and later attempts to be admitted to the all-male Harvard Law School, along with her two autobiographies—used *embodied discourse* and, more specifically, the schisms around how she experienced her own embodiment, as a textual and social praxis that allowed her both to demonstrate her fitness for received social categories and also alternately to challenge those same gender and sexual categories. Though transgender people existed, the contemporary category of transgender or *trans* simply did not exist in any medically ascertainable form by 1940.[14] By challenging existing categories of sexual orientation, gender identity, and biological sex, Murray's struggle presaged the very debates that would take place one decade later between John Money and other sexologists who began to grapple with the meaning of homosexuality, the relationship of gender to sex, the meanings of intersexuality and hermaphroditism, and a whole host of other terms. Unfortunately, Murray's own ascent to race leadership outpaced advances in the scientific scholarship on biological sex and transgender identity, limiting her options and forcing her to make difficult decisions about her identity.

She also struggled to reconcile her gender conflicts with her racial identity, wondering if perhaps she was really experiencing some kind of sublimated race conflict and an emotional response to racial segregation and repression.[15] But, she rejected this initial idea and reaffirmed her pride in her racial origins. Murray's question about the ways her racial identity related to her gender and sexual identity is an important one. Her body, which she frantically and actively sought to define within some acceptable scientific language, including early inchoate iterations of intersexuality, had already been marked as a particular kind of racial subject. As Marlon Ross observes, if it is true that "by the eighteenth century, race is already marked 'on the body' as a totalizing sign of invisible anatomical species difference, then what happens in the nineteenth century when, as Foucault argues, homosexuality is marked on 'the body'" in precisely the same way?[16] Foucault fails to answer this question by assuming that the homosexual bodies of which he speaks "are *not* already marked as Negroid or Oriental; that is, in other words, because they are silently, invisibly already marked as unspecified Anglo-Saxons."[17] Murray's body and her struggles to characterize and, indeed, *authorize* its various modes of being, marked "the uneven discursive development of race, gender, and sexuality" and invited the question, "What does it mean for a racialized body to be named before a gendered or homosexualized one?"[18]

Becoming Jane Crow

Just two weeks after being committed to Bellevue in March 1940 by her friend Adelene (Mac) McBean, the two were arrested in Petersburg, Virginia, for defying a bus segregation statute. Forced to spend three days in a squalid jail cell with five other women, Murray reflected in her notebook on the mixed emotions that she felt as a "Negro woman," of educated and respectable origins being forced to endure filthy conditions on account of her fierce commitment to racial freedom.[19] Murray recounted this experience in *Song in a Weary Throat*, as a pivotal one, marking her as a race activist; but there is no mention of the harrowing hospital confinement that had plagued her just weeks before. During that confinement, Murray had written in her notes that her desire to embrace her maleness was so strong, that she simply could not reconcile herself to any notion of womanhood.[20] Yet by March 25, 1940, Murray was waxing eloquent about the peculiar plight of the Negro woman-turned-activist.[21]

Song also does not mention that Murray was passing as male when she and Mac were arrested.[22] When asked by the police at the scene for her name and address, she told them, "Oliver Fleming." Glenda Gilmore recounts that one of the passengers on the bus that day was a white sociology graduate student from UNC named Harold Garfinkel. The incident made such an impression on Garfinkel that he wrote an essay recounting it called "Color Trouble," which was published two months later in *Opportunity* magazine.[23] The fact of Pauli Murray's femaleness was so undetectable as to entirely escape Garfinkel's notice.[24] The complicated gender performances that underlie Murray's "respectable" autobiographical narration of this incident evince some tensions concerning how dissemblance operates within Black women's leadership memoirs versus how it operates in public space. Murray's self-presentation on the bus was an unapologetic public performance of gender nonconformity and female masculinity within the very racialized space—a segregated bus—that adherents to the culture of dissemblance and the politics of respectability would argue demanded Black women's silence and allegiance to prescribed heterosexual and *cisgender* (one's biological sex and gender performance are congruent) norms. However, when she narrated the events years later, Murray left out critical details, rendering her gender performance subordinate to the larger narrative of racial segregation. Though Garfinkel perceived them as a heterosexual couple, it is unclear whether Mac was Murray's romantic partner. What is clear is that these two young racial activists engaged in gender nonconforming behaviors in the public sphere. Their performances invite us to rethink the limits of the culture of dissemblance and its regulation of Black women in the Black public sphere. Though it is true that nineteenth-century ideas about dissemblance and respectability had shifted significantly by the 1940s, it is also true that there was a demand for women in the civil rights era to be morally upstanding and without reproach. Gender nonconformity and any appearance of queer sexual identity would have been a significant violation of socially acceptable norms for Black women, especially those engaged in activist work. What emerges, then, is a more dynamic picture of the range of ways race women engaged in the public sphere and a challenge to the notion that women who aspired to race leadership never performed intimate subjectivity in public.

The regime of respectability, which called into being a culture of dissemblance, proceeded upon the fundamental belief that it was detrimental for Black women to actively signal a sexual or erotic self in public, because such significations would make them vulnerable to rape. But Murray's performance raises the question of gender passing as a form of resistance to the immediate threat of rape. It also highlights the inherent heteronorms and cisgender identity performances implied by respectability politics. How do these two women's very public performances of queer Black female sexuality disrupt the narrative of racial (hetero)respectability? How did sexuality affect one's ability to become a successful race woman?

First, it bears noting that Pauli Murray did not automatically see herself as a woman. Her gender nonconformity, then, did not only create what Harold Garfinkel called "color trouble." It also exemplifies Judith Butler's now-classic formulation of gender performativity as "gender trouble." In *Gender Trouble*, Butler codifies the production of the category of *women* by delineating the ways that "juridical power"–the power of law–"inevitably 'produces' what it merely claims to represent." She suggests that there might not be an actual subject, woman, *prior* to the law, awaiting representation by the law. Rather, the law names women as a group that must have certain rights, privileges, and protections, and in doing so, creates a category of individual called *woman*. Borrowing from Simone de Beauvoir, Butler concludes, then, that "one is not a woman, but rather *becomes* a woman." From this, "it follows that *woman* itself is a term in process, a becoming, a constructing that cannot rightfully be said to originate or to end."[25] This observation has an important implication for gender, which becomes ultimately a "performance" in the sense that the gendered body "has no ontological status apart from the various acts which constitute its reality."[26] Thus, gender is defined as "the repeated stylization of the body, a set of repeated acts within a highly rigid regulatory frame that congeal over time to produce the appearance of substance, of a natural sort of being."[27] Murray certainly approached gender performatively, considering her description of those *actions* that marked her as male, including her preference for pants over dresses and her desire to do things that she perceived to be male social amusements. At the same time, Murray's encounter with law enforcement offers us a picture of what it meant for Black women in the Civil Rights era to be interpellated by the law as women, even when their own sense of gender identity was in conflict with official definitions.

In the case of eventual race women activists like Murray, the dictates of respectability politics, coupled with the demands of race leadership, came to constitute the "highly rigid regulatory frame" through which categories of race manhood and race womanhood were produced. To say it differently, respectability politics, which were taken up as a full-scale political program after the end of Reconstruction, not only regulated African American gender performance, but also acted to *produce* the gender categories themselves, giving political and cultural shape and meaning to what it meant to be a race man or race woman, race boy or race girl. For these racialized categories of gender were still in flux just thirty years after the end of slavery; so the cementation of Jim Crow, and eventually Jane Crow, and the politics of respectability that arose in response, constituted a racialized production of a gender schema, rather than merely regulating existing schemas. By the time Murray began to negotiate these historical notions of racialized gender and black manhood and womanhood, she understood the "regulatory frame" to be "highly rigid."

Murray's masculine gender performance caused problems for her in both her activism and in her education. In 1938, she attempted to desegregate a University of North Carolina graduate program, ironically the same program in which Garfinkel would become a student. Denied admission because of her race, Murray sought to become one of the NAACP's test cases under the Plessy segregation statute. Murray pursued admittance to UNC with her characteristic fervor. She wrote letters to the UNC president, the campus newspaper, and other local opponents like James Shepard, president of North Carolina College for Negroes.[28] But her unapologetic boldness was perceived as a dangerous, if naive, brashness by the NAACP's leadership, especially Roy Wilkins. Glenda Gilmore notes that Roy Wilkins actively lobbied against the NAACP taking Murray's case because "since she has gone this far [in writing letters], she should be allowed to proceed by herself."[29] Officially, the NAACP declined Murray's case on the grounds that her college attendance and subsequent employment in New York made her state residency claim shaky. However, I concur with Gilmore's assessment that Wilkins's decision was motivated by more personal matters, including Murray's less-than-secret lesbian associations, and even perhaps her bouts with mental illness.

Murray's refusal to comply, at least during her college and young adult years, with the compulsory heterosexuality demanded of all respectable race figures, especially its women, became costly as she sought to champion racial causes. Her leadership style was precocious, aggressive, combative, unrelenting, and intellectual. With regard to her intellectual and rhetorical ability, Murray never suffered from a lack of confidence. She often registered her protest at various and sundry injustices through lengthy letters that she referred to as "confrontation by typewriter."[30] During her work with A. Philip Randolph on the first March on Washington Movement in the early 1940s, Murray told him that she considered herself one of his "lieutenants" in the struggle against racial repression.[31] Wilkins himself was undoubtedly exasperated by what he and Marshall referred to as Murray's "maverick spirit."[32] This sense of self-possession and her sense of wanting to be classed as a man among men caused Murray to be off-putting to figures like Wilkins and Marshall, who were not known for their progressive attitudes on gender.

Hoping that Petersburg would provide her another opportunity to become a test case for the NAACP, Murray made contact again with her acquaintances Leon Ransom and Thurgood Marshall. But the judge, sensing an impending struggle, dismissed the segregation violation and simply charged Murray and Mac with disturbing the peace. Convicted and forced to serve a brief jail sentence, the two young women had indeed disturbed the peace in more ways than one: first, by disrupting the very silences that presumed a willing acquiescence to racial segregation, and second and more subtly, by disrupting those silences that enshrouded compulsory heteronormative self-expression. The refusal of the NAACP to take Murray's case underscores the broad reach of respectability politics, the ways in which respectability politics has played a role in constructing Black gender performances of manhood and womanhood, and the extent to which the regime of respectability circumscribed and limited the strategies of political resistance available to those in the broader African American freedom struggle.

Murray maintained her relationship with Ransom who, as Dean of the Howard University Law School, helped her secure a scholarship there in 1941. At Howard, Murray encountered a male-centered learning culture rife with "discriminatory sex bias," which she named "Jane Crow," "a twin evil" of Jim Crow.[33] Women were often the butt of sexist jokes, much to Murray's dismay, and as the only woman in her class and in the entire student body (the other female student had dropped out), Murray was routinely excluded from class discussions—not because professors "deliberately ignored" her, but because

FIGURE 5. Pauli Murray. Schlesinger Library, Radcliffe Institute, Harvard University

"their freewheeling classroom style of informal discussion allowed the men's deeper voices to obliterate [her] lighter voice."[34] This alleged obliteration of voice, coupled with the assumption that Murray "had nothing to contribute," left her feeling "condemned to silence."[35] The use of the term *obliterate* might have been hyperbolic on Murray's part, given her reputation for aggressive questioning and her willingness to confront male opponents, but her sense of her experience there attests to the ways in which her masculine-of-center gender performance was summarily rejected.

The function of Jane Crow on Howard's campus further incensed and aggravated Murray because of the increasing commitment of Howard's female students to lead desegregation efforts at home in solidarity with Black male soldiers who were fighting abroad. When Pauli's friend Ruth Powell and three other Howard women were arrested on U Street for refusing to overpay for a cup of coffee, their actions galvanized the campus chapter of the NAACP. Murray's women-centered account of the Howard desegregation campaign provides a direct challenge to the male-centered historiography that has dominated civil rights literature. Powell's arrest undoubtedly reminded Murray of her own 1940 arrest in Petersburg. But Murray also personally felt an additional responsibility to "help make the country for which our Black brothers were fighting a freer place in which to live when they returned from wartime service" since it was merely "an accident of gender [that had] exempted me from military service and left me free to pursue my career." [36] Murray's "accident of gender," loomed insistently in the background, creating a "dis-ease" that was exacerbated by the repeated encroachments of Jim Crow outside of Howard and Jane Crow inside of Howard.

During the 1930s, Howard's programs in humanities and social sciences housed the most prominent Black public intellectuals of the day, including economist Abram Harris, sociologist E. Franklin Frazier, political scientist Ralph Bunche, philosopher Alain Locke, literary scholar Sterling Brown, and theologian Howard Thurman. [37] By the 1940s, Howard Law had taken up a similar model, becoming the premiere national laboratory in which the legal strategies of the civil rights movement were being formulated and tested. Murray explained:

> Many of the briefs in key cases before the Supreme Court were prepared in our law library, and exceptionally able students were rewarded for excellence by being permitted to research on a brief under the supervision of a professor. When a major case was to be presented to the Supreme Court, the entire school assembled to hear dress rehearsal arguments. Faculty members and alert students subjected the NAACP attorneys who argued these cases to searching questions, and by the time the attorneys appeared before the nine justices they were thoroughly prepared to defend their positions. [38]

Despite the auspiciousness of Howard's intellectual and political culture, Murray also bore the brunt of deeply ingrained sexist practices. The only female student in her class, she was excluded from joining the campus legal fraternity. When she confronted Ransom about this obviously exclusive process, he told her to start her own legal sorority. Murray perceived her exclusion from the "fraternity of lawyers who would make civil rights history" not as an isolated case of sexism, but rather a representative case of a larger practice of sexist exclusion among many of the most notable civil rights pioneers. "The discovery," wrote Murray, "that Ransom and other men I deeply admired because of their dedication to civil rights, men who themselves suffered racial indignities, could countenance the exclusion of women from their professional association aroused an incipient feminism in me long before I knew the meaning of the term 'feminism.'"[39]

Her experience within the intellectual and political culture at Howard involved a kind of cultural disciplining and gender policing designed to *force* Murray into her "place." Still beset with conflicts over her gender identity, Murray herself struggled to know what her place was. In May of 1943, the summer before her final year at Howard Law, she found herself again hospitalized with depression, this time in Freedman's Hospital on Howard's campus. Dealing with the kinds of racial masculinity propagated at Howard, and the deliberate exclusion from certain privileges on account of her femaleness, certainly did not help matters. When Murray confronted the politics of racial manhood in operation at Howard, she also confronted a kind of racial disciplining that encoded a demand for strict gender conformity. Racial respectability demanded not only heteronormative gender role performances and sexual relations, but also cisgender identity performances as well. Though she was clearly committed to the uplift of her race, Murray struggled to "become a woman."

Though Murray first named Jane Crow at Howard, her experience of sexism in legal circles radiated outward. In 1944, she applied to do graduate work at Harvard Law, a tradition for the top student in the Howard graduating class. This time, she was rejected not because of race, but because Harvard Law did not admit women. Yet again undaunted, Murray wrote to the Dean of Harvard Law School, outlining the reasons that she should be granted admission. Among her laundry list of appeals, she noted that even though she was a woman, she typically took a male perspective on things and that this might account for her persistence in applying for admission to Harvard.[40] Though it is unclear why Murray thought it a good idea to highlight her biological femaleness when her goal was to have Harvard overlook it, it is clear that by the end of her tenure at Howard Law, she had medically confirmed herself to be biologically female and had begun to assimilate some notion of gender identity as a woman. The specter of exclusion on the basis of her sex undoubtedly made the process of accepting herself as a woman all the more difficult and exasperating.

Murray's own personal process of "becoming" a woman coincided with her recognition and increasing acknowledgment of sexism and embrace of feminism as a response to it. Feminism and, in particular, her experience and naming of Jane Crow, helped Murray to reconcile herself with femaleness and womanhood. But her quip to the admissions committee at Harvard Law School points to an ongoing disidentification with dominant gender ideology. In exactly the same moment that she admitted to being female, she also claimed the positionality of having a "male perspective" on things. José Esteban Muñoz argues that disidentification is "a mode of dealing with dominant ideology, one that neither opts to assimilate within such a structure nor strictly opposes it."[41] Disidentification in this regard is different from identification or counter-identification. Identification encodes a notion of wholesale acceptance, while counter-identification encodes a notion of wholesale rejection. Disidentification means that one identifies with some aspects of an oppressive system and rejects others, in pragmatic ways that allow one to live and thrive. In Murray's case, on the one hand, she did not fully see herself as a woman. On the other, she recognized that the discrimination she experienced had everything to do with her being female. So at exactly the same moment that she named Jane Crow as a form of sexist discrimination that she experienced as a woman, she was frequently being hospitalized for depression related to her struggle with her gender identity. But she chose to acknowledge the biological fact of her femaleness and came to believe in a set of political commitments that challenged sexism. She always resisted a strict feminine gender performance, but she did come to identify as a woman. In this way, her strategies of negotiation and survival constitute a form of disidentification with the dominant gender norms she encountered during the 1930s and 1940s.

Because scientific thinking about transgender identity would not fully emerge until the 1950s, Murray turned to feminism to help her think more critically about what it meant to be both female and a woman. Though the biological fact of her femaleness indexed a range of problems related to her personal identity construction, feminism helped her to articulate concretely, if partially, some of the oppressions that she experienced as a female-bodied person. Though it could not, at the time, provide an adequate framework for negotiating her own emergent—and perhaps arrested—transgender identity, feminism did allow Murray to think productively about being a female-bodied person, since an overt male gender-queer performance would not be an option in the circles of racial leadership.

Jane Crow is also one of the earliest articulations of intersectional theory within Black feminist thought. When she served on one of the subcommittees of President Kennedy's President's Commission on the Status of Women, Murray wrote a memorandum and personally walked it around to key senators on Capitol Hill, whose votes were necessary to make sure the word *sex* remained in the 1964 Civil Rights Act. She was responding to several different groups of critics. Some groups opposed the inclusion of the word because they thought it would eliminate special legal protections for women, in much the same way that those who opposed the Equal Rights Amendment thought. Some liberal critics believed that racism was Black women's primary problem and could not see how sexism affected Black women as well. One woman, on the other hand, supported the amendment because the inclusion of the word *sex* would somehow inexplicably "protect" white women from Black women's economic competition. Murray exposed the obvious flaw in her thinking by pointing out that Black women experienced sex discrimination as well, and that frankly "it was exceedingly difficult for a Negro woman to determine whether or not she is being discriminated against because of race or sex."[42] As Julie Gallagher notes, "[T]hese forms of discrimination were deeply interconnected, a reality 'that Negro women are uniquely qualified to affirm.'"[43] Not only did Murray's advocacy on behalf of the Civil Rights Act help ensure the inclusion of legal protections against sex discrimination, but she also laid the legal scaffolding for Kimberle Crenshaw's intersectional arguments about Black women's status as a protected legal class a quarter-century later. Moreover, Murray's assertion that Black women were "uniquely qualified to affirm" the interconnectedness of race and sex discrimination echoed the same assertions from her race women forebears like Anna Julia Cooper and Mary Church Terrell. In so doing, her legal theorizing concerning black women and race and sex discrimination is the most direct precursor to the emergence of intersectional thinking within the law and within Critical Race Theory two decades later.

Murray also pioneered the use of the race-sex analogy in her thinking. For instance, she encouraged organizations like the National Organization of Women (NOW), which she cofounded, and the ACLU with whom she worked to pursue anti–sex discrimination cases under the fourteenth amendment Equal Protection clause as civil rights attorneys had done in the fight against racism. In 1970, in an article entitled "Constitutional Law and Black Women," Murray argued that Black women have a dual stake in antiracism and antisexism legislation because they are both Black and women. The use of the race-sex analogy became one of Murray's most signal contributions to legal thought and civil rights activism.[44]

She used the race-sex analogy to demonstrate that Black women were viable juridical subjects capable of both legal recognition and remedy. With regard to "the status of the Black woman under the law," Murray argued that she "is affected not merely by her relationship to a Black male but also by the position of women in the total society."[45] Black women's historical relationship to the law has been as a "brood mare." Thus, "the forcible rape of a female slave by another person other than her master was not considered a crime but only trespass upon and injury to the property of her master."[46] Given the precarious status of Black women within the law, Murray concluded that they "have an important stake in the present movement to make the guarantee of equal rights without regard to sex part of the fundamental law of the land."[47] Murray called this strategy of using the race-sex analogy, "reasoning from race." As I demonstrate later in the chapter, Murray didn't just "reason from race" in her legal career. She worked out the social implications of this analogy in her own life, reasoning that like racism and sexism, the same things that could be true about racial identity could also be true about sexual identity.

Beyond its intersectional implications, Jane Crow also named a socio-spatial race and gender formation that shaped Black women as knowledge producers and intellectual leaders.[48] Whereas intersectional approaches have always sought to make Black women socially and juridically legible, Jane Crow exposed the ways in which the culture of legal institutions in the Civil Rights era, metonymically symbolized by Howard University Law School, militated against Black women's ability to resist damaging institutional definitions of Black womanhood. Thus, Jane Crow is also deeply rooted in a Black intellectual history context that sought not only to institutionalize particular definitions of racial freedom but also to formalize a narrative of proper race manhood and womanhood. Consequently, it was at Howard that Murray became, not only a woman, but also a *race woman*.

Why Negro Girls Stay Single: Compulsory Heterosexuality and the Politics of Respectability

Just as in the heyday of Mary Church Terrell, Black marriage politics have residually dominated Black cultural and political conversations among Black intellectuals. Black women's negotiation of the politics of their intimate lives provides an important layer to the discussion of how otherwise public women inhabited their personal daily lives. Pauli Murray entered an ongoing debate about Black marriage and gender roles with her 1947 essay—really, a manifesto—entitled "Why Negro Girls Stay Single," which appeared in the pages of *Negro Digest*, the forerunner to *Ebony Magazine*. Dayo Gore notes that Murray's piece was part of a long-running conversation among African American public intellectuals. Some of the more notable pieces included Ann Petry's "What's Wrong with Negro Men?" and Roi Ottley's reply, "What's Wrong with Negro Women?" St. Clair Drake responded to Murray's piece with an essay entitled "Why Negro Men Leave." Gore notes that these articles "provide a glimpse of how debates over black womanhood and the black family took shape among African American public intellectuals."[49] By 1947, Murray, a graduate of Howard and newly named woman of the year by the National Council of Negro Women and *Mademoiselle* magazine, had indeed become a public figure.

Murray took the opportunity in her article to further develop her conception of what Ayesha Hardison terms "Jane Crow discourse," a way of speaking about "black female subjectivity under a specific set of social conditions: mass migration, changing gender relations, class anxiety and racial strife."[50] Murray proclaimed that the Negro woman was in a "state of revolt" against a dual "framework of 'male supremacy' and 'white supremacy' [in which] the Negro woman finds herself at the bottom of the socioeconomic scale."[51] The revolt was being "felt most keenly among Negro college-trained and professional women." Such a woman, who in many cases had outpaced her male counterpart in educational achievement, could not "find a mate with whom she can share all the richness of her life in addition to its functional aspects." Murray averred that these women's advanced educational skills and increased earning power "were a social handicap if [the woman] wanted marriage." Men would shy away from such relationships, because "it is too great a threat to their security." And since Black women could not look to these relationships for economic security, they might still find in them a modicum of emotional security. "But here again," Murray declares, "she [the Negro woman] is defeated." "The American Negro male is not prepared to offer emotional security because he has rarely, if ever, known it himself. . . . His submerged status in American life places unnatural stresses and strains upon his already inadequate equipment inherited from our immature democracy."[52]

Notwithstanding the clear dig at Black men's "inadequate equipment," a dig that is shot through with Murray's own anxieties regarding her "equipment," she nailed the analysis of the ways that racism and the failures of liberal American democracy had stunted and entrapped Black men in retrograde ideas about Black masculinity. This frustrated masculine (and gender) development equated to a "general mis-education of the sexes," which, when coupled with "outmoded social tabus [*sic*] . . . have helped to form rigid moulds into which the sexes are poured and which determine in advance the role men and women are to play in community life." The politics of racial manhood compelled Black men to "act as if they are the lords of creation, the breadwinners and warriors of our time and of all time." But, Murray assessed, "they play the role with varying degrees of hamacting and success" and really "are as frightened and insecure as modern women are."[53]

In Murray's estimation, Black men were frustrated patriarchs, not full-fledged patriarchal figures. In terms of Black feminist assessments of patriarchy, that intellectual distinction is important. The Negro male, she wrote, is "the victim of constant frustration in his role as a male because socially he is subordinate to the white woman although he is trained to act as a member of the dominant sex. He is required to fit his human emotions into a racially determined pattern which may have nothing to do with his desires."[54] On the one hand, Black men want to dominate white women as true and proper males; on the other hand, they are sometimes sexually attracted to them. In both cases, the logic of racial segregation denies them the opportunity to exercise these male prerogatives. It is surprising that Murray does not further interrogate the problematic relationship implied here between Black men and white women, especially since she indicates early in the essay that white women are Black women's allies around issues of sex discrimination. Instead, she focused her attention on the ways that experiences of subordinate masculinity[55] precipitated the abuse of Black women, leading to Black men that would "vent [their] resentments upon the Negro woman who may become [their] sex partner."

At the same time, however, she argued that the constant conflicts between white men and Black men over their respective treatments of Black women and white women "contributes to a jungle of human relationships, aggravates among Negroes the alienation of the sexes, intensifies homosexuality and often results in a rising incidence of crimes of passion, broken homes and divorces."[56] This clear endorsement of the compulsory heterosexuality that undergirds racial respectability politics and shunning of sexual "deviance" demonstrates the tensions that animated Murray's own ascent into public race womanhood.[57] By 1947, Murray had had a few passionate romantic relationships with women, and a very brief failed marriage to a man. In this regard, she absolutely did not follow the dictates of respectability around heteronormative marriage. However, her experience of patriarchy and sexism directed at her female body demanded a sophisticated and extensive critique of sex roles. Femaleness had disrupted both her professional and personal aspirations, by foreclosing access to top institutions like Harvard on the one hand, and by making it impossible for her to pursue fully without censure the love relationships she wanted with women, on the other. She could demonize homosexuality, because she, too, viewed it as a deviant practice. In her estimation, if she were attracted to women, then she must be male, an assessment that points to ways she lived in the tension between biological sex, sexual orientation, and gender identity. Thus, her adoption of a feminist politic is fraught with her own continued struggles with gender—on the one hand, not identifying with womanhood, and on the other, not accepting male sexism and patriarchy.

Working within a heteronormative framework, Murray advocated for healthier relationships between men and women: "We desire that the Negro male accept the Negro female as his equal and treat her accordingly and that he cease his ruthless aggression upon her and his emotional exploitation of her made possible by her admittedly inferior position as a social human being in the United States." Murray also called for the Black man to "strive for emotional maturity himself," to "see the Negro woman as a personality," and to "maintain the dignity and respect for human personality with relation to the Negro woman." Although her progressive prescriptions are laudable, they also reinscribe social norms that place queer identity and racial respectability at odds.

In many ways, Murray's capitulation to respectability politics speaks less to a personal failing and more to the recalcitrance and relentlessness of gender norms in Black communities, especially for those who wanted to assume the mantle of race leadership. In a 1943 letter to Lillian Smith, Murray attested to the unyielding heteronormativity she encountered among members of her own race, indicating that much of the social conservatism around sexuality that she experienced among Black people made her absolutely miserable.[58] Evelyn Hammonds argues that "Black lesbians are 'outsiders' in Black communities," and that this outsider status is conferred by straight Black women acting in service of a politics of respectability or silence. "If we accept the existence of the 'politics of silence' as an historical legacy shared by all Black women," Hammonds avers, "then certain expressions of Black female sexuality will be rendered dangerous, for individuals and for the collectivity. From this it follows that the culture of dissemblance makes it acceptable for some heterosexual Black women to cast lesbians as proverbial traitors to the race."[59]

Straight Black women particularly vexed Murray, despite her fervent defense of them in her manifesto. Murray was repeatedly rebuffed by putatively heterosexual Black women who, when they became attracted to her, told her to obtain psychiatric help and treated her as a deviant. Because of these conflicts, Murray did not always move unencumbered through the Black female social networks that characterized earlier generations of Black female leadership. For while the larger society viewed Black people as racial deviants, her own community viewed her as a sexual deviant. Murray's failure to gain broad acceptance in African American communities informed her tendency to pursue friendships, leadership, and political consciousness outside of distinctively African American organizations and networks, though she did not eschew them altogether.[60]

Consequently, Murray's inability to *embody*—to reconcile—the discourses available to her regarding her biological sex, her gender identity, and her sexuality alongside respectable notions of Blackness, placed her in the uneasy position of defending racial respectability politics. As a political and textual praxis of resistance invoked by race women, embodied discourse offers a set of tools through which they attempt to cohere their bodily self-presentation with transformative social discourses in order to make the case for the inherent value of Black womanhood and personhood. However, for Murray, embodied discourse had its limits. "The rigid moulds into which the sexes are poured," and the compulsory heterosexuality portended by such molds became a social Goliath that she could not slay.

While Murray's private sexual life suggested far more fluidity and nonconformity to heteronorms, her desire to move into public life subjected her to the disciplining forces of racial heteronormativity. The proper performance of the politics of respectability was a nonnegotiable prerequisite for race women's ascent to leadership, and while the discourse of respectability emerged specifically to combat notions about Black women's hypersexuality and (hetero)sexual deviance—a charge which left them vulnerable to rape—respectability demanded an allegiance to the proper performance of functional heterosexual unions as evidence of African American's fitness for citizenship, and also for race women's leadership. In fact, presumptive heterosexuality has been so normatively entrenched in the study of Black women's lives that there has been very little sustained public dialogue about the lack of traditional heterosexual relationships in the lives of race women like Anna Julia Cooper, Mary McLeod Bethune, or Ella Baker, all of whom were widowed or divorced, and apparently disinterested in remarrying.[61]

Acknowledging the complicated and inextricable relationship between race and sexuality is critical to understanding Murray's conflicts and the ways it informed her public and private personas. Candice Jenkins argues that "in fact the 'political' and the 'intimate' may be mutually constitutive signs for the Black subject," so much so, that "it may not be possible, or sensible, to think about racial identity without thinking, simultaneously, of intimate subjectivity for African Americans." The larger implication is that "the 'public' and 'private' faces of Blackness cannot and perhaps should not, be distinguished with any great ease."[62]

Murray had become a victim of a racial ideology that Candice Jenkins refers to as the *salvific wish*, an iteration of the politics of respectability, which is "best defined as the desire to rescue the Black community from racist accusations of sexual and domestic pathology through the embrace of bourgeois propriety."[63] The salvific wish is a "response to the peculiar vulnerability of the

Black subject with regard to intimate conduct," which leaves "Black bodies, understood as sites of sexual excess . . . [as] doubly vulnerable in the intimate arena—to intimacy itself as well as to the violence of social misperceptions surrounding Black intimate character."[64] Murray's own stated allegiances to heterosexuality might therefore more appropriately be read in the context of the salvific wish and its beguiling possibilities for combating Black social ills.[65]

But if intimacy itself has such potential for violence—here understood as denial and exclusion—then it might be more useful to consider Murray's struggles with queer identity in terms of the exclusions for various breaches of racial conduct that respectability mandated within Black communities. More specifically, we might read the generalized Black female subject of her 1947 manifesto as a kind of stand-in for Murray's own struggles with the gender politics of Black communities. This leads to two questions that I want to spend the final section of this chapter answering: What does it mean if "the salvific wish, with its attempts to repress and discipline Black intimate conduct [by] limiting that conduct to patterns of respectability" becomes a site for the repression of Black intimacy and subjectivity? And, more importantly, how do Black female race leaders negotiate these exclusionary and repressive cultural politics?

Irreconcilable Differences: Toward Multiracial Peculiarity

Bested by the recalcitrance of social discourses on sex and gender, Pauli Murray turned her attention to the question of racial identity. As mentioned earlier, she published *Proud Shoes* in 1956, the first of two autobiographies. Her historical impulse to set the record straight as it related to issues of Black participation in the Civil War and her own American origins fits within the range of impulses that have characterized race women's turn to autobiography, including a need to revise "official," exclusionist historical narratives; a desire to theorize about race and gender identity as they relate to Black female subjectivity; and an opportunity to explore forms of embodied discourse that might allow them to counter the sexual silences demanded by the politics of respectability and the culture of dissemblance. However, the text also had a more immediate aim: to recuperate Murray's public image after she became a target of the Red Scare.

In 1952, Murray applied for a job as "research assistant to the Director of the Codification of Laws of Liberia," "the program President Truman initiated to provide technical assistance to underdeveloped nations."[66] Participation in this project was at the heart of Murray's own emergent understanding of African American racial identity. In the unpublished prologue to *Proud Shoes*, Murray wrote that she was drawn to Liberia because it had cultural traditions that drew upon both American and African roots. Thus, the research position would offer a chance to study how African Americans who had expatriated to Liberia dealt with the challenge of both losing and regaining elements of their African heritage.[67] For Murray, Liberia was evidence not of Black or African resistance to failed American idealism, but rather evidence of Black Americans fundamental affinity for their American homeland.[68] In the introduction to the 1978 edition of *Proud Shoes*, Murray noted that despite a sojourn to Ghana in the ensuing years between the book's first publication, she remained firm in her "conviction that [she] was of the New World, irrevocably bound to the destiny of [her] native America."[69]

Nevertheless, Murray's participation in her twenties with the Socialist party and the Lovestoneite Movement made her candidacy unviable and caused her "past associations" to be subjected to relentless scrutiny.[70] Murray chose to respond to these aspersions by upending and refiguring what was meant by "past."[71] Her white ancestors had been a part of the North Carolina planter class, and one of them had donated much of the land on which the University of North Carolina now sits. Enamored of her white forebears, Murray believed that her family's relationship to the peculiar institution of slavery had given her a "peculiarly American background," a long and identifiable procession of mixed race ancestry of which she was quite proud. Recuperating Fannie Barrier Williams's language of peculiarity and its invocations of the ways that slavery had affected Black women's reproductive choices, Murray chose to use her mixed race heritage for decidedly different ends. These "past associations" would give her the necessary racial currency in her quest to be what she termed "an unhyphenated American."[72]

The desire to be unhyphenated was not only a claim against racial demarcations but also a gesture toward the sexual identity conflicts that haunted Murray throughout her young adult life. By foregrounding her multiracial heritage, Murray hoped to neutralize polarizing discourses of racial *and* sexual binarism via a claim to multiplicity. Jared Sexton argues that "conceptions of the multiracial cannot help but imply a production of race in the field of heterosexuality, nominating, more specifically, the reproductive sex act as the principal site of mediation for racial difference itself."[73] Consequently, in the choice to foreground her family's mixed-race heritage and the consensual interracial relationships of some of her ancestors, Murray made visible and even celebrated the quotidian nature of interracial sex. Consensual interracial relationships did not merely subvert the binary racial logic that undergirded *heterosexual* practices in the American context; consensual interracial relationships also exposed the racializing function of heteronormativity itself. As Aliyyah I. Abdur-Rahman argues, "[N]ot only does sexuality fundamentally underlie racial logics, but, more to the point, racial identity is itself conceived, regulated, and disciplined through sexuality—through sexual practices, violations, and norms."[74]

Heteronormativity does not just demand sexual difference, but also racial difference. In the American heteronormative context, heterosexual acts between consenting *white* parties have historically been viewed as the most appropriate and permissible expression of sexual activity. Thus, in pointing to her own family's "peculiar" American past of multigenerational mixed-race relationships, Murray offers a queer reading of her racial past and America's racial and sexual past. Here again, Ross's point about the uneven history of racial and sexual development is instructive.[75] Because racialized discourse marked Black bodies as deviant before homosexuality as a discursive concept actually existed, then it would be critical to disentangle and dismantle the racial logic of heteronormativity before one could dismantle its sexual logic.[76]

It was precisely this uneven development of discourses on race and sex that seemed to create an impossibility for Murray as she sought to understand and make legible her own sexual identity within the scientific discourses available to her. Because racial discourses had a longer history in the U.S., Murray inherited both a larger national narrative and a family narrative that had disrupted notions of biological fixity, in that so many people in her family had passed for white. As Albert Murray has said, "American culture, even in its most rigidly segregated precincts, is patently and irrevocably composite. It is, regardless of all the hysterical protestations of those who would have it otherwise, incontestably mulatto."[77] Thus, Murray possessed a set of discursive resources, backed up by cultural support, to push back against the binary logic of race.

Murray's aunts vigilantly inculcated an appreciation of the broad racial dimensions of their heritage. They recounted, for instance, how Murray's great-grandfather Thomas was the progeny of Irish royalty. Having "Fitzgerald ancestors from County Kildare, Ireland, . . . strengthened the growing shell of pride used to protect the soft underbelly and wobbly legs of a creature learning slowly to navigate in a cruelly segregated world."[78] Here, Murray uses this corporeal image of her childhood self to enact the textual praxis of embodied discourse by writing her body, in its formative stages, into the text as a vulnerable subject caught between racial fixity and malleability. That young Pauli proudly identifies with her white ancestor is meant to signal, not an internalization of racial self-hatred, but rather a disidentification with the binary racial logic of segregation and white supremacy.

Many of her relatives changed their racial status in census counts at will, identifying one way in one decade, and differently the next. The fact that her "people traveled back and forth through this corridor of mixed bloods as they chose,"[79] gave Murray a clear sense of how identity could operate in fluid terms. Whereas the law became a place that fixed gender identities through the recognition of the category "woman," Murray's ancestors' refusal of static racial identification across time, particularly on the census, defied legal attempts to impose fixity upon their racial identities. Her celebration of her family's refusal of official, externally imposed racial boundaries reinforced her lifelong resistance to institutional definitions of race, gender, and sexuality. Though she relied on the law's official recognition of Black people and women in order to advocate for civil rights, her approach was more pragmatic than ideological. She firmly believed that the attempt to force human beings into "rigid" categories of racial and gender identification was dehumanizing, not to mention an inaccurate way to characterize the range of human experiences. Yet, she also understood that "being caught 'betwixt and between' the races" was a space of "doing battle."[80] This contested space, which the Fitzgeralds, Murray's mulatto relatives, occupied, was a "no man's land between the whites and Blacks, belonging wholly to neither yet irrevocably tied to both."[81] Adding her own racial theorizing to the broad tradition of Black feminist thought, Murray concluded that racial malleability and fluidity are the logical telos to America's peculiar racial history.

Even so, racial malleability was not a foregone conclusion. For although knowledge of her noble white ancestry provided a "shell" of protection for Murray, it also "more than anything else, kept me," she writes, "from an acceptance of my lot. I would always be trying to break out of the rigid mold into which I was being forced. I would always be in rebellion against the crushing walls until people no longer needed legends about their ancestors to give them distinctiveness and self-respect."[82] Her return to the image of the "rigid molds into which [she] was being forced," invoked her discussion a decade earlier about the mis-education of the sexes. This similarity in language is not accidental; rather it points us to sublimated and subversive sexual desires that remained dangerous for a race woman to articulate in public.

In a letter written in March 1973 to her friend Peg Holmes, a white woman with whom Murray had a romantic relationship in the late 1930s, Murray told Peg that she was returning pictures, most probably of Peg and a masculine-performing Pauli, in telling romantic poses. One picture was particularly difficult for Murray to return, and she noted that it had inspired a passage in *Proud Shoes*.[83] The passage in question was a description of the massive attempts at familial reconciliation among separated Black families that took place in the immediate aftermath of the Civil War:

> In this restless movement were those for whom freedom meant an unending quest for loved ones. Years before, they had been parted; wives sold one way and husbands another, children separated from their parents and [the] aged separated from their children. When the parting came, each had carried with him an image of his loved one and the place where he had left him. All his remaining years he would be inquiring of people if they had heard of a slave called "Black Cato" or "Yellow Sam" or "Sally," and trying to get to that place where they had been separated. He would describe the loved one in the intimate way he remembered him—a charm worn about the neck, a dimple in the cheek, a certain manner of walking or smiling. It did not matter that children had grown up and white haired. The description remained the same.[84]

The narrative of familial reconciliation after slavery is a powerful and important moment in Black people's quest for freedom. Its invocation here demonstrates that even before she pioneered the legal strategy of reasoning from race, Murray used deeply significant racial narratives to embed her own ideas about sexual freedom and kinship. The intentional submersion of her sexual narrative into the larger racial narrative, via use of what Drury refers to as "invisible footnotes," stitches Pauli and Peg's interracial same-sex relationship to the backing of America's mulatto heritage and to Black people's queer past.[85] Murray demonstrates that a racial past necessarily encodes a sexual past, but her account of multiracial American identity resists the normativizing imperatives of the official American binary classification of race. By forcing her readers to think simultaneously about racial identity and intimate subjectivity, she forces us to consider America's peculiar racializing imperative as a queer practice all its own.[86] Murray's weaving of her own queer sexual past into a collectively resonant racial narrative suggests a deep disidentification with the heteronormative dictates of respectable African American society and simultaneously demonstrates Candice Jenkins's point about the inextricability of racial identity and intimate subjectivity.[87] This passage, and Murray's archival letter about its origins, attest to the ways that she intentionally stretched racial narratives to make room for herself.

Writing about the quest for racial reconciliation in a way that fundamentally acknowledged the human longing for kinship, Murray created space within a broader racial narrative to acknowledge her own sublimated longings for a certain kind of relational connection to a loved one. In this regard,

Proud Shoes tills new ground in terms of race women's revisionist historical project, namely inserting an unspeakable sexual past into a poignant and residual community narrative that marked the shift from unfreedom to freedom by the ability to be with the ones you loved.[88] It is important, too, that the passage refers to the ways that kinship and connection is marked on the body—through dimples, a kind of smile, a particular kind of walk. Murray's argument grounds her challenge to the rigid identity molds fundamentally within the body, largely because she understood her sexuality and gender identity in terms of a struggle both within and around her body.

The corporeal imagery in this text, coupled with Murray's textual interpellations of her own queerness, constitutes a new iteration of embodied discourse in Black women's autobiography. Like her nineteenth-century forebears, Murray celebrates the bodily memories of the newly free, but she also uses these bodies as textual vehicles for her own sexual and bodily pleasures and remembrances. Hardison argues that "the mandates of middle-class respectability demanded Murray's silence on her sexuality in her memoir, as the politics of Jane Crow circumscribed not only black women's literal bodies but also their textual representation."[89] Thus, Murray's particular appropriation of this racial narrative queers the narrative of multiracial identity and familial connection within the U.S. context. And her use of embodied discourse as a form of textual activism against respectable silence provides a way for us to read women's autobiographies "as negotiations in naming the unspeakable."[90] Moreover, the narrative allows us to "claim a critical location from which to read the sexual unspeakable from outside a polarized framework in which normative heterosexuality and oppositional homosexuality operate as authorized and mutually exclusive discourses."[91] By narrating her own irreconcilable differences through the carefully chosen surrogate race narratives of Emancipation and reconciliation, Murray refracted her own "unending quest for loved ones" through the queered prism of a wholly racial experience. Her refusal of the racial binary constituted a rejection of its narrative authority over her history, both sexual and racial. She understood the static racial boundary to be an obstacle whose swift and sure removal was the necessary first step in her quest to authorize herself.

Pauli Murray, a mid-twentieth-century race woman problematizes our easy imposition of the categories of race and womanhood on her body. While she is critically important to the intellectual histories of Civil Rights, the Women's Movement, and Black feminism, she herself was also deeply ambivalent about what it meant to be Black and what it meant to be a woman. Thus, she attempted to understand her actual corporeal body within available social and scientific discourses, with limited results. Ultimately, while she demonstrated the gendered dimensions of Jim Crow segregation by pointing us to Jane Crow, and while she demonstrated that America's past is more peculiar than exceptional, she also confronted profound limitations as she attempted to embody the social discourses around race and gender through which she was supposed to understand herself. Thus, she reasoned from race, through American peculiarity, toward a profoundly queer and embodied conception of what it meant to be Jane Crow.

At the height of her struggle over what it meant to Black, African American communities renewed their debate about the role of women in intellectual and political struggle. Murray's own defiant opposition to the racial and sexual politics of the Black Power era serve as a backdrop for the next chapter, which offers a picture of how Black communities both contested and constructed leadership roles for women during the shift from Civil Rights to Black Power.

CHAPTER 4

The Problems and Possibilities of the Negro Woman Intellectual

Negro women intellectuals share two responsibilities:
to really be an intellectual (although she may not eat
well, have friends and be credited with loose screws)
and to help shape a new definition of femininity.
—Ponchitta Pierce, *Ebony Magazine* (1966)

In 1966, the year that "Black Power" replaced "Freedom Now" as the dominant slogan of the Civil Rights movement, Black communities struggled to determine the best leadership strategies for racial advancement. One year earlier, the infamous Moynihan Report had branded Black women as the denizens of Black racial pathology because of their alleged iron-fisted matriarchal rule of Black families. Whereas Black women's ideas about building strong Black families had been the driving force of their political organizing in women's clubs in the first half of the twentieth century, the Moynihan report indicated that the uplift infrastructure Black women had so carefully built had crumbled. Along with it came a resurgence of the cultural distrust of Black women's political ideas and leadership abilities. The performance of respectable racial manhood and womanhood had failed to foster Black people's full assimilation into U.S. civil society.

Indicative of this cultural upheaval, an *Ebony Magazine* special issue on "The Negro Woman" contained an article entitled "Problems of the Negro Woman Intellectual."[1] It began with this observation: "The Negro woman intellectual is easily one of the most misunderstood, unappreciated and problem-ridden of all God's creatures. In fact, if it were left to many Negro males alone to decide, she would not even exist."[2] Cultural hyperbole aside, being a Black woman intellectual apparently constituted the stuff of existential crisis.

Though Black communities may have been in crisis because of shifts in Black leadership and damaging national discourses, *Ebony Magazine* chose to place that crisis at the feet of Black women, even though the author acknowledged that it was Black men who were most uncomfortable. Black men were quick, wrote Ponchitta Pierce, to "deprecate the woman intellectual," even though "few really know this object of their discontent."[3] Black women intellectuals defied existing categories of cultural and racial identity, creating both a political and intellectual problem within Black communities that, since the nineteenth century, had responded to political instability by reasserting the primacy of traditional gender roles.

The escalation of the intergenerational conflict between Martin Luther King Jr. and Stokely Carmichael (Kwame Ture) in the summer of 1966 dramatized not only two kinds of Black political possibilities, but also two potential kinds of Black masculine gender performance—the respectable racial manhood of old and the revolutionary militant Black manhood of the present. The fact that the constitution of Black gender categories was at stake in these political battles was obscured by the more pressing problem of choosing a political path.

By 1967, in response to this cultural and political upheaval, Harold Cruse proclaimed Black intellectuals to be in full-scale crisis, in his now-classic polemic *Crisis of the Negro Intellectual*. With the notable exception of Lorraine Hansberry, whom he lambasted along with the rest of his targets, Cruse's procession of Negro Intellectuals was all male. They included Frederick Douglass, Martin R. Delany, Edward Blyden, Alexander Crummell, Henry M. Turner, George Washington Williams, Booker T. Washington, Marcus Garvey, and W. E. B. Du Bois.[4]

The overarching narrative of *crisis* has been a salient feature of Black political life at least since Du Bois began serving as editor of the NAACP magazine of the same name. This recourse to the narrative of Black political crisis frequently obscures an attendant upheaval over gender politics, particularly a broad discontent over the opportunities to pursue certain kinds of respectable racial manhood. Consequently, resolutions to Black political crises are frequently pursued through the insistence on prescribing traditional gender roles for Black communities. *Ebony*, however, repackaged the cultural crisis over racial manhood as a crisis over Black femininity and Black womanhood, obscuring the political stakes of this battle for Black men. This repackaging laid the responsibility for rectifying the crisis at the feet of Black women who simply needed to figure out their role and play it.

This kind of cultural discombobulation over the role of intellectuals in racial leadership dramatizes a continuing crisis of racial manhood, and of the construction of Black gender identities more generally, that underwrites most of the major shifts in Black leadership throughout the twentieth century. However, I am less interested in what such dramas mean for Black men and more interested in the ways that Black women responded to these accusations. In this chapter, I consider how political movements, specifically Civil Rights and Black Power, and Black women's responses to them have shaped the intellectual geography of Black thought and influenced the intellectual genealogies that are bequeathed to us. Through close readings of a range of cultural texts—the *Ebony* article, the civil rights autobiographies of Anna Arnold Hedgeman and Pauli Murray, and Toni Cade Bambara's edited volume *Black Woman*—I map the broad cultural debates about Black women's role in race leadership. Unlike more recent works in Civil Rights and Black Power Studies that are concerned with recovering Black women's contributions to the struggle, I examine the ways that debates over the conceptual category of the intellectual illumine the gender politics of the shift from Civil Rights to Black Power. These cultural anxieties over the meaning of the intellectual also dovetail cultural anxiety about the ways Black men and women performed gender identity. Thus, such debates restage earlier twentieth-century debates within Black communities and Black organizations about the meanings of race womanhood and race manhood.

Because these debates were not merely tactical, Black women not only responded politically but also intellectually, by conceptually reframing the terms of race womanhood. Toni Cade Bambara's preface and essay, "On the Issue of Roles," in her 1970 book, *Black Woman*, played a lead role in Black women's attempts to articulate a coherent narrative about Black female identity and Black women's leadership against the angst-ridden backdrop of Cruse's proclamation of crisis. My examination reveals the ways in which battles over race leadership are always deeply tied to contestations over gender and demonstrates that these moments of cultural upheaval frequently urge a refiguring of existing categories of gender within Black communities.

This chapter concludes the intellectual genealogy and geography of Black women's public intellectual work that I have been mapping throughout *Beyond Respectability*. I argue that the kinds of Black feminist intellectual projects that emerge during the 1970s are, by and large, products of Black women's public work rather than, for instance, traditional academic theorizing. By the 1980s, with the ascent of women like Mary Helen Washington, bell hooks, Beverly Guy-Sheftall and Patricia Hill Collins, Black feminism moved solidly into the academy, benefiting from a newly available and unprecedented set of institutional resources for Black women to professionalize public intellectual work. But the work of literary and creative intellectuals in the 1970s retained what Farah Jasmine Griffin has called an "extra-academic" tenor that allowed for a range of conversations and contestations about the nature of Black womanhood in the public sphere.

We Have a Dream:
The Masculinist Politics of the Big Six

The only woman to serve on the 1963 March on Washington for Jobs and Freedom organizing committee, Anna Arnold Hedgeman was a reluctant Black intellectual. In 1933, Hedgeman was invited, as part a new generation of "young Negro intellectuals," to Joel Spingarn's Second Amenia Conference in Troutbeck, New York.[5] She recalled being both "flattered and disturbed to be called an intellectual because," as she reflected, "my recent experience with the problems of the masses of people made me fear words which might separate us."[6] Though a few women were invited to Amenia II, she mostly remembered the prominent men: "Abram Harris, Charles H. Houston, Ralph Bunche, Marion Cuthbert [a woman], William Hastie, James Weldon Johnson, Walter White, and W. E. B. Du Bois." Those "last three," she noted, "represented a link with the past." But "we had ideas of our own, however, and insisted, as youth always does, that the progress of the Negro had been too slow."[7] Hedgeman was especially enamored of the young economist Abram Harris and how his approach might help Black people struggling to recover from the Depression. She also recalled an excited "Charles Hamilton Houston, fresh from Amherst and Harvard, [filled] with plans for the development of the Howard University Law School [who] was discussing the role of the law in the struggle for Civil Rights." What they came to agree on was that "increased training and specialization of the Negro would help him make new openings for other Negroes" . . . in particular, "college graduates [with] specialized training in the liberal arts could bring new strength."[8] Despite her reservations about the inherent elitism of being classed among the "intellectuals," Hedgeman supported the broad liberal vision put forth by the "Young Turks" at Amenia II.

This liberal vision informed her work as the first Black woman to serve on a New York mayoral cabinet under the Wagner administration in the 1950s.[9] And in the 1960s, she was invited by A. Philip Randolph to complete the work she had begun with him in the 1940s in New York during the first March on Washington Movement, where she also worked with a young Pauli Murray. For the 1963 March, she teamed up with the "Big Six": A. Philip Randolph, Roy Wilkins, Martin Luther King, James Farmer, Whitney Young, and John Lewis.

FIGURE 6. Anna Arnold Hedgeman. Courtesy of Moorland Spingarn Research Center, Manuscripts Division, Howard University, Washington D.C.

However, one week before the March she realized that "no woman [was] listed as a speaker" on the program. So "it was proposed that Mr. Randolph, as chairman, would ask several Negro women to stand while he reviewed the historic role of Negro women, and that the women would merely take a bow at the end of his presentation." Internally, she balked at this dismissive attempt to silence Black women by not even allowing them to speak, while claiming to celebrate them. She found it "significant that not even the rebellious youth leader [presumably John Lewis] thought of the role which woman had played in the present phase of the continuing Negro revolution."[10] She thus marshaled her forces and sent a memo to Randolph: "In light of the role of Negro women in the struggle for freedom and especially in light of the extra burden they have carried because of the castration of our Negro man in this culture, it is incredible that no woman should appear as a speaker at the historic March on Washington Meeting at the Lincoln Memorial." She went on to request "that a Negro woman make a brief statement and present the other Heroines just as you have suggested that the Chairman might do."[11] She suggested two potential women: Myrlie Evers, widow of Medgar Evers, and Diane Nash Bevel. But the male organizers remained resistant about female participation. Because of consistent advocacy and agitation on the part of Hedgeman, Pauli Murray, and Dorothy Height, on the day of the March "Daisy Bates was asked to say a few words," but even then A. Philip Randolph limited her time at the microphone. Hedgeman noted that "Mrs. Rosa Parks, the courageous woman who had refused to 'move to the back of the bus,' in Montgomery was presented, but almost casually."[12] That elicited a shared knowing among many of the women there: "[W]e grinned; some of us, as we recognized anew that Negro women are second-class citizens in the same way that white women are in our culture."[13]

Published in 1964 just one year after the March, Hedgeman's "memoir of Negro leadership," *Trumpet Sounds*, acts as an intervention in a recalcitrant masculinist narrative of racial leadership. The gender politics of the March on Washington demonstrate firsthand the ways in which this symbolic show of the Black freedom struggle was inherently gendered and fraught with Black men's own investments in dominating the direction of racial leadership. Not only did Hedgeman call the Civil Rights establishment publicly to task, but she also took specific aim at King. She acknowledged that King's "speech on that day has been reprinted and sent across the world, for all men understand the 'dream.'"[14] As he addressed the crowd, King reminded her of President John F. Kennedy. "Both of these young men," she wrote, "had somehow seemed to detach themselves from all sense of their own relationship to the past. President Kennedy had done it with his announcement that the younger generation would establish the new frontier and Martin Luther King had seemed to bring the same message with his beautifully poetic description of his dream." Inscribed in her own words on her program from JFK's inauguration, she had written "Dear Mr. Kennedy, your dream of a new frontier is bound up in the dreams of all men who have had a vision beyond the moment; a vision of some men in the world sense the beginning of time." She "wanted desperately to say these same words to Martin Luther King, standing in front of 250,000 people who had come to Washington because they had a dream." "In the face of all the men and women of the past who have dreamed in vain, I wished very much that Martin had said, 'We have a dream.'"[15]

Acutely aware of the multigenerational nature of the Black freedom struggle, Hedgeman pointed to the ways that the politics of King's dream were predicated on an active erasure of long histories of collective Black dissent. While the March on Washington has come to symbolize the moment when King donned his role as official "charismatic leader" of the Black freedom struggle, Hedgeman was neither swayed nor seduced by his charismatic masculinism. Erica Edwards powerfully argues that

> [c]harisma is founded in three forms of violence: the historical or historio-graphical violence of reducing a heterogeneous Black freedom struggle to a top-down narrative of Great Man leadership; the social violence of performing social change in the form of a fundamentally antidemocratic form of authority; and the epistemological violence of structuring knowledge of Black political subjectivity and movement within a gendered hierarchy of political value that grants uninterrogated power to normative masculinity.[16]

Hedgeman's resistance to the charismatic race man leadership model personified by the Big Six exposes all that is wrong with the predominating force of charisma. On the one hand, The March exemplified magnificently what I term the *black radical spectacular*, wherein Blackness and black radical politics are placed on spectacular display and deployed for radically disruptive and productive ends. When a spectacle is being politicized to call attention to injustice, the charisma of those who speak for the crowd is important for political efficacy. On the other hand, this moment reinscribed the subordination of Black women's political issues to the more pressing concerns of a Black male-centered liberation narrative.

In line with Edwards's observations, Hedgeman's memoir resists both the historical and historiographical attempt of Black men, literally and figuratively, to write Black women out of the story and make them merely ornamental on stage; it exposes the power-laden gender relationships that informed the most symbolic of all Black marches; and it demonstrates the ways in which women attending the March were attuned in the immediate moment to the gendered hierarchy they witnessed. Hedgeman presciently connected Black women's marginalization within the March to the burgeoning white feminist movement, a connection that would not resound fully for Black women until later in the decade. Therefore, her race leadership memoir is an important site in Black women's intellectual geography because it contests and makes quite plain the fictive, yet violent, nature of accounts of Black leadership built upon recourse to the most charismatic, well-known Black leadership figures. That all these things were apparent to Hedgeman, and that she then fought back by telling her own story of Black political belonging, adds yet another dimension to the story of twentieth-century Black political leadership. Though Hedgeman's book was called *Trumpet Sounds*, her bugle calls went largely unnoticed. Her book foretold an approaching problem: How would Black men make space for Black women within the bounds of racial leadership? Though Hedgeman tried to intervene, she confronted a deep cultural resistance to even acknowledging Black women's intellectual capacity and contribution to discussions of movement building.

The Negro Woman Intellectual as Problem

Ponchitta Pierce's *Ebony* article, which appeared just two years after Hedgeman's book, provides compelling insight into how Black communities thought about intellectual Black women at the height of the Civil Rights era. First, the article is entitled "Problems of the Negro Woman Intellectual," though it might just as easily have been titled "*The Problem* of the Negro Woman Intellectual." In a late-twentieth-century remix to Du Bois, the magazine article essentially asked of Black women intellectuals, "How does it feel to be a problem?" The designation of Black women as intellectuals was so perplexing as to constitute a conceptual anomaly. By way of comparison, a content analysis of the rest of this special issue on women reveals that in the range of articles that profiled women in the arts, politics, and entertainment, this article is the only one in the issue that constructed its titular category and subject matter as "a problem."

Gwendolyn Brooks, interviewed for the article, asserted that though there were many Black women whom we might call "bright or brilliant, productive, effective, intelligent, creative, eminent, discerning, distinguished . . . the right to such adjectives [would not] automatically entitle them to the security also of the title, 'intellectual.' That is something else."[17] At face value, her final declaration that "intellectual" was "something else" effectively suggested that an intellectual is something else other than a Black woman—that no matter how many commendable traits a Black woman might possess, being an intellectual was a feat just beyond her reach. It is unsurprising then that Brooks excluded herself from the designation of "intellectual" as well.

To read slightly against the grain of Brooks's sentiment, I would suggest that there is also another moment of possibility in the space of the "something else." I say this, not wholly in terms of a notion of the Other, but in terms of the cultural vernaculars by which the Southern Black communities of my youth might say to a young woman who was audacious, and unapologetically self-possessed, "Girl, you are something else!" To be an intellectual is to be "something else." Black women are "something else!" It is that space of possibility, that unique Black women's cultural conceptualization of the "something else" as a form of energized, audacious, vivifying engagement with the world, that can, if we let it, animate conceptions of the Black woman intellectual.

Like her nineteenth-century forebears, Brooks then invoked the practice of listing that I discussed in the introduction, a practice in which Black women name the names of other Black women that are doing the work as a way to resist historiographical silencing. Brooks's list included just five women whom she considered intellectuals: novelist Paule Marshall, playwright Lorraine Hansberry, journalist and memoirist Era Bell Thompson, poet and professor Margaret Walker, and educator and author Margaret Just Butcher. Brooks's parsing of the term *intellectual* echoed Frederick Douglass's parsing of the term *famous*" back in 1892, when he cautioned Monroe Major, "[W]e have many estimable women of our variety but not many famous ones. . . . Many of the names you have are those of admirable persons, cultivated, refined, and ladylike. But it does not follow that they are famous. Let us be true and use language faithfully."[18] The right to simply even be called intellectual was a hard-fought battle.

Brooks's reluctance to classify any Black women as intellectuals left Pierce with the task of creating some kind of classificatory schema for defining Black women intellectuals. She formulated a continuum with four types of intellectuals. The woman at the pure end of the continuum was a "woman whose primary commitment is the search for knowledge. She delights in intellectual activity. . . . 'She doesn't flirt with or court ideas, she marries them.'"[19] This woman isolated herself in pursuit of ideas. Yet Pierce noted, "few Negro women, if any, know such experience." Black women rarely have had the luxury of solely pursuing the life of the mind and instead are expected—compelled even—to make their ideas "functional to aid in the social revolution of the Negro."[20] This, then, necessitated a second type of intellectual, "whom circumstances have thrust into the limelight." She had certain characteristics: "morality, creative vision, objectivity-integrity and a disciplined mind." As secondary characteristics, she should have "wit, urbanity, sound education, grasp of the humanities, appreciation of the arts, travel background. She is also expected to be action-oriented, to translate the ideas she creates into practical, socially useful programs."[21] This type of intellectual constituted the quintessential definition of a public intellectual.

There was also a third type, "a woman, who, while not refined by a solid education and sufficient exposure to culture, often because of poverty, more often because of segregation, does have an incisive and critical mind and a certain strength of conviction which makes her willing to live for her ideas rather than on them. Her whole life is one of ideas, [but] she acts them out rather than writing them down." Fannie Lou Hamer is an exemplar of this type of what we may term, a *pragmatic intellectual*. The pseudointellectual, "who spends more time talking than thinking, who spews out clichés and commonplaces, rather than ideas," bookended Pierce's spectrum.[22]

She also used the work of famed scholar Richard Hofstadter to distinguish between intelligence and intellect: "Intellect is the critical, creative and contemplative side of mind. Whereas intelligence seeks to grasp, manipulate, reorder, adjust, intellect examines, ponders, wonders, theorizes, criticizes, imagines. Intelligence will seize the immediate meaning in a situation and evaluate it. Intellect evaluates evaluations, and looks for the meanings in situations as a whole."[23] One woman, Mary Turner, quoted in the article suggested: "[T]he intellectual brings another capacity besides memory and learning to the field of knowledge. She must create entirely new elements."[24] And finally, Pierce returned to Gwendolyn Brooks, who said, "[A]n intellectual is one who observes and/or claws out facts and ideas, worries them, turns them inside out, assembles them, relates them, and—on the *highest* level— enhances or nourishes them."[25] Ranging from pure, to public, to pragmatic, to pseudo, Pierce imagined a far more dynamic world of possibilities for Black women intellectuals than other Black thinkers had managed to do.

Certainly, Black women have worried ideas, turned them inside out, and enhanced and nourished the constellation of terms that shape how we think about contemporary Black life. But even if Negro women intellectuals could be found, and this, it appears, was debatable, they faced age-old problems, the primary one being (apparently): Who would marry them? Just as Anna Julia Cooper, Ida B. Wells, Mary Church Terrell, and Pauli Murray had done at some point in their careers, Pierce had to grapple with the effect of Black marriage politics on Black women's intellectual work. In a section of the article, reminiscent of Murray's "Why Negro Girls Stay Single," interviewee Mary Turner lamented the tendency of Black women intellectuals to marry "beneath their intellectual levels." At the same time, however, she argued that "intellectualism should not be an excuse for ignoring care of the family." In her estimation, husbands and wives should negotiate these challenges such that "in the case of any working woman, the husband should be willing to pitch in where needed, without regarding each effort as a threat to his masculinity."[26] If all efforts at finding a suitable mate failed, Black women, Pierce argued, could pursue a range of other outlets: "She may turn to another race, often giving more than she receives. She may wind up with a 'shadow' husband who, while not her equal, at least doesn't impede her progress. . . . Failing in any of the above, the Negro woman generally decides to bypass marriage completely (by becoming Lesbian or celibate) or to take a lover."[27] Despite Pierce's assumption that heterosexual, companionate marriage was the desired end for all professional, intellectual women, she does at least gesture toward the possibility of other intimate arrangements. That the private lives of intellectual women were even up for such scrutiny indicates the extent to which Black women's bodies were fully conscripted for racial service, and their intimate lives subject to racial policing and cultural disciplining.

In fact, despite a largely positive reception of the Negro Woman special issue from both male and female readers of *Ebony*, one male reader wrote an angry letter in the October 1966 issue:

> As I sit here in my matriarchal home (father deceased) awaiting a divorce from my potentially power-mad wife of four months, I started reading the special issue of the August, 1966 edition of Ebony featuring Negro Women. I will not argue the point that Negroes are where they are now primarily because of the efforts of Negro women, since Negroes are still *nowhere*. . . . When the Negro woman realizes that real progress will come only when she decides to get in behind her Negro man, and not on top of him, freedom will come in a matter of years and not in hundreds of years.[28]

This clearly devastated reader blamed the dissolution of his marriage on his wife's failure to perform socially prescribed gender roles, a phenomenon that he suggested also militated against the broader Black freedom struggle. One woman quoted in the article mentioned that "potential suitors . . . also rebuked [her] for being more intellectual than emotional."[29] In many ways, then, high achieving Black women threatened and upended traditional gender role ideology, creating cultural anxiety about proper performances of masculinity and femininity and challenges for themselves in intimate contexts. As Brooks noted, "It is hard for the world to believe that a female is capable of thought. That she may possess an excellent brain is often unpalatable, sometimes a frightening and infuriating, distraction. And the brain-owner herself is steadily interrupted by demands on other parts of her body."[30] Brooks implicitly acknowledged the embodied nature of intellectual work, arguing that the cultural resistance to allowing Black women to become fully formed intellectuals happens largely upon the ground of exacting other kinds of bodily labor from them. This was not merely racial discrimination, but "another kind of discrimination—that of sex."[31]

Pierce argued that this continual onslaught of negative repercussions toward intellectual Black women produced a sense of defensiveness and aggressiveness and a set of cultural perceptions that cause Black women's performance of gender and femininity to be a source of cultural anxiety (and policing). As one commenter in the article put it, "I don't know if she is aware of it, but she tends to be neither masculine nor feminine."[32] For some, intellectual pursuits made Black women's gender identities illegible. Moreover, many Black people perceived the pursuit of intellectualism as a direct affront to the gendered goals of the project of respectability, which implicitly took as a goal the feminizing of Black womanhood in ways that made Black women legible as ladies worthy of protection in the public sphere.

Black women's intellectual pursuits produced a kind of cultural alienation in which "the educated Negro intellectual faced with a gap between herself, the world of intellectualism and the Negro community" could never fully go home again: "[T]he woman returns home from college and finds herself alienated from her home culture." Despite what Stephanie Shaw has called the carefully cultivated "ethic of socially responsible individualism"[33] instilled in Black women since their earliest days of educational access, by the middle of the twentieth century, Black women had to learn how to negotiate this access in the context of communities uncomfortable—not only with the elite access that education had provided but also with apparent gender performances that could not be culturally apprehended. Battles over the meaning and definition of the intellectual necessarily implicated an ongoing Black cultural project of constructing and reconstructing Black gender identity. Just as Pauline Hopkins had laid out the "duties" of the "true-race woman" in 1902, *Ebony* made clear the duties of Black women intellectuals in the 1960s: "[N]egro women intellectuals share two responsibilities: to really be an intellectual (although she may not eat well, have friends and be credited with loose screws) and to help shape a new definition of femininity." Much as Mary Church Terrell's college pals believed that taking the gentlemen's course would make her "unwomanly," nearly a century later, Black communities still worried about whether intellectual work would degrade the carefully crafted meanings of Black womanhood and femininity that the NACW School had fought so hard to inscribe within Black communities. Black women intellectuals like Pauli Murray and Toni Cade Bambara took on these battles for a new generation.

The Apostles of Black Consciousness and the Battle for Black Studies

Murray was one of the Negro women intellectuals featured in Pierce's *Ebony* article. In 1965, she became the first Black woman to receive the Doctor of Juridical Science degree from the Yale School of Law. She had also served on one of the subcommittees of John F. Kennedy's President's Commission on the Status of Women. In 1969, Murray was in her first year as professor of American Studies at Brandeis. Her time at Brandeis coincided with the 1969 student takeover of the campus as part of a push for a Black Studies curriculum. She had been recruited, in part, because of her activist background and the administration's hopes that students would view the hiring of Murray as an olive branch in their struggles to institute a Black Studies curriculum. In that position, she was forced to directly confront her deep ambivalence about the tactics and goals of the Black Power Movement. As she wrote, her "loyalties were divided between professional integrity and racial sympathy." Murray felt "light-years apart" from her students who "were engaged in a collective search for an acceptable identity, which took the form of pride in *Blackness*."[34] As I demonstrated in chapter three, Murray's concerns over race acted as surrogate discourse for her concerns over gender politics within Black communities. Thus, what her time at Brandeis reveals is not only a resistance to the racial politics of Black Power but also its gender politics.

Whereas Murray's militant descendants, whom she referred to in personal correspondence as the "apostles of Black consciousness," affirmed their identity by an allegiance to *Blackness*, Murray writes, "I had chosen to affirm my identity by anchoring myself firmly in the immediate American past, which had produced my mixed racial origins. . . . 'Black is beautiful' had no personal meaning for me. I had come to appreciate the beauty of American Negroes in all their rich variety of features, hair texture, and skin tone . . . revealing the harmonious genetic blending of several races."[35] Moreover, Murray writes:

> My strong individualism worked against tendencies toward a too strong alliance with a racial group to the exclusion of others not so identified. . . . To thrive, I need a society hospitable to all comers—Black as well as white, women as well as men, "the lame, the halt, the blind," the browns and yellows and reds—a society in which individuals were free to express their multiple origins and to share their variety of cultural strains without being forced into a categorical mold.[36]

Although they might have appreciated her ideals, Murray's students resented her choice to "anchor herself firmly in the American past," and they treated her like the relic that she unwittingly proclaimed herself to be. One student even kept a tally during Murray's lectures of how often she used "Negro" versus "Black."

Her insistence on integrationism, as the tides among Black youth turned toward nationalist aims, made Murray summarily ineffective at negotiating the increasingly hostile racial campus climate at Brandeis in 1969. One of her prized pupils, a senior honors student named Patricia Hill, boldly walked out of class, yelling "Black solidarity," as the campus erupted into widespread protest over the battle to adopt a Black studies curriculum in 1969.[37] In Murray's view, this "new phase of the struggle . . . confused and distorted the earlier goals" that "had been more universal, emphasizing the international solidarity of the working classes, the racial component of which had been a fire burning underground with only an occasional spurt of smoke and flame becoming visible."[38]

In 1942, Murray had written a passionate article entitled "Negro Youth's Dilemma" that captured all the angst and anger that characterized the young upstarts of her generation. In it she asked, "Am I to forget the festering sores of racial intolerance, injustice, brutality and humiliation eating at the core of my national allegiance?" In response to the critics who felt that Black people should "fight a white man's war" (WWII), Murray riposted, "[P]erhaps we are foolish in not realizing that Hitlerism would destroy us utterly while our fellow citizens in Sikeston, Missouri, would merely burn a few of us each year. But men who confront death and women who see the frustrations of their youth cannot be expected to distinguish between brutalities."[39] Murray had been attuned to the "the impatience of young people, the desire for action, whether or not they are informed and trained."[40] But she became increasingly bewildered, intimidated, and angered by this youthful impatience during its second iteration in the 1960s and '70s. Not only did the separatist rhetoric of Black Power "grate upon [her] sensibilities," she wrote, but she literally felt that she was "living in a world turned upside down [with] a complete reversal of the goals that had fired her own student activism."[41] Murray's narrative of Black female subjectivity and her political allegiances were predicated upon a very particular notion of Negro or Black racial identity, which foregrounded the mixed racial heritage and American values and aspirations of people of color. In this respect, her more assimilationist values found her embracing and reinscribing the politics of respectability for a later generation, rather than resisting it, as she had done earlier. At the bottom of a copy of "Negro Youth's Dilemma," Murray mused during her time at Brandeis on her generation's response to a new generation of discontented youth, wondering what, if anything, they could say to young people when conditions had changed so little.[42]

Murray's classroom at Brandeis—a veritable battleground within the space of the university between two different generational approaches to the Black freedom struggle—serves as an important site for mapping the intellectual geography and genealogy of Black feminist intellectual work. Her student Patricia Hill, whom we know today as Black feminist scholar Patricia

Hill Collins, deeply impacted Murray through her rejection of Murray's outmoded racial conservatism. Murray saw herself within the liberal civil rights traditions, which exemplified the kind of proper, dignified agitation of people like Mary Church Terrell. Patricia Hill represented a new school of thought altogether. For us, the schism between the two women, that is, Hill's clear rejection of Murray's race politics, indicate that race women intellectuals did not merely contend with gender politics. They also had differing ideas about racial identity that informed their approaches to combating racism and to the intellectual work of studying Black people. At the same time, this conflict connects in a literal, embodied way the academic origins of Black feminism to the larger project of Black Studies. This battle in Murray's classroom at Brandeis brings us back to the initial set of concerns that have driven this book. Their battles demonstrate the ways in which the categories of gender and race are imbricated by the institutional state of racial knowledge production.

As Murray would come to write just one year later in her essay, "The Liberation of Black Women": "[R]eading through much of the current literature on the black revolution, one is left with the impression that for all the rhetoric about self-determination, the main thrust of black militancy is a bid of black males to share power with white males in a continuing patriarchal society in which both black and white females are relegated to secondary status." Though she did not fully articulate her concerns in 1969, by 1970, her later critique made clear the political stakes of the masculinism of the Black Power Movement. In that regard, she helped to clarify one of the major critiques of Black Power that precipitated the development of a clearly articulated Black feminist political stance in the ensuing years, as articulated by groups like the National Black Feminist Organization and the Combahee River Collective, and by self-described "cultural workers" like Toni Cade Bambara.

The Negro Woman and Revolutionary Possibility

Toni Cade Bambara took up the politics of revolution, family, and knowledge production with decidedly less ambivalence than Murray. Her 1970 collection of essays, poetry, and cultural criticism, *Black Woman*, offered a resounding response to the cultural and intellectual discombobulation that had framed the works of Pierce and Cruse. Exemplary of Brooks's definition of a Negro woman intellectual, "who observes and/or claws out facts and ideas, worries them, turns them inside out, assembles them, relates them, and—on the *highest* level—enhances or nourishes them," Bambara and her colleagues considered a range of issues relevant to Black women's lives, turning them inside out, interrogating their relevance, discarding the ideas that were not useful, and offering a new set of conceptual frames for thinking and writing about Black women's lives and organizing for Black liberation. Bambara and her comrades did not see Black women's lives through the framework of a problem. Rather, like Cooper, they looked at Black women's lives and their embodied experience as a space of possibility.

The year 1970 was auspicious in terms of increasing Black women's cultural and intellectual legibility. With the publication of first novels by Alice Walker and Toni Morrison, Maya Angelou's publication of *I Know Why the Caged Bird Sings*, the posthumous editing and publication of Ida B. Wells's autobiography, *Crusade for Justice*, and the launch of *Essence Magazine*, Black women created a veritable Black women's literary renaissance. Echoing the creative literary and political ferment of the early 1890s, these women challenged existing institutional categories of knowledge production, storming the gates and making a way for themselves. At the same time, the placing of Angela Davis on the FBI's Ten Most Wanted List made clear the violent material conditions that Black women faced and the consequences of having Black radical politics. Bambara's text entered into a cultural moment eager to articulate and celebrate the multiplicity of Black women's lives. But the clarity that animates the intellectual project of *Black Woman* should be seen as a corrective to the crisis narrative that Harold Cruse propagated in *Crisis of the Negro Intellectual*. As her forebears like Williams and Terrell and Victoria Earle Matthews had done, Bambara's introduction to *Black Woman* laid out an ambitious plan of study about Black women's lives, while the essays pressed the case for a vibrant, burgeoning, politically informed, and culturally conscious Black women's movement.

Beverly Guy-Sheftall has written about her incredulity at the fact that it had never "occurred to Cruse that a comprehensive discussion of Black intellectuals should not have been an exclusively male discourse."[43] In addition to Cruse's egregious oversight, scholars of Black intellectual history have also placed Cruse's work within the tradition of landmark Black texts including "Du Bois's *The Souls of Black Folk*, Alain Locke's *The New Negro*, Carter G. Woodson's *The Mis-Education of the Negro*, and E. Franklin Frazier's *Black Bourgeoisie*."[44] The problem is that all of these texts were written by Black men.

Black Woman disrupts this all-male intellectual fraternity of texts both by signaling a set of past practices and by marshaling in an intellectual future for Black women. Proclaiming from the first line of the preface, "[W]e are involved in a struggle for liberation," Bambara goes on to clarify that the "first job is to find out what liberation for ourselves means, what work it entails, what benefits it will yield." "To do that," Black women often initially turned "to various fields of studies to extract materials, data necessary to define that term in respect to ourselves." However, their searches yielded little information. Much like Fannie Barrier Williams had recognized in 1893, Bambara and her contributors "note[d], however, all too quickly the lack of relevant material."[45] Psychiatry as a field continued to prescribe conservative definitions of womanhood and gender and to reduce the quest for liberation to the freedom of women "to enjoy orgasm." Moreover, much of the research on Black people tended to "clump the men and women together and focus so heavily on what white people have done to the psyches of Blacks, that what Blacks have done to and for themselves is overlooked, and what distinguishes the men from the women forgotten."[46]

In short, one major problem was that "'the experts' are still men, Black or white. And the images of the woman are still derived from their needs, their fantasies, their secondhand knowledge, their agreement with other 'experts.'" And it remained unclear to what extent the work of the few white women experts would be applicable to Black women: "[H]ow relevant are the truths, the experiences, the findings of white women to Black women? Are women after all simply women? I don't know that our priorities are the same, that our concerns and methods are the same, or even similar enough so that we can afford to depend on this new field of experts (white, female)."[47] Contesting the idea of the "expert" was critical to making space for Black women as intellectuals and combating decades of epistemic subjugation. Bambara worked from the premise that Black women's experiences, and their ability to articulate them, trumped questionable forms of external "expertise." She concluded, like the women of the NACW had done over three-quarters of a century earlier, that Black women must study themselves.

And they had been "forming work-study groups, discussion clubs, cooperative nurseries, cooperative businesses, . . . women's caucuses within existing organizations, [and] Afro-American women's magazines" with the goal of studying and making legible various kinds of Black female selfhoods. By celebrating the profusion of community spaces in which Black women were conducting self study, Bambara resisted a top-down account of racial knowledge production, demonstrating a range of horizontal spaces in which Black women were coming together to make sense of their own lives. Like the Club era, these community-based spaces, wherein Black women produced knowledge about themselves, constituted a kind of Black female counter-public space that allowed Black women to contest official, dominant narratives that undermined them morally, intellectually, and politically. However, unlike the clubwomen, Bambara did not seek to bring these groups under an organizational umbrella. Instead, she took a more traditional discursive approach, producing an anthology of writings through which Black women could testify to their embodied experiences. Farah Jasmine Griffin notes that the multiplicity of voices in this text, the dialogues between a range of differently situated Black women, is one of the most remarkable features of *Black Woman*: "[I]ts chorus of voices reminds us of the extra-academic origins of black women's intellectual work and of its concern with something other than curriculum, canons, fields, careers and academic publication. And while the academy is certainly an important site of struggle, it is not the only place where socially and politically engaged intellectuals ought to find themselves."[48] In short, the text reminds us that within Black women's intellectual history, "the sites of intellectual work are always shifting."[49] The extra-academic nature of the text and its willingness to offer a range of perspectives—both feminist and nonfeminist, nationalist and antinationalist—within its pages offers a discursive representation of a robust Black women's public sphere. Moreover, it demonstrates in practice that Black women's knowledge production is not beholden to the academy. By drawing on the works of a range of women to constitute her anthology, Bambara offered a robust model for what Black women's public intellectual work looked like.

Her text also marked one of the clearest generational shifts in the rhetoric about race womanhood. She noted that "unlike the traditional sororities and business clubs," her contributors "[seemed] to use the Black Liberation struggle rather than the American Dream as their yardstick, their gauge, their vantage point."[50] This represented a marked shift from the rhetoric of liberal race women like Williams and Murray, whose lives bookend the paradigmatic frame of American peculiarity as a critique of American exceptionalism. Unlike Murray, whose primary quest was for American acceptance, Bambara's race women used Black freedom as the measuring stick for determining racial progress, noting that, in fact, these two ideals were not congruent. Moreover, the textual debate between Black nationalist women and Black feminist women challenged the distinctive integrationist versus nationalist binary that Cruse had set forth in *Crisis*.[51]

Ironically, however, the major gains made by Black women in politics in the 1970s signals that public Black women, in fact, *were* using the American Dream as a yardstick. In 1972, Shirley Chisholm ran for president on the Democratic Party ticket. That same year, Barbara Jordan was elected to the House of Representatives, becoming the first woman ever to represent the state of Texas. By the mid 1970s, Barbara Jordan became a kind of guardian of the public trust. Her well-known eloquent speech in the wake of the Watergate scandal and her keynote address at the 1976 Democratic convention relied upon the most traditional of American liberal values. In defense of Nixon's impeachment and the U.S. Constitution, which she felt his crimes had undermined, Jordan famously declared:

> Earlier today, we heard the beginning of the Preamble to the Constitution of the United States, "We, the people." It is a very eloquent beginning. But when the document was completed on the seventeenth of September 1787 I was not included in that "We, the people." I felt somehow for many years that George Washington and Alexander Hamilton just left me out by mistake. But through the process of amendment, interpretation and court decision I have finally been included in "We, the people." . . . My faith in the Constitution is whole, it is complete, it is total.[52]

Jordan's rhetoric was decidedly centrist and steeped in a kind of American civic nationalism that has characterized Black women's public thought for as long as they have had access to the public stage. However, Jordan's words also signaled a different moment, one in which Black women were asked to step into the national imaginary as a keeper of the public trust and an arbiter of the nation's moral consciousness.

Shirley Chisholm's rhetoric was very different. Though her commitment to electoral politics placed her solidly within the liberal democratic tradition, her speeches were peppered with rhetoric from the radical Black women that Toni Cade Bambara highlighted. At a 1974 speech for a conference on Black women in America, Chisholm argued that Black women like "Ida Wells [who] kept her newspaper free by walking the streets of Memphis, Tennessee in the 1890s with two pistols on her hips" and other women like "Mary McLeod Bethune, Mary Church Terrell, Daisy Bates, and Diane Nash" had played "a crucial role in the total fight for the freedom of this nation."[53] In the same speech, she quoted from Frances Beale's essay, "Double Jeopardy," which appeared in *Black Woman*. And then, as if echoing Bambara, Chisholm averred:

> It is very interesting to note that everyone—with the exception of the Black woman herself—has been interpreting the black woman. It is very interesting to note that the time has come that black women can and must no longer be passive, complacent recipients of whatever the definitions of the sociologists, the psychologists and the psychiatrists will give to us. Black women have been maligned, misunderstood, misinterpreted—who knows better than Shirley Chisholm?[54]

Chisholm encouraged her audience not to accept this state of affairs but "to stand up and be counted." In this charge, she echoed the same kind of organized anxiety, or as Bambara termed *impatience*, that had driven Black women over the last several years to begin to study themselves. Bambara had noted Black women's impatience with the white women's liberation movement and with "all the 'experts' zealously hustling us folks for their doctoral theses or government appointments." To their great chagrin, and again "impatience," (a word that Bambara repeated six times in one paragraph), "in the whole biography of feminist literature, literature immediately and directly relevant to us, wouldn't fill a page."[55] Chisholm's direct engagement with Bambara's text through the work of Frances Beale demonstrates the very kind of critical feedback loop that women like Fannie Barrier Williams had called into existence through their work in women's clubs. Chisholm then used the practice of listing, calling the names of many race women, including Wells and Terrell, to construct her own intellectual and political genealogy through their life and work.

Bambara's text attempted to rectify this need for self-study, but she soon realized the perhaps too-ambitious scope of the book. Among a few of the topics in her twelve-point list were to "set up a comparative study of the woman's role as she saw it in all the Third World Nations; examine the public school system and blueprint some viable alternatives; explore ourselves and set the record straight on the matriarch and the evil Black bitch; pay tribute to all our warriors from the ancient times to the slave trade to Harriet Tubman to Fannie Lou Hamer to the woman of this morning; interview the migrant workers and the grandmothers of the UNIA; analyze the Freedom Budget and design ways to implement it; thoroughly discuss the whole push for Black Studies programs and a Black university; get into the whole area of sensuality, sex (and is not in original); and finally "chart the steps necessary for forming a working alliance with all nonwhite women of the world for the formation of, among other things, a clearing house for the exchange of information." As this "list grew and grew," she came to understand it as a "lifetime of work," of which the anthology constituted "just a beginning."[56]

In many ways, though, Black women who hoped to fulfill the ambitious intellectual projects she laid out were beginning *again*. Fannie Barrier Williams, Gertrude Bustill Mossell, and Victoria Earle Matthews had been calling for racial knowledge production about Black women since 1893. Over three-quarters of a century later, however, Black women still were not seen as experts on their own social condition, and, indeed, if *Ebony* is to be believed, not capable of any appreciable expertise at all. Bambara's list of items of study, however, did offer a set of priorities for Black and women-of-color feminisms that have been taken up across a range of disciplines at the present date. The priorities she laid out continue to inform new avenues of study within the broader fields of Black feminism and Black Studies.

Black Woman did effectively take up the charge from Pierce's *Ebony* article to lay out a "new definition of Black femininity." So, for instance, in Bambara's oft-cited essay "On the Issue of Roles," she faced head-on the question of "the Black woman's Role in the Revolution," by questioning both the binary definitions of masculine and feminine and offering up her own structural account of Black gender categories. Calling stereotypical notions of masculine and feminine "a lot of merchandising nonsense," Bambara argued that gender binaries militated against "what revolution for self is all about—the whole person." These questions about the relations of gendered identities to revolutionary politics implicated each other, for "the usual notion of sexual differentiation in roles is an obstacle to political consciousness, [because] the way those terms are generally defined and acted upon in this part of the world is a hindrance to full development. And that is a shame, for a revolutionary must be capable of, above all, total self-autonomy."[57]

Sounding a note of concern similar to that expressed by Murray twenty years earlier, Bambara complained about Black women being "jammed in the rigid confines of those basically oppressive social contrived roles," arguing that these investments were rooted in the economic demands made on men to accumulate property in a capitalist system and with the imposed cultural dictates of Christianity. If precolonial African societies were an indicator, Bambara argued (despite her skepticism over white anthropological accounts of Africa), "no rigid and hysterical separation based on sexual taboos" existed.[58] Still, Black men frequently remained invested in the idea "that Black women must be supportive and patient so that Black men can regain their manhood. The notion of womanhood—they argue . . . is dependent on his defining his manhood. So the shit goes on." These men, she accused, were "obsessive," about their "lost balls." But revolution "entails at the very least cracking through the veneer of this sick society's definition of 'masculine' and 'feminine.'"[59] Not only would engagement with revolution transform the self, and implode gender role ideology, but it would necessarily transform family structures. Invoking Fanon's *A Dying Colonialism*, Bambara argued that when willfully engaged in a revolutionary freedom struggle, "the 'family' was no longer a socially ordained nuclear unit to perpetuate the species or legitimize sexuality, but an extended kinship of cellmates and neighbors linked in the business of actualizing a vision of a liberated society."[60] As Brooks demanded of intellectuals, Bambara turned the notion of family on its head and then offered up a completely reconfigured concept that she viewed as more relevant to the aims of Black revolutionary struggle. Black women, particularly Black clubwomen, had been the original theoreticians of the Black family as an institution. Like Cooper who argued that "a race is but a total of families," Bambara connected family configuration to the articulation of racial identity or "Blackhood."[61] But she rejected the respectable ideas of family that Cooper and early race women believed in. Bambara entered into that long intellectual legacy of theorizing race and family, cultivated by Black women, showing more concretely the linkages between one's racial goals and the ways in which that directly related to the structure of the Black family. However, she rejected the liberal, assimilationist paradigms that Murray and others adopted by associating binary configurations of gender with hierarchical ideas propagated by white supremacy, capitalism, and Christianity. Bambara thus insisted on the need for a political and economic revolution.

But that revolution could begin only with Black men and Black women obtaining a "sound analysis." This sound analysis regarding "roles" would lead Black people "to submerge all breezy definitions of manhood/womanhood (or reject them out of hand if you're not squeamish about being called neuter) until realistic definitions emerge through a commitment to Blackhood."[62] Bambara thus concluded that Black communities would create structures to govern gender based upon racial dictates and political priorities, but those structures could not in any way be predicated on the subordination of femininity vis-à-vis female bodies to masculinity or male bodies. Moreover, her conception of Blackhood disentangled respectable gender categories from the articulation of Blackness. She argued for a new way to articulate and make legible Black humanity, not predicated on an investment in binary gender identities or limiting notions of man*hood* and woman*hood*. If the end of Reconstruction had made the articulation of respectable gender identities an urgent project, the immediacy of the political concerns of the Black Power era urged and necessitated new articulations of Blackness and gender. Though Bambara does not elaborate any further here on the meaning and function of "Blackhood," she implicitly argues that the ways we understand race are inextricably linked to the ways we understand and articulate gender. Black communities needed entirely new conceptions of gender, ones rooted in the primacy of preserving Black life, in order to move toward liberatory articulations of Black identity. Ironically, though Bambara's clear commitment to Black national politics might have been off-putting to Murray, undoubtedly Murray would have reveled in Bambara's calls to throw off the strictures of traditional gender roles. Indeed, both women attempt to retheorize and expand Black women's gender possibilities by offering up new (though wholly different) conceptions of racial identity. Murray embraced the multiracial, whereas Bambara opted for an identity rooted in peak Blackness. Bambara's notion of Blackhood constitutes a twentieth-century attempt at defining the very kind of racial sociality that Fannie Barrier Williams had been concerned with in the late 1890s. Antirespectable in its rejection of traditional gender roles, Blackhood as a form of revolutionary, queer, Black racial sociality, had the potential—and indeed even the intrinsic demand—to formulate new ideas about the performance of Black gender identities.

Putting Black Women on the List

The intellectual work of *Black Woman* as text is important because it reconstituted Black women's historic practice of listing through the form of the literary anthology. Black women had employed edited compendiums of coauthored biographies as a form of intellectual history since the nineteenth century. Gertrude Mossell's *Work of the Afro-American Woman* (1894) proclaimed, "[T]he intellectual history of a race is always of value in determining the past and future of it," and she believed Black women's lives should be a documented part of Black intellectual history. Hallie Quinn Brown's *Homespun Heroines* (1925) and Sadie Daniel's *Women Builders* (1931) continued this work of profiling prominent African American women leaders well into the twentieth century. However, we should also understand Bambara's turn to the anthology composed of actual writing by multiple Black women authors as its own kind of Black feminist intellectual method that could disrupt the supremacy of lists dominated by men.

Alice Walker reminds us that Zora Neale Hurston was almost relegated to obscurity because of the inherent sexism in received lists and canons of important Black thinkers. She writes: "[T]he first time I heard Zora's *name*, I was auditing a Black literature class taught by the great poet Margaret Walker, at Jackson State College, in Jackson, Mississippi. . . . The class was studying the 'usual' giants of Black literature: Chesnutt, Toomer, Hughes, Wright, Ellison, and Baldwin with the hope of reaching LeRoi Jones very soon. Jessie Fauset, Nella Larsen, Ann Petry, Paule Marshall . . . and Zora Neale Hurston were names appended, like verbal footnotes, to the illustrious all-male list that paralleled them."[63] Black women's repeated encounters with the "all-male list" have structured every facet of our intellectual lives.

Walker and other women, including literary scholar and Combahee River Collective cofounder Barbara Smith, countered the intellectual tyranny of the "all-male list" when they taught the first courses on Black Women Writers in the early 1970s. Walker taught the first Black women writers courses at Wellesley and at the University of Massachusetts around 1971 or 1972. Her list included "Nella Larsen, Frances Watkins Harper (poetry and novel), Dorothy West, Ann Petry, [and] Paule Marshall, among others." Smith taught Hurston's work in a Black women's writers course in 1973.[64] These first courses, taken together with literary criticism from scholars like Barbara Smith and Mary Helen Washington, provided the intellectual scaffolding for the Black Women's Literary Renaissance and for the reemergence of the Black woman literary intellectual as another iteration of the race woman figure. Frances Harper had been the first.

Black feminists' anthological practice of listing reminds us that putting Black women's names on the list simultaneously constituted putting Black women's thoughts on the map and making space for the work of a range of Black women thinkers to be taken seriously. Bambara's work gave birth to several women of color feminist anthologies, including *All the Women Are White, All the Blacks Are Men: But Some of Us Are Brave* (1982), *This Bridge Called My Back: Radical Writings by Women of Color* (1983), and *Home Girls: A Black Feminist Anthology* (1983). These works did not attempt to constitute canons of new thinkers, but rather to demonstrate the breadth of existing Black and women-of-color thinkers.

As literary intellectuals, Bambara, Toni Morrison, and Alice Walker took on the task of reformulating the late-twentieth-century landscape of Black women's intellectual thought, not only by writing groundbreaking novels like Morrison's *The Bluest Eye* (1970) and *Sula* (1973), and Walker's *The Third Life of Grange Copeland* (1970) and *Meridian* (1976), but also by using a range of positions in influential institutions to shift the course of Black women's creative intellectual production and intellectual history. As an editor at Random House, Toni Morrison was responsible for launching the careers of Gayl Jones and Gloria Naylor; all three women's novels have become canonical in the study of African American women's literature.

Walker took it upon herself to excavate Zora Neale Hurston's literary intellectual legacy as both a novelist and an anthropologist. In 1973, she traveled to Hurston's hometown of Eatonville, Florida—in what has become one of the origin stories of contemporary Black feminism—in order to locate Hurston's grave and place a marker on it. Standing in a snake-infested graveyard, with over grown weeds, Walker calls out "Zora! I'm here. Are you?"[65] When she found herself standing in a sinkhole that seemed to fit the description of where Hurston is buried, she placed a grave marker there.

In many ways though, her looking, her calling out, her naming of her own presence, and her questioning of the presence of her intellectual and creative forebear is emblematic of the contemporary quest of Black feminist intellectuals to retrieve Black women's intellectual history. Walker's story is well known among Black feminist scholars, who for the last four decades have excavated and created a viable discipline of Black feminist literary criticism. Because of her insistence on telling Zora's story, many of Hurston's books are back in print, and her most well-known novel, *Their Eyes Were Watching God*, has even been made into a movie. As a scholar from a newer generation, I am taking my cues not primarily from Hurston, but rather from Walker, who sojourned through the field looking until she found Hurston.

The field of African American Women's Intellectual History is strewn about with unrecognized Black female genius. Walker's generation of scholars has done a great job of marking the graves of these women, so to speak, of making the case for their value and their presence. Yet, it is also true that too many of our intellectual genealogies and geographies begin and end in overgrown graveyards, amid a silent cacophony of unmarked graves. It is my generation's job not only to make sure those markers remain meticulously landscaped and in full view but also to dig deeper, to think seriously about the material conditions and intellectual terms upon which our thinkers are memorialized, and to retrieve and revisit their work with renewed vigor and scrutiny. In this book, I seek to take seriously the intellectual formulations and methods put forth by these women; the range of methods they employed and deployed to challenge masculinist narratives of Black intellectual production; and the range of ways that they sought to throw off the dictates of Black respectability politics, to create new formulations of gender, and to offer new ideas of what a Black public might look like. Black women's intellectual work has been bound integrally to our understanding of notions of the public and notions of gender politics and what they allow and disallow. The term *race woman* has no uniform meaning. But it does name and help to make visible multiple generations of Black women who dedicated their lives to the Black freedom struggle, not only by theorizing and implementing programs of racial uplift but also by contesting the gendered politics of racial knowledge production and pushing back against limiting notions of Blackness and womanhood. In so doing, these women created a robust and enduring tradition of Black public intellectual work.

Epilogue

Straight men, unintentionally or intentionally, have
taken the work of queer Black women and erased our
contributions. Perhaps if we were the charismatic
Black men many are rallying around these days, it
would have been a different story, but being Black
queer women in this society (and apparently within
these movements) tends to equal invisibility and non-
relevancy. We completely expect those who benefit
directly and improperly from White supremacy to try
and erase our existence. We fight that every day. But
when it happens amongst our allies, we are baffled,
we are saddened, and we are enraged.

—Alicia Garza (2014)

In July 2013, organizers Patrisse Khan-Cullors, Alicia Garza, and Opal Tometi used social media to proclaim that #BlackLivesMatter (BLM) after
George Zimmerman was acquitted of the murder of seventeen-year-old
unarmed Florida teen Trayvon Martin. By the next summer, August 2014,
these young Black women found themselves at the helm of a new national
civil rights movement as Black people in Ferguson, Missouri, and around
the country took to the streets to protest the slaughter of eighteen-year-old
Michael Brown by Ferguson police officer Darren Wilson. Wilson claimed
that the unarmed youth attacked him in his police car after Brown and his
friend allegedly refused the officer's command to "get the fuck up on the
sidewalk" instead of walking in the middle of a residential street in his neighborhood. By October 2014, Alicia Garza wrote a herstory of the burgeoning
BLM Movement, after early attempts at co-optation threatened to erase the
intellectual and political labor undertaken by these three Black women. Much
like Anna Arnold Hedgeman, Pauli Murray, and other race women who
had come before her, she called out and stridently critiqued the continued
celebration of heterosexual, charismatic Black male leadership.[1] Moreover,

her comments appeared at *Feminist Wire*, an online site founded by two Black feminist academics, Tamura Lomax and Hortense Spillers, in order to highlight conversations of relevance to women of color about social justice. In the streets, in the academy, and online, Black women thinkers continue to reimagine and reshape the terms upon which Black women's knowledge production takes place. It is, therefore, befitting that the intellectual geography and genealogy that I have been building in this book end at the beginning of this new, dynamic, and powerful women-led Movement for Black Lives.

The largely Black female leadership of the Movement for Black Lives has the potential to usher in a new era in our thinking about the most effective models of racial leadership. Both Garza and Khan-Cullors are queer Black women, and they have insisted that the Black Lives Matter leadership and organizing model move, as Garza mentioned in her herstory,

> beyond the narrow nationalism that can be prevalent within some Black communities, which merely call on Black people to love Black, live Black and buy Black, keeping straight cis Black men in the front of the movement while our sisters, queer and trans and disabled folk take up roles in the background or not at all. Black Lives Matter affirms the lives of Black queer and trans folks, disabled folks, Black-undocumented folks, folks with records, women and all Black lives along the gender spectrum.[2]

In this regard, these new Black women leaders—including Johnetta Elzie, Brittany Packnett, Brittany Ferrell, Alexis Templeton, Charlene Carruthers, Samantha Master, Elle Hearns, Jasmine Abdullah Richards, and Melina Abdullah[3]—are shaping a movement that rejects the kind of masculinist posturing that caused so much grief for women like Ida B. Wells in the nineteenth century and Pauli Murray in the twentieth century. This movement is inherently Cooperian in its insistence that Black women's bodies and lives (cis and trans) offer a space of possibility and place through which to cathect our best thinking about how to get free. Yet, Garza's fears about the erasure of Black women's intellectual and political labor are well-founded and avoiding this common trap with Black women's contributions requires a critical vigilance to document, respect, engage, and take seriously the thinking of Black women who continue to lead our movements.

My goal in *Beyond Respectability* is to take seriously the work of Black women thinkers and to demonstrate the value that Black women's long histories of knowledge production on behalf of Black people can have to contemporary intellectual conversations. Despite the fact that Black feminism, as a critical locus of Black women's twentieth-century knowledge production, has become a fully institutionalized field of academic specialization since the late 1970s, my contention in this book is that there is still a requisite and tacit failure to take Black women's work, as thinkers and theorists on broader questions affecting Black people, seriously. Yes, Black feminist women's arguments about the centrality of gender to racial concerns have gained major academic currency, as evidenced by the broad use of intersectional discourse in numerous fields and disciplines. And yes, this new Black Lives Matter Movement, particularly as conceived by Garza, Tometi, and Khan-Cullors has made Black feminist politics the currency of Black radical thought. But the fact that Alicia Garza's comments written in the second decade of the twenty-first century, sound eerily similar to commentary from Anna Julia Cooper writing in the nineteenth century, and Pauli Murray, Toni Cade Bambara, and bell hooks writing in the twentieth suggests that not enough has changed.

bell hooks attended college in the early 1970s, just as Women's Studies programs and courses on Black women's literature and history entered the academy. By the late 1970s, figures like Barbara Smith and Mary Helen Washington were steering Black feminism into academic spaces and by 1991, more than ten years after she published her first book, bell hooks became the poster child for a new generation of professional Black feminist women who had obtained doctoral degrees, written books, and taught courses about differential aspects of Black women's lives. In a collection of essays and interviews that she coauthored with Cornel West entitled *Breaking Bread*, hooks reflected on the working conditions and livelihoods of Black women intellectuals in an essay of the same title. hooks, very much in line with Pierce, made clear that the continued challenge of seeing Black women as intellectuals is rooted in our understanding of what it means to be an intellectual:

> Moreso than any group of women in this society, black women have been seen as "all body, no mind." . . . To justify white male sexual exploitation and rape of Black females during slavery, white culture had to produce an iconography of Black female bodies that insisted on representing them as highly sexed, the perfect embodiment of primitive, unbridled eroticism. . . . Seen as sexual sign, Black female bodies are placed in a category that, culturally speaking, is deemed far removed from the life of the mind.[4]

As Black women in the current moment lead street protests in major cities to combat police brutality, they continue to confront the possibility that their labors will be perceived as "all body, no mind."

hooks's observation clarifies both the fervent embrace of respectability politics among historic Black women thinkers and the reason that respectability politics remain a deeply contested ground among Black feminist thinkers, especially in the current movement. Her observation makes clear why Anna Julia Cooper's formulation of embodied discourse constitutes a radical act. Cooper, whose theorization of embodiment I discuss in the prologue, placed the material condition of the Black female body at the center of her understanding and theorization of Black life, politics, and intellectual possibility. In doing so, she disrupted the tacit and prevailing logic of Western thought that Black women's bodies are merely there to do reproductive and service labor within Black communities. These questions about embodiment and reproductive labor surface over and over again in the lives of women examined in this book. Whether it is concerns about how public intellectual work made Black women unfit for marriage or other kinds of regulation of Black female sexuality, particularly of the unmarried and nonheterosexual varieties, the work of being a race woman demands an engagement with the politics of the black (female) body. Consequently, the black female body takes center stage in much of the thought work produced by Black women, as they discuss the material effects of poor social conditions on African American life chances.

I argue within these pages that Black feminist thought is at a critical disadvantage because of failure to robustly engage the rich intellectual legacies bequeathed us by race women of the NACW School of Thought. Thus, I challenge the continued use of the paradigms of respectability and dissemblance as the only ways to read the historic Black female body as it shows up in race women's texts, politics, and theorizing. In addition to situating Cooper and other race women's use of embodied discourse as a corrective to these foregoing frameworks, I discuss in chapter two the ways in which Mary Church Terrell crafted a model of what she termed *proper, dignified agitation* to contest racism and sexism. Though the tactics were grounded in respectable forms of protest, Terrell's written and spoken advocacy against the perils and pitfalls of racism in a democratic republic invoked the best traditions of militant racial agitation. Though she was one of the twentieth century's foremost architects of respectability politics, particularly among African American women, her whole story does not rise and fall upon the dictates of respectability, and my challenge in this book has been to take her political theorizing seriously.

Moreover, I suggest that one of the challenges of doing the kind of histori-cally grounded Black feminist theorizing that I call for necessitates resisting the gendered and raced dimensions of terms and concepts like "intellectual." By challenging the racial and gender exclusivity of the term *intellectual*, this book opens up a space to reimagine Black women's political and activist work as work rooted deeply in a set of shared intellectual concerns about Black humanity and personhood, about the problem of violence, about sexual politics, about getting a job, about putting together strong Black families, and about notions of community and unity. Thus, I argue for reconsidering the National Association of Colored Women as its own school of racial thought committed to training Black women to become public intellectuals and students of their own social condition. Though in the twenty-first-century academy it might seem like a foregone conclusion that Black women can be, are, and have been intellectuals, this book reminds us, that unlike for race men, the right to assume the mantle of the "intellectual" among race women has been a contested battleground, and that a critical part of their knowledge production in the nineteenth *and* twentieth centuries was writing against any formulation of the intellectual that attempted to construct Black women outside its parameters.

Despite an explosion of Black women academics in the ensuing two decades and a wholesale institutionalization of Black feminist studies in the academy where the study of intersectionality is now almost considered so regular as to be passé, there is still a dearth of real knowledge about Black women public intellectuals. If pressed to name the most prominent Black thinkers of our day, the list looks remarkably like it did nearly twenty-five years ago. Most of the people named would be men like Cornel West and Henry Louis Gates, Michael Eric Dyson, Marc Lamont Hill, and Robin D. G. Kelley.

However, the list of women would still primarily include Toni Morrison, Alice Walker, bell hooks, and Patricia Williams. The one remarkable addition would be Melissa Harris-Perry.

Harris-Perry, a full professor of political science at Wake Forest University, hosted a popular weekend cable news show offering overtly Black feminist cultural and political commentary on everything from politics to popular culture from 2012 to 2016. Her show absolutely transformed the landscape of possibility for Black women intellectuals by routinely highlighting the important intellectual contributions of a range of other Black women thinkers inside and outside the academy. In November 2015, Melissa Harris-Perry and Valerie Jarrett, the director of the White House Council on Women and Girls convened a historic summit at the White House called "Advancing Equity for Women and Girls of Color."[5] This work is directly attributable to the organizing undertaken by Professor Kimberlé Crenshaw and a group of academics, activists, and philanthropists, after President Obama pledged in 2014 to address the social injustices facing only men and boys of color through an initiative called My Brother's Keeper. Black women were outraged at the President's attempt to exclude Black women and girls, who experience racial injustice right alongside Black men and boys. In addition to an open letter organized by Crenshaw's African American Policy Forum (AAPF) and a national traveling series of town halls featuring testimonies of women and girls of color organized by Crenshaw and Joanne Smith of Girls for Gender Equity, the AAPF issued a series of reports documenting the unique inter-sectional jeopardies faced by Black girls.[6] Harris-Perry took up this cause by featuring stories about this counter-organizing against My Brother's Keeper on her show and then using the Anna Julia Cooper Research Center, which she founded at Wake Forest University, to partner with the White House in a ten-year research project about Black women and girls.

These efforts to make visible and legible the plight of Black women and girls, this campaign to rescue them from political and social obscurity, fits within the long history, documented in this book, of Black women making the case that Black women's lives are worthy of study and that their struggles are worthy of social remedy. The organizing of Crenshaw, Harris-Perry, Smith, and others also places these race women within a history of Black women using institutional access and resources to make the plight of Black women and girls visible. It is frustrating that Black women have to keep fighting such battles in every generation. But this book demonstrates that they have a very robust and multigenerational playbook to aid their efforts.

Harris-Perry's time as a host at MSNBC was nothing if not embattled. In 2014, when Ta-Nehisi Coates, an editor at *Atlantic,* wrote that Harris-Perry is "America's foremost public intellectual," there was a firestorm of controversy after Dylan Byers, a journalist at *Politico,* suggested that such assertions damaged Coates's credibility.[7] Though Harris-Perry achieved what no other tenured Black woman professor has ever achieved in being the eponymous host of her own major cable network show, Byers still called her intellectual credentials into question. When Harris-Perry departed her show in February 2016 after a contentious struggle with the network over editorial control of her show, she wrote in an email to her staff: "I will not be used as a tool for their purposes. I am not a token, mammy, or little brown bobble head. I am not owned by [Andy] Lack, [Phil] Griffin, or MSNBC. I love our show. I want it back. I have wept more tears than I can count and I find this deeply painful, but I don't want back on air at any cost."[8] Harris-Perry's dignified and costly stance against a major corporation reflects the enduring battles for dignity and self-authorship that have characterized Black women's in-tellectual work in the public sphere. But her decision to make visible both the love and the pain caused by the decision to leave on her own terms also reflects a long history of Black women naming the embodied and affective sacrifices that shape their advocacy work on behalf of Black communities. It also reflects the ways that Black women thinkers in the public sphere continually move beyond the politics of respectability and the dictates of dissemblance, when situations warrant it, opting to make their pain, their anger, and their contempt for injustice visible and palpable. The resolute defiance contained in Harris-Perry's statement, that "I will not be used as a tool for their purposes," reminds us of Black women's continuing quest for what Anna Julia Cooper called "undisputed dignity" and the right to have one's voice and one's humanity respected as equal to that of white men with power.

In his 2008 book *Betrayal: How Black Intellectuals Have Abandoned the Ideals of the Civil Rights Era*, Vanderbilt University Professor and literary critic Houston Baker offers a scathing assessment of those engaged in Black thought leadership in the forty years since the passing of the Civil Rights era. Interestingly enough, Baker returns to the figure of the "race man/woman" as a Black leadership ideal, reasserting the primacy of both a race-centered analysis and a certain level of racial kinship and loyalty in defining this aggregate group that he terms *race people*. The problem, to wit, is that the intellectuals who have taken center stage in the post–Civil Rights era fall into two lamentable categories according to Baker: "black centrists and black neoconservatives."[9] Taking on black celebrity public intellectuals, including Princeton professor Cornel West, Harvard Professor Henry Louis Gates, and Georgetown Professor Michael Eric Dyson, among others, Baker accuses them of the high crime of racial *betrayal*. More specifically, they have refused or failed (it is unclear which) to carry forth the legacy of Dr. Martin Luther King, whom Baker characterizes as "not only the most exemplary race man ever born in the United States, but also the greatest black public intellectual leader of the liberation struggle our world has ever known."[10] Although Baker raises a number of important concerns about the ways in which the radical messaging of the contemporary Black intellectual elite has been co-opted by mainstream forces and the seduction of celebrity, his turn back to King should give us pause.

Most notably, Baker's chapter "After Civil Rights: The Rise of Black Public Intellectuals," manages not to mention even one Black woman public intellectual from the past or present. This is in part a problem of numbers, because the rise of prominent Black female public intellectuals did not keep pace in the post–Civil Rights years with the rise of figures like West, Gates, or Dyson. This is precisely why folks like hooks and Harris-Perry (who came to prominence after Baker's book) are so visible. Their brilliance and intellectual skill is undeniable, but they also have a level of visibility available to only a select and elite few Black women scholars. However, the refusal to even acknowledge the work and career of bell hooks is an egregious error on Baker's part. Not only has she maintained a strident critique of structures of *white supremacist capitalist patriarchy*, a term she coined and popularized, but she has resisted formal structures of elitism in a number of ways that dovetail the kinds of radical political critique for which Baker calls. Baker also offers a paragraph of acknowledgment to Angela Davis, particularly her work on prison abolition, in the final chapter of *Betrayal*. But other than cursory gestures to the work of women like Davis and Tricia Rose, Black women are absent from Baker's account of Black intellectual leadership in the twentieth century. Though Baker claims gender inclusivity in his use of the term *race people*, it is clear that he thinks race men have failed us and that a deliberate turn back to the race man model of the King era is the only thing that has the potential to save us. But Baker's account of the problems in Black leadership say much more about the persistence and limitations of the politics of racial manhood in defining and mapping effective forms of Black leadership than they do about the actual state of Black leadership. The story shifts dramatically when we look toward the work of race women.

In *Beyond Respectability*, I join with other scholars such as Erica Edwards in her book, *Charisma and the Fictions of Black Leadership*, and Robert Patterson in his book, *Exodus Politics: Civil Rights and Leadership in African American Literature and Culture*, in calling for a sure end to the charismatic race man model of leadership with which folks like Baker, West, Gates, and others continue to enjoy a tortured romance. Edwards writes against a thoroughgoing Black community investment in charismatic male leaders, and Patterson argues that this investment informs a broad-based belief in "exodus politics," a Black cultural paradigm rooted in the biblical Moses narrative which, "disallows the possibility of Black female leadership" and "produces a gender hierarchy that prioritizes black men, black men's leadership, and black men's political interests."[11] By (re)turning to the figure of the race woman, *Beyond Respectability* interrogates the persisting cultural and gender narratives that continue to circumscribe Black women's leadership possibilities within African American communities and the broader public sphere. I maintain that at the center of this debate is a kind of skepticism about Black women's ability to be creative and broad *thinkers* about race issues. Certainly, Black women are viewed as committed, devoted, reliable, and dependable *workers*, but in the twenty-first century we still believe far too often that the thinking should be left up to men.

Accounts like Baker's engage in just the sort of Jane Crow politics that have shaped Black male intellectual practices and which Pauli Murray called out during her time as a law student at Howard University. Murray's invocation of the term *Jane Crow*, which I excavate and examine in chapter three, offered a thorough and unrelenting critique of the kinds of sexist practices that shaped the vaunted male leadership class of the Civil Rights generation, the very leadership class that Baker uncritically supports. Those practices almost silenced the brilliant Pauli Murray, not only through explicit sexism, but also through covert forms of homophobia and heterosexism couched in the language of respectability. These Jane Crow politics concretized a racial leadership model that allowed only (putatively) straight, middle-class men to lead. Part of what it must mean to be a race man in the twenty-first century is to radically disavow the politics of Jane Crow. That would mean, for instance, rejecting the kind of all-male list practices that constitute *Betrayal* and that Black women public intellectuals have written against since the 1890s. The barrier of the all-male constituted leadership list is something that Black women have challenged by offering their own lists of important female leaders. I discuss the importance of this practice of listing in the introduction and chapter four. But it is the refusal of Baker and others to acknowledge the ways in which Black women have offered new and productive ideas to uplift Black communities, and the desire to resituate Black leadership squarely within the hands of a committed, if radical, male few that makes projects like *Beyond Respectability* intellectually and politically necessary.

The election of President Barack Obama has also contributed to a resurgence of discussions about Black leadership and about the kinds of models that are most effective in uplifting African American communities. Certainly, the landscape of twenty-first-century Black political and intellectual leadership looks monumentally different than it did even thirty years ago. Patricia Hill Collins argues that "black public intellectuals differ from their historical counterparts and from their domestic contemporaries in several ways."[12] They have "unprecedented access to print media" and broadcast media; they are not necessarily "in daily contact with African American communities or African Americans"; and they have benefited from America's fascination and obsession with questions of race. Broad levels of access to media have shifted the meaning of the term *public* among these well-known intellectuals. Imani Perry notes that "from the late-19th until the mid-20th century, it was a matter of course that African-American intellectuals engaged in public life in a multitude of ways. They developed school curriculums, worked in and for civil-rights organizations like the NAACP, and participated in civic organizations, churches, and professional societies."[13] For instance, Anna Julia Cooper not only earned a doctorate and wrote scholarly books, but she also served as principal of the M Street School in Washington, D.C.

Written in 2005, Collins's reflections are all the more salient given both President Obama's election (and reelection) and the astronomical proliferation of social media sites like Facebook and Twitter and digital content-sharing platforms like YouTube. Perry, too, points out that "the democratizing power of new digital forms of communication and 24-hour cable television news networks has renewed the role of the black public intellectual." Perry therefore attempts to steer junior academicians back to the older model of public scholarship, which means direct forms of community engagement, encouraging them not to view public as being synonymous with doing media.

This continued investment in doing scholarship that is accessible for communities of color outside of the academy exists as a long-standing value among Black women public intellectuals. For example, in *Breaking Bread*, bell hooks discusses the backlash she received when she chose to publish her books without footnotes. She discovered from talking to folks outside the academy, that footnotes often signaled to them that a book "wasn't for them," but for "an academic person." However, academics were initially resistant to her claim that the choice to footnote or not was a "choice informed by questions of class, access, and literacy levels" rather than "shoddy, or careless scholarship."[14] Moreover, the commitment to accessible writing showed up as a concern even among nineteenth-century black women public intellectuals. Ida B. Wells noted in her autobiography that she "wrote in a plain, common-sense way on the things which concerned our people." Furthermore she argued, "knowing that their education was limited, I never used a word of two syllables where one would serve the purpose."[15] I argue that young Black feminist intellectuals have taken up this charge to do accessible scholarship through the massive proliferation of feminist blogs and "hashtag syllabi" that offer cultural and political commentary in an accessible and engaging style.[16] Given the commitment of women like Ida B. Wells and Alice Walker to eschewing the traditional dictates of knowledge production in their respective generations, I am aware that *Beyond Respectability* is in many respects a traditional book of academic scholarship. My hope is that this book further opens the door for other kinds of books about Black women intellectuals to be written and that it encourages us to look anew not just at the labor of institution building, educating, nurturing, organizing, and serving that Black women performed, but also at their thought labor. Thus, in each chapter, I choose to focus on theoretical concepts put forth by race women in hopes that these concepts, in all their richness, will be taken up in future volumes. Rather than offering a definitive word on the women under examination here, I suggest that the field is ripe to really take these women on as thinkers and see how their intellectual work can inform contemporary thinking.

The renewing of conversations about Black leadership means the time is especially ripe for correcting the historical politics of exclusion that has kept these and other Black women public intellectuals relegated to the margins of Black leadership. In chapter one, I discuss at length Fannie Barrier Williams's contention that the Club Movement was the "organized anxiety of women." The term *organized anxiety* is especially generative for contemporary conversations about leadership. A focus on the ways in which anxiety can animate our organizing or, when misdirected, lead Black communities into disarray, offers a far more productive model for thinking about where leaders should direct their attention than accusing people of betrayal. At the same time, much of the broad external support of Barack Obama, coupled with internally (and secretively) voiced dissent, can be understood through Williams's dual anxiety framework, which catalogues an anxiety of aspiration and an anxiety of aversion. We are anxious for leaders that represent the interests of Black communities and are averse to the continuation of social conditions that disfranchise our communities. Barack Obama's presence encompasses both these anxieties, perhaps causing folks to offer both bombastic levels of criticism and bombastic levels of support. In this regard, Williams's call for a new racial sociality, rooted not in class relations or in easy deferrals to race unity, but in a deliberate and radical empathy for other Black people, is an idea whose time has come. Surely, her understandings of the affective relationships between black people can inform our perennial conversations about terms like *the Black community* and *Black unity*. Toni Cade Bambara, whom I examine in chapter four, issues the call for new forms of racial sociality again through what she terms a commitment to "Blackhood." And, indeed, Alicia Garza's herstory of the Black Lives Matter Movement suggests that this new generation of Black leaders, including the many queer, trans, and gender nonconforming leaders among them, are working out in praxis Bambara's notions of revolutionary Blackhood, unencumbered by the traditional dictates of respectable gender ideology.

Throughout this book, I talk about the named lists of Black women that other Black women intellectuals created as a form of archive and memorial to their colleagues who joined them in the project of uplifting African American communities. It is fitting to end this study, in which I interrogate how exclusionary gender politics and conservative ideas about knowledge production continue to shape our ideas about Black intellectual life, by offering a named list of my own. These are women whose lives and work did not make it into this study in any substantive way. They are women that I encountered in various forms along the way—newly discovered archival material, a mention in a book or newspaper article, or another encounter with their already prodigious legacy—but whose lives and thought work I could not do justice to within the bounds of this study. Still they are a part of the story that this book tells. Their names and their work constitute additional markers in the intellectual genealogy and geography that this book has built, and they provide some direction as to where future scholarship might proceed:

Sojourner Truth. Sarah Mapps Douglass. Hallie Quinn Brown. Jane Edna Hunter. Mary McLeod Bethune. Sadie Daniel. Sadie Tanner Mossell Alexander. Ella Baker. Fannie Lou Hamer. Lorraine Hansberry. Jessie Fauset. Callie House. Gertrude Elise Johnson MacDougald Ayer. Dorothy Height. Era Bell Thompson. Ellen Tarry. Claudia Jones. Fanny Jackson Coppin. Alice Dunbar-Nelson. Lucille Clifton. Maritcha Lyons. Angela Davis. Assata Shakur. Frances Beale. Patricia Roberts-Harris.

The women under examination in this book and the women listed here attest that Black women's intellectual leadership traditions are long, robust, multigenerational, and continuing. Still, the intellectual contributions of many of these women languish in relative obscurity because of an enduring politics of racial manhood that places the mantle for race leadership in the hands of men—always men—who are deemed more capable, more critical, and more *appropriate*. I hope that through the careful excavation of Black women's ideas, this book reinvigorates and augments the study of Black women's intellectual traditions pioneered by Gertrude Mossill, Victoria Earle Matthews, Alice Walker, Barbara Smith, Mary Helen Washington, bell hooks, Patricia Hill Collins, Beverly Guy-Sheftall, Hazel Carby, and others. Black women are serious thinkers, and it is our scholarly duty to take them seriously.

Notes

Prologue

1. Cooper, *Voice from the South*, 31.

2. Hine, "Rape and the Inner Lives," in *Hine Sight*. See also Higginbotham, *Righteous Indignation*, the chapter titled "The Politics of Respectability." More recently, Candice Jenkins coined the term *salvific wish* to describe "Black, largely female, generally middle-class desire [and] longing to protect or save Black women, and Black communities more generally, from narratives of sexual and familial pathology, through the embrace of conventional bourgeois propriety in the arenas of sexuality and domesticity." Jenkins, *Private Lives, Proper Relations*.

3. Cooper, *A Voice from the South*, 31.

4. Edwards, *Charisma and the Fictions of Black Leadership*.

5. Cooper, *A Voice from the South*, 30.

6. Martin Delany, "Political Destiny of the Colored Race on the American Continent," in *Life and Public Services of Martin R. Delany* (New York: Arno Press and the *New York Times*, 1969), 335. Delany understood racial identity primarily in biological terms, arguing that Black people had "inherent traits, attributes, so to speak, and native characteristics, peculiar to our race, whether pure or mixed blood."

7. Cooper, *A Voice from the South*, 30.

8. For a more thorough discussion of Martin Delany's political philosophy of Black Nationalism, see Tommie Shelby's *We Who Are Dark: The Philosophical Foundations of Black Solidarity* (Cambridge: Harvard University Press, 2005). Shelby argues that Delany was less a "classic Black nationalist" and more a "pragmatic Black nationalist" primarily committed to strategic invocations of racial unity that would make it possible for Black people to achieve justice and equality in the U.S.

9. W. E. B. Du Bois, *The Souls of Black Folk (Vintage Books Edition)* (New York: Library of America, 1986), 8–9. This discussion appears in the first chapter of *Souls*, "Of Our Spiritual Strivings."

10. Cooper, *A Voice from the South*, 143–44.

11. Cooper's clarity about what the intersection makes possible for Black women is important, especially in a scholarly moment where there is a shift past intersectionality into other accounts of both power and identity. Those accounts suggest that the paradigmatic focus on Black women in intersectionality studies is a retrograde position and a position potentially violent to other women of color. For examples of scholars pushing to move past intersectionality, see Robyn Wiegman, *Object Lessons* (Durham: Duke University Press, 2012), chapter 5. See also Jasbir Puar, *Terrorist Assemblages: Homonationalism in Queer Times* (Durham: Duke University Press, 2007).

12. Cooper, *A Voice from the South*, 144.

13. Ibid., 26–27.

14. Alexander, "We Must Be," 338.

15. Cooper, *A Voice from the South*, 96.

16. Alexander, "We Must Be," 344.

17. Ibid., 345.

18. Ibid., 338.

19. Cooper, *A Voice from the South*, 91. Wells actually sued the rail line for segregating her, won, and was awarded damages. However, the Tennessee Supreme Court overturned the case.

20. Karen Baker-Fletcher, *A Singing Something: Womanist Reflections on Anna Julia Cooper* (New York: Crossroads Press, 1994), 1993. See also May, *Anna Julia Cooper*.

Introduction

1. Hopkins, "Some Literary Workers," in Dworkin, *Daughter of the Revolution*, 142.

2. See Jones, *All Bound Up Together*.

3. For more on Pauline Hopkins's life, see Lois Brown, *Pauline Elizabeth Hopkins: Black Daughter of the Revolution* (Chapel Hill: University of North Carolina Press, 2012).

4. Bay et al., *Toward an Intellectual History*, 5.

5. Ford, *Liberated Threads*, 3.

6. The "cult of domesticity," also referred to as the "cult of true womanhood," promoted a belief that women should be chaste, pious, private, homemakers and mothers who were overseers of the moral conscience of their families. See Welter, "Cult of True Womanhood."

7. Morgan, *Women and Patriotism*, 9–10.

8. Hopkins, "Some Literary Workers," in Dworkin, 142.

9. Ibid.

10. Arguably, Black women weren't the only women who could be called race women. The mothering work that white women were called on to do certainly was tethered to ideas about the reproduction of whiteness.

11. Ibid.

12. Quoted in Mary Hawkesworth, *Political Worlds of Women: Activism, Advocacy and Governance in the Twenty-First Century* (Boulder: Westview Press, 2012), 89.

13. Ibid.

14. Lucy Craft Laney, "The Burden of the Educated Colored Woman," (1899), accessed May 17, 2013. http://www.blackpast.org/?q=1899-lucy-craft-laney-burden -educated-colored-woman.

15. Lucindy A. Willis, *Voices Unbound: The Lives and Works of Twelve American Women Intellectuals* (Delaware: Scholarly Resources, Inc., 2003), xiii–xiv.

16. Williams, "Club Movement," 127.

17. Ibid.

18. Tommy J. Curry, "The Fortune of Wells: Ida B. Wells-Barnett's Use of T. Thomas Fortune's Philosophy of Social Agitation as Prolegomenon to Militant Civil Rights Activism," *Transactions of the Charles S. Peirce Society* 48.4 (Fall 2012): 479, n. 53.

19. Williams, "Club Movement," 118.

20. Ibid.

21. Ibid.

22. Ibid.

23. Martha Jones's *All Bound Up Together* and Michele Mitchell's *Righteous Propagation: African Americans and the Politics of Racial Destiny after Reconstruction* (Chapel Hill: University of North Carolina Press, 2004) both point to vibrant Black women's intellectual cultures in the church (Jones) and in public life (Mitchell). Jones's work maps the public debates and sites of gender activism for nineteenth-century Black women seeking to move the needle toward gender inclusivity in Black public culture and in the church. Mitchell maps conversations about eugenics, vitality, and sexuality in Black public discourse, with significant attention given to Black women's contributions to these public conversations.

24. Williams, "Club Movement," 130.

25. See Glenda Gilmore, *Gender and Jim Crow: Women and the Politics of White Supremacy in North Carolina, 1896–1920* (Chapel Hill: University of North Carolina Press, 1996) for more on the New Woman. See also Deegan, *New Woman of Color.*

26. Williams, "Club Movement," 117.

27. Ibid.

28. Collins, *On Intellectual Activism*, ix.

29. Victoria Wolcott, *Remaking Respectability: African American Women in Interwar Detroit* (Chapel Hill: University of North Carolina Press, 2001). Wolcott argues that in the context of Detroit, although respectability does emerge as a form of intraracial, interclass policing, as a strategy it has limited effectiveness and falls increasingly out of favor as strategy for social reform by the 1920 and 1930s. See introduction.

30. Hortense Spillers, "Mama's Baby, Papa's Maybe: An American Grammar Book," in *African American Literary Theory: A Reader*, ed. Winston Napier (New York: New York University Press, 2000), 259.

31. Ibid., 261.

32. McKittrick, *Demonic Grounds*, 44–45.

33. Ibid., 45.

34. See Gaines, *Uplifting the Race*, introduction and chapters 1 and 5.

35. E. Frances White, Dark Continent of Our Bodies: Black Feminism and the Politics of Respectability (Philadelphia: Temple University Press, 2001), 14 and 36–37.

36. Darlene Clark Hine, "Rape and the Inner Lives of Black Women in the Middle West," *Signs* 14, no. 4 (Summer 1989): 912–20.

37. Morris, *Close Kin and Distant Relatives*, 3.

38. Danielle McGuire, *At the Dark End of the Street: Black Women, Rape, and Resistance—A New History of the Civil Rights Movement from Rosa Parks to the Rise of Black Power* (New York: Knopf, 2010), 76–78 and 160.

39. Hine, "Rape and the Inner Lives," 918.

40. Drake and Cayton, *Black Metropolis*, 394–95.

41. Ibid.

42. For example, see Beverly Guy-Sheftall's essay, "Where Are the Black Female Intellectuals?" on the framing of Black intellectual work in Harold Cruse's *The Crisis of the Negro Intellectual Reconsidered*, ed. Jerry Watts (New York: Routledge, 2004), 223–26.

43. See Williams, *In Search of the Talented Tenth*. Chapter 3 includes the most substantive discussion of women at Howard.

44. Martin Kilson, *Transformation of the African American Intelligentsia* (Cambridge: Harvard University Press, 2014), 5.

45. See all these descriptions of literary workers in Hopkins, "Some Literary Workers," in Dworkin, *Daughter of the Revolution*, 140–55.

46. Cooper, *Voice from the South*, 140–42.

47. Black women's listing practices persist well into the twenty-first century. In 2002, when Halle Berry won the Academy Award for Best Actress, becoming the first and only Black woman to date to have won the award, she began her speech, saying, "This moment is bigger than me. This moment is for Dorothy Dandridge, Lena Horne, and Diahann Carroll. It's for the women that stand beside me. Jada Pinkett, Angela Bassett, Vivica Fox and it's for every nameless, faceless, woman of color that now has the chance because this door tonight has been opened." At Oprah Winfrey's Legend's Ball in 2005, novelist Pearl Cleage presented a poem called, "We Speak Your Names," to honor the scores of Black women pioneers in artistic and creative fields. In one stanza, Cleage wrote, "We are here to speak your names / because we have sense enough to know / that we did not spring full blown from the / forehead of Zeus / or arrive on the scene like Topsy, our sister once / removed, who somehow *just growed* / We know that we are walking in footprints made / deep by confident strides / of women who parted the air before them like / forces of nature you are." Pearl Cleage and Zaron Burnet Jr., *We Speak Your Names: A Celebration* (New York: One World, 2005).

48. Gore, Theoharis, and Woodard, *Want to Start a Revolution?* 8.

49. Carla Peterson's *Doers of the Word* also played a critical role in considering the

intellectual contributions from 1830 to 1880, but she focused solely on Black women living up North. See Peterson, *Doers of the Word*.

50. Kristin Waters and Carol B. Conaway, *Black Women's Intellectual Traditions: Speaking Their Minds* (Lebanon, N.H.: University of Vermont Press, 2007), 3.

51. Bay et al., *Toward an Intellectual History*, 2.

52. White, *Dark Continent*, 16.

53. May, *Anna Julia Cooper*, 38.

54. McGuire, *At the Dark End*. See also Carole Boyce Davies, *Left of Karl Marx: The Political Life of Black Communist Claudia Jones* (Durham: Duke University Press, 2008). Barbara Ransby, *Eslanda: The Large and Unconventional Life of Mrs. Paul Robeson* (New Haven: Yale University Press, 2014). Giddings, *IDA*. Bay, *To Tell the Truth Freely*. Jeanne Theoharis, *The Rebellious Life of Mrs. Rosa Parks* (New York: Beacon Press, 2014). Hendricks, *Fannie Barrier Williams*. Scanlon, *Until There Is Justice*.

55. Dayo Gore's *Radicalism at the Crossroads: African American Women Activists in the Cold War* (New York: New York University Press, 2011) and Erik McDuffie's *Sojourning for Freedom: Black Women, American Communism, and the Making of Black Left Feminism* (Durham: Duke University Press, 2011) focus on contributions of women involved in the labor movement and the Communist Party.

Chapter 1. Organized Anxiety

1. Williams "Club Movement," 119.

2. Du Bois, "Two Negro Conventions," *Independent*, September 7, 1899. In *What Gender Perspectives Shaped the Emergence of the National Association of Colored Women?* Thomas Dublin et al., eds. (Binghamton: State University of New York at Binghamton, 2000), accessed May 22, 2013. http://asp6new.alexanderstreet.com .proxy.libraries.rutgers.edu/was2/was2.object.details.aspx?dorpid=1000688677.

3. Ibid.

4. Williams, "Club Movement," 124.

5. Ibid.

6. Ibid.

7. Ida B. Wells had also written about the relation of convict leasing to lynching in the pamphlet she sold at the Chicago World's Fair.

8. Williams, "Club Movement," 124.

9. Hendricks, 119.

10. May, *Anna Julia Cooper*. For further discussion of Anna Julia Cooper's intellectual legacy in the field of education, see also Stephanie Y. Evans, *Black Women in the Ivory Tower, 1850–1954: An Intellectual History* (Gainesville: University Press of Florida, 2007).

11. Hendricks, *Fannie Barrier Williams*, 133.

12. See White, *Too Heavy a Load*, for more on the ways that race women centered nation-building efforts on the experiences of black women.

13. See Wanda Hendricks, *Gender, Race, and Politics in the Midwest: Black Clubwomen in Illinois* (Bloomington: Indiana University Press, 1998). See also Anne Meis Knupfer, *Towards a Tenderer Humanity and a Nobler Womanhood: African American Women's Club in Turn-of-the-Century Chicago* (New York: New York University Press, 1998). Shaw, *What a Woman Ought to Be*. Cynthia Neverdon-Morton, *Afro-American Women of the South and the Advancement of the Race, 1895–1925* (Knoxville: University of Tennessee Press, 1989).

14. See Hendricks, *Gender, Race, and Politics*. See also Hendricks, *Fannie Barrier Williams*.

15. See Kristie Dotson, "Knowing in Space." labrys, études féministes/estudos feministas janvier/juin 2013 - janeiro/junho 2013, accessed May 26, 2013. SSRN: http://ssrn.com/abstract=2270343.

16. Williams, "Intellectual Progress," 696.

17. Ibid.

18. Ibid., 698.

19. Ibid.

20. Ibid.

21. Williams, "Club Movement," 122.

22. Ibid., 122–23.

23. Ibid., 123.

24. Ibid., 119.

25. Darlene Clark Hine, "Rape and the Inner Lives of Black Women in the Middle West," *Signs* 14, no. 4 (Summer 1989): 915.

26. Ibid., 918.

27. Ibid., 917.

28. Harris-Perry, *Sister Citizen*, 48.

29. Matthews, "Value of Race Literature," 126.

30. Ibid.

31. Ibid., 127.

32. Ibid., 128.

33. Matthews's charge for the deliberate creation of a distinctive African American literary tradition should absolutely inform contemporary debates about whether such a tradition exists. Literary scholars like Kenneth Warren and Hazel Carby have rejected the idea of a cohesive tradition, claiming that the idea of tradition is an academic notion imposed by contemporary scholars upon a prior body of disparate texts. Matthews conceived of an African American literary tradition as being disparate from the very beginning, explicitly noting that not all "race literature" had to deal explicitly with questions of race. The African American literary tradition was a concept projected forward rather than one imposed backward. See Carby, "Woman's Era: Rethinking Black Feminist Theory," in *Reconstructing Womanhood*, 7–16. See Kenneth Warren and Adolph Reed Jr., eds., *Renewing Black Intellectual History: The Ideological and Material Foundations of African American Thought* (Boulder: Paradigm Publishers, 2010), introduction. At the same time, this call for the creation of

a robust body of literature should be read as one of the origin points for the creation of institutionalized Black Studies.

34. Terrell, *Colored Woman*, 274.

35. Gertrude Mossell, *The Work of the Afro-American Woman* (Philadelphia: Geo S. Ferguson Company, 1894), 49.

36. Tate, *Domestic Allegories*, 134–38. Tate concludes that "roughly two decades before white American literature achieved canonical status, [Anna Julia] Cooper and [Gertrude] Mossell canonized African American literature and identified specific characteristics as ennobling of Black novelistic ventures." While Tate takes up the implications of these arguments for the creation of African American women's novels, I am interested primarily in the ways these political aims are taken up in autobiography and other nonfiction works.

37. Matthews, "Value of Race Literature," 129.

38. Ibid., 145.

39. Ibid., 146.

40. Schuller, "Taxonomies of Feeling," 281.

41. Cooper, *Voice from the South*, 145.

42. Schuller, "Taxonomies of Feeling," 278, 281.

43. Williams, "Intellectual Progress," 710.

44. Ibid., 705.

45. Ibid., 707.

46. Charles H. Wesley, *The History of the National Association of Colored Women's Clubs, Inc.: A Legacy of Service* (Washington, D.C.: Mercury Press, 1984), 27.

47. Williams, "Intellectual Progress," 706.

48. Ibid., 703.

49. Ibid., 696.

50. Ibid., 697.

51. See Dotson, "Knowing in Space."

52. Fannie Barrier Williams, "The Colored Girl," *Voice of the Negro* 6, no. 2 (1905): 400–403.

53. Williams, "Intellectual Progress," 704.

54. Viscount James Bryce, *The American Commonwealth,* with an introduction by Gary L. McDowell (Indianapolis: Liberty Fund, 1995), Vol. 2. Chapter: *chapter 76: The Nature of Public Opinion,* accessed January 30, 2013. http://oll.libertyfund.org /title/697/188343.

55. Ibid.

56. Deegan, *New Woman of Color*, 87.

57. Williams, "Club Movement," 124.

58. Bryce, *American Commonwealth*, Vol. 2. Chapter: *chapter 79*.

59. Jurgen Habermas, *The Structural Transformation of the Public Sphere* (Cambridge: MIT Press, 1991) is the definitive work of political theory on the creation of public spheres. However, I am not debating Habermas's failure to consider gender and race, so much as offering a different historical entry point into understanding

how Black women participated in forming and shaping an operational Black public sphere. For feminist and race critiques of Habermas, see Nancy Fraser, "Rethinking the Public Sphere: A Contribution to the Critique of Actually Existing Democracy," in *Habermas and the Public Sphere*, ed. Craig Calhoun (Cambridge: MIT Press, 1992), 109–42. See also *The Black Public Sphere: A Public Culture Book* (Chicago: University of Chicago Press, 1995).

60. Jones, *All Bound Up Together*, 5.

61. Mossell, *Work of the Afro-American Woman*, 100.

62. Williams, "Club Movement," 127.

63. Ibid.

64. Ibid. The rabid class politics and elitism of Williams and other clubwomen is indeed troubling. Even as we continue to acknowledge and disavow this kind of elitism, it is important not to let this become the grounds upon which we dismiss the important intellectual work being done here. Just as the class politics of Du Bois's "Talented Tenth" idea have not curtailed our scholarly examinations of his work, the class politics of the NACW does not mitigate its import as a school of thought.

65. Gaines, *Uplifting the Race*, 21.

66. Mary Church Terrell, "The Duty of the National Association of Colored Women," in Riggs, *Can I Get a Witness?* 73.

67. Gaines, *Uplifting the Race*, 42, 45.

68. Williams, "The Awakening of Women," in Riggs, *Can I Get a Witness?* 115.

69. Ibid.

70. Ibid.

71. Ibid.

72. Ibid.

73. Ibid., 114.

74. Harris-Perry, *Sister-Citizen*, 37.

75. Megan Watkins, "Desiring Recognition, Accumulating Affect," in *The Affect Theory Reader*, ed. Melissa Gregg and Gregory J. Seigworth (Durham: Duke University Press), 273.

76. My thinking about affect is informed by a range of scholars. In particular, Raymond Williams's well-known idea of "structures of feeling" and notions of emergence seem to be at play. Lawrence Grossberg does a good job of connecting Williams's "structures of feeling" to notions of affect in an interview called "Affect's Future: Discovering the Virtual in the Actual," in Gregg and Seigworth, *Affect Theory Reader*, 310, 317–18.

77. Williams did not always maintain an overly sanguine view of the NACW. By 1904, she cautioned the leadership against descent into "petty envies and jealousies that are purely womanly peculiarities," or it "will be in danger of losing the co-operation of the women who are capable of everything, except bickering and small personalities." See Williams, "The Club Movement Among the Colored Women," in Deegan, *Collected Writings*, 48.

78. Williams, "Club Movement," in Riggs, 128.

Chapter 2. "Proper, Dignified Agitation"

1. Mary Church Terrell, "Misrepresentation of Colored People," MCT Papers, Box 102-3, Folder 85, page 5 (ca. 1913).

2. Mary Church Terrell, "Victory at Kresge's" Letter, January 15, 1951, MCT Papers, Box 102-9, Folder 233.

3. Kimberlé Crenshaw, "Mapping the Margin: Intersectionality, Identity Politics, and Violence against Women of Color," in *Critical Race Theory: The Key Writings that Formed the Movement*, ed. Kimberlé Crenshaw et al. (New York: The New Press, 1995).

4. Perkins, *Autobiography as Activism*. There are certainly earlier memoirs and slave narratives from Black women, but this is the first leadership memoir published from a Black woman of Terrell's public stature.

5. Terrell, *Colored Woman*, 147.

6. Ibid.

7. Giddings, *IDA: A Sword among Lions*, 242.

8. Wells, *Crusade for Justice*, 72.

9. Dorothy Sterling, *We Are Your Sisters: Black Women in the Nineteenth Century* (New York: W. W. Norton and Co., 1997), 436.

10. Giddings notes that this was not an easy transition and that on a few occasions Douglass failed to offer Wells the support she needed to transition into leadership. In fact, it seems he actively undercut her sometimes, but the two continued to enjoy great affection for each other until his death. See Giddings, *IDA*, chapter 11, "St. Joan and Old Man Eloquent," 283–310.

11. Mary Church Terrell, "The Mission of Meddler," *Voice of the Negro* (August 1905): 567.

12. Ibid., 566.

13. Ibid., 567.

14. Ibid.

15. Ibid., 568.

16. Ibid.

17. For more on the contradictions of uplift politics, see Gaines, *Uplifting the Race*.

18. Terrell, "Misrepresentation," 4.

19. Ibid.

20. Ibid.

21. Ibid.

22. Ibid., 5.

23. Ibid.

24. Ibid.

25. For a great discussion of Fortune's influence on Wells, see Tommy J. Curry, "The Fortune of Wells: Ida B. Wells-Barnett's Use of T. Thomas Fortune's Philosophy of Social Agitation as a Prolegomenon to Militant Civil Rights Activism," *Transactions of the Charles S. Peirce Society* 48, no. 4 (2012). I agree with Curry that Wells was deeply

influenced by the radical philosophies of T. Thomas Fortune. The historical record supports that reading. But her connection to Fortune in no way removes Wells from the intellectual traditions of Black feminist thought, as Curry argues. Wells developed much of her thinking in consultation with many race women including Fannie Barrier Williams, Mary Church Terrell, Victoria Earle Matthews, and Maritcha Lyons. All of these women, of whom Wells was a great admirer (she called Lyons her mentor, in fact) had significant and explicit gender analyses of both white and Black sexism in their work from the 1890s forward.

26. See Giddings, *IDA*, Chapter 16.

27. Terrell, "Victory at Kresge's," 234.

28. Ibid.

29. See Harlan, *Booker T. Washington*, 372–73, for a discussion of Mary Church Terrell's brief career as a "double agent."

30. David Levering Lewis, *W. E. B. Du Bois: Biography of a Race, 1868–1919* (New York: Henry Holt and Company, 1993), chapters 12 and 14.

31. Ida B. Wells, "The Lynchers Winces," *New York Age.* September 19, 1891, in *The Light of Truth: The Writings of Ida B. Wells*, ed. Mia Bay (New York: Penguin Classics, 2014).

32. Ida B. Wells, "Freedom of Political Action: A Woman's Magnificent Definition of the Political Situation," in Bay, *Light of Truth*, 42–43.

33. Terrell, "Misrepresentation," 6.

34. Terrell, *Colored Woman*, 29.

35. Ibid., 30.

36. Ibid., 29.

37. Ibid., 30.

38. Terrell, *Colored Woman*, 461.

39. Peterson, *Doers of the Word*, 14.

40. Nellie McKay, "The Narrative Self: Race, Politics, and Culture in Black American Women's Autobiography," in *Women, Autobiography, and Theory: A Reader*, ed. Sidonie Smith and Julia Watson (Madison: University of Wisconsin Press, 1998), 96.

41. Mostern, *Autobiography and Black Identity Politics*, 12.

42. Terrell, *Colored Woman*, 31.

43. Ibid., 39.

44. Ibid., 64.

45. Ibid.

46. Cooper, *Voice from the South*, 68.

47. Terrell, *Colored Woman*, 126.

48. Ibid., 127.

49. Ibid.

50. Ibid., 128.

51. Wells, *Crusade for Justice*, 72.

52. Ibid., 73.

53. Terrell, *Colored Woman*, 196.

54. Ibid., 197.

55. Ibid., 142. There is some discrepancy in how Terrell narrates the loss of her son in her memoir. By 1892, the year Tom Moss was lynched, she had lost her first child. But the baby boy to whom she refers in this passage would have been born in 1896, four years later. See Giddings, 416 for more on Terrell's struggle with depression after miscarriage.

56. Ibid., 143.

57. Ibid., 85.

58. Ibid.

59. Ibid., 451.

60. Ibid., 187.

61. Ibid., 185.

62. See Sarah Haley's extensive discussion of Terrell's advocacy against convict leasing in *No Mercy Here*, 132–41.

63. Mary Church Terrell to Robert Terrell, August 18, 1900. Mary Church Terrell Papers, Library of Congress, Reel 3.

64. Dennis Brindell Fradin and Judith Bloom Fradin, *Fight On! Mary Church Terrell's Battle for Integration* (New York: Clarion Books, 2003), 71. Although this book was written for a young adult audience, it is one of the few books on Terrell and drew on extensive archival sources that seemed important enough to reference here.

65. Terrell, *Colored Woman*, 200.

66. Ibid., 281.

67. Ibid., 201.

68. Ibid., 52.

69. Henderson, "Speaking in Tongues," 350.

70. Terrell, *Colored Woman*, 238.

71. Ibid.

72. Ibid., 243.

73. Ibid.

74. "Shade" is a colloquial term that refers to the subversive ways that Black queer and Black women's communities signify upon and indirectly implicate the racist, sexist, and homophobic presumptions of others.

75. See Henderson, "Speaking in Tongues.

76. Terrell, *Colored Woman*, 244.

77. Dotson, "Knowing in Space.

78. Terrell, *Colored Woman*, 337.

79. Ibid., 346.

80. Ibid., 287.

81. Ibid., 471.

82. Mary Church Terrell, "Mass Meeting, June 15, 1951," MCT Papers, Box 102–3, Folder 83, 5.

83. Terrell, "Mass Meeting, June 15, 1951," 8.

84. Fradin and Fradin, *Fight On!*

85. Murray, *Pauli Murray*, 205.

86. Ibid., 224–25.

87. Terrell was also a leader in the effort to desegregate Hecht's Department Store Lunch Counters in 1951 and 1952.

88. Terrell, "Mass Meeting, June 15, 1951," 4.

89. Ibid., 5.

90. Ibid., 1.

91. Ibid.

92. Ibid.

93. Ibid., 5.

94. Ibid., 6.

95. Ibid., 6–7.

96. Ibid., 7.

97. Ibid., 8.

98. Eleanor Holmes Norton, quoted in Murray, *The Autobiography*, 229.

99. Ibid., 232.

Chapter 3. Pauli Murray's Quest for an Unhyphenated Identity

1. "Questionnaire, Sunday," December 14, 1937, Pauli Murray Papers, Schlesinger Library, Radcliffe Institute, Harvard University Box 4, Folder 71 (hereafter Pauli Murray Papers are cited as PMP). I draw extensively upon Murray's archive at the Schlesinger in this chapter and chapter 4, but restrictions prevented me from quoting from this material directly. Researchers can find all materials that I referenced using the citations provided here.

2. Even though Murray seemed to reject scientific assessments, she actually believed that experimental treatments with hormones were a viable option. Doreen Drury has written extensively about the ways that Murray was influenced by the scientific discourses of her time. See Drury, "Experimentation on the Male Side," chapter 3.

3. "Questionnaire Tuesday, December 16, 1937," PMP, Box 4, Folder 71. See also Drury, "Experimentation on the Male Side": "As Murray was well aware, discourses on homosexuals often attributed same-sex attraction to a weakness of mind and morals. Her problem, she desperately sought to prove, was *not* 'in the brain' but in her 'glands.' (106). Drury also writes that Murray was greatly interested in the "naturalist position" on homosexuality, which viewed it as "a benign but inborn anomaly, linked to an organic congenital predisposition" (108). This view held that there was a third sex.

4. *Song in a Weary Throat* was retitled and published by the University of Tennessee Press in 1989 as *Pauli Murray: The Autobiography of a Black Activist, Feminist, Lawyer, Priest and Poet*, and it is referred to as *The Autobiography*.

5. See Drury, "Experimentation on the Male Side." See also the more recent article "Love, Ambition, and 'Invisible Footnotes,'" 297.

6. Ibid.

7. "Questionnaire," Wednesday, December 17, 1937, PMP, Box 4, Folder 71.

8. Murray had a short-lived marriage to William Roy Wynn that began in 1930 and fizzled out very quickly. The marriage was not annulled until 1948.

9. "Memorandum to Dr. Helen Blount," March 8, 1940, PMP, Box 4, Folder 71.

10. Ibid.

11. This term refers to a person that has biological chromosomes designating them as male *or* female, and genitalia that reflect either both sexes or the opposite sex. See Anne Fausto-Sterling, *Sexing the Body: Gender Politics and the Construction of Sexuality* (New York: Basic Books, 2000), chapter 3.

12. "Questionnaire," Wednesday, December 17, 1937. I use the pronoun "she" here because Murray never made the shift to referring to herself using masculine pronouns.

13. Foucault, *History of Sexuality*, 43.

14. Much of our contemporary thinking about the distinctions between biological sex and socially constructed gender don't emerge until the latter half of the twentieth century. David Rubin argues that many of these distinctions emerge from John Money's work on hermaphroditism and treatment of intersex patients beginning in the 1950s. See David Rubin, "'An Unnamed Blank That Craved a Name': A Genealogy of Intersex as Gender," *Signs Journal of Women in Culture and Society* 37, no. 4 (Summer 2012): 883–908. I use *trans* with an asterisk to signal the range of identities contained in this moniker including gender nonbinary, gender nonconforming, and transgender.

15. Murray, Questionnaire, 1937.

16. Ross, "Beyond the Closet," 165.

17. Ibid., 167.

18. Ibid., 166.

19. "Prison," PMP, Box 4, Folder 85.

20. Memo to Dr. Blount, March 8, 1940, PMP, Box 4, Folder 71.

21. In the years between 1937 and 1940, she had come to locate the problem as a conflict over her biological sex rather than as a conflict over her sexuality and gender. In today's terms, we would understand Pauli Murray to be articulating an experience as a transman. However, this language did not exist in 1940 and is reflected in the difficulty of determining whether her initial conflict was over gender identity, sexual identity, or her biological sexual orientation.

22. Glenda Gilmore recounts this entire incident in her book *Defying Dixie*, 315–29.

23. Ibid., 322.

24. Ibid., 536, n. 120. "Color Trouble" was mistaken for fiction and republished in *Best American Short Stories of 1941*.

25. Butler, *Gender Trouble*, 45.

26. Ibid., 185.

27. Ibid., 45.

28. Gilmore, *Defying Dixie*, 265–66. Shepard had impeded past attempts to desegregate UNC in order to lobby for additional funds for his own school's graduate programs.

29. Ibid., 285.

30. Murray, *The Autobiography*, 96. In her sixties, Murray wrote a long letter to a Baltimore police officer who had given her a parking ticket. She was older and frail and needed to carry several heavy books into her apartment. She berated him for his insensitivity to her plight and paid the ticket.

31. "Pauli Murray Letter to Brother Randolph," July 24, 1942, PMP, Box72, Folder 1265.

32. Gilmore, *Defying Dixie*, 287.

33. Murray, *The Autobiography*, 183.

34. Ibid.

35. Ibid., 184.

36. Ibid., 205.

37. See Williams, *In Search of the Talented Tenth*; Jonathan Holloway, *Confronting the Veil: Abram Harris, Jr., E. Franklin Frazier, and Ralph Bunche, 1919–1941* (Chapel Hill: University of North Carolina Press, 2002), and Eben Miller, *Born along the Color Line: The 1933 Amenia Conference and the Rise of a National Civil Rights Movement* (New York: Oxford University Press, 2012).

38. Murray, *The Autobiography*, 182.

39. Ibid., 184.

40. Pauli Murray Letter to Mr. Smith, June 24, 1944, PMP, Box 18, Folder 415.

41. José Esteban Muñoz, *Disidentifications: Queers of Color and the Performance of Politics* (Minneapolis: University of Minnesota Press, 1999), 11.

42. Gallagher, *Black Women and Politics*, 137.

43. Ibid., 138.

44. Mayeri, *Reasoning from Race*, chapter 1.

45. Murray, "Constitutional Law and Black Women," 43.

46. Ibid.

47. Ibid.

48. Hardison, *Writing through Jane Crow*. Hardison points to this broader socio-spatial formation as also producing "a rupture in twentieth-century African American literature," as Black women writers in the post–WWII period produced a series of "Jane Crow texts" that attempted to "redefine black female agency within public and private spheres" and to "imagine new identity formations for black female subjectivity within literary and social contexts." See Loc 128–29 of the Kindle edition.

49. Dayo Gore, *Radicalism at the Crossroads: African American Women Activists in the Cold War* (New York: New York University Press, 2011), 51–52.

50. Hardison, Introduction. Loc 128 of the Kindle edition.

51. PauliMurray, "Why Negro Girls Stay Single," PMP, Box 85, Folder 1469. Originally published in *Negro Digest*, July 1947, 5.

52. Ibid., 6.

53. Ibid.

54. Ibid., 7.

55. Patricia Hill Collins explicates the relationship between hegemonic and subordinate masculinities in *Black Sexual Politics: African Americans, Gender, and the New Racism* (New York: Routledge, 2004), chapter 6.

56. Murray, "Why Negro Girls Stay Single," 8.

57. Adrienne Rich, "Compulsory Heterosexuality and Lesbian Existence," in *Blood, Bread, and Poetry: Selected Prose* (repr. New York: W. W. Norton and Company, 1994). Rich argues that it is fallacious to understand homosexuality, specifically lesbianism, as the "mirror image of heterosexual or male homosexual relations." It is also incorrect to marginalize lesbianism as "alternative," "deviant," or "unnatural." Such characterizations are intrinsic results of a system that views heterosexuality as normative and compels others to do so. Evelyn Brooks Higginbotham introduced the term "politics of respectability" in her doctoral dissertation and later in her book *Righteous Discontent*. She writes, "Black Baptist women . . . infused concepts such as equality, self-respect, professionalism, and American identity with their own intentions and interpretations. In the dialogic sense of multiple and conflicting meanings, these concepts became new, resistant pronouncements against white public opinion. The Black Baptist women's opposition to the social structures and symbolic representations of white supremacy may be characterized by the concept of the 'politics of respectability.'" She points out that "adherence to respectability enabled Black women to counter racist images and structures," but because of its "assimilationist leanings," it led to "an insistence upon Blacks' conformity to the dominant society's norms of morals and manners" (186–87).

58. Pauli Murray to Lillian Smith, June 21, 1943, PMP, Box 80, Folder 1402.

59. Hammonds, "Black (W)holes and the Geometry," 491. See also Cole and Guy-Sheftall, *Gender Talk: The Struggle for Women's Equality in African American Communities* (New York: One World, 2003), chapter 6.

60. Lillian Smith and her partner Paula Snelling, and Candice Stone (great niece of Lucy Stone) and her partner Jean were genuine allies to Murray as she navigated her own path to race womanhood.

61. The sexual discourses surrounding each of these women are interesting for a variety of reasons. Anna Julia Cooper was widowed just two years after marrying in her twenties, and she never remarried. But she was implicated in the early 1900s in a sexual scandal with one of her students, a scandal which led to her losing her job. Mary McLeod Bethune had a troubled relationship with her husband who had problems with her independent spirit. She was also rumored to live openly with a female partner. Ella Baker was the most silent about her marriage and eventual divorce. Thus many students in the Civil Rights Movement didn't know she had been married, and she seemed committed to the idea that this wasn't inherently public knowledge. Gloria Hull affirms my concerns here about the "hidden nature of women's sexual lives in general," and more specifically, "lesbian invisibility" which creates particular challenges for doing "lesbian-feminist scholarship, where the subjects feel constrained even in their private utterances from expressing themselves clearly and fully." See Gloria Hull, *Color, Sex, and Poetry: Three Women Writers of the Harlem Renaissance* (Bloomington: Indiana University Press, 1987), 21.

62. Jenkins, *Private Lives, Proper Relations*, 33.

63. Ibid., 43.

64. Ibid., 44.

65. See also Hardison's discussion of Murray and the salvific wish in *Writing through Jane Crow*. Loc 444 of the Kindle edition.

66. Murray, *The Autobiography*, 295.

67. Murray, "Prologue, Draft 4," 1–2, PMP, Box 77, Folder 1365.

68. Ibid., 2.

69. Murray, "Introduction 1978," *Proud Shoes*, xx.

70. For a brief time in the 1930s, Murray was a member of the Lovestonite Communist Opposition faction, led by Jay Lovestone, a former member of the Communist Party who eventually headed the AFL-CIO. See Gore, *Radicalism at the Crossroads*, 53, and Murray, *The Autobiography*, 102–3.

71. Murray, "Prologue," 6.

72. Ibid.

73. Jared Sexton argues in *Amalgamation Schemes: AntiBlackness and the Critique of Multiracialism* (Minneapolis: University of Minnesota Press, 2008), 7. Sexton's project is more concerned with debunking the intrinsic heterosexuality implied in discourses around racial admixture, in order to open up space for the discussion on interracial sex in nonheterosexual unions. Murray's project does not go quite so far in deliberately opening up a space for queer sexual practices, but she does offer a "queer" reading of what it means to be American and what it means to embrace any sort of racial identity, Black or white.

74. Aliyyah I. Abdur-Rahman, *Against the Closet: Black Political Longing and the Erotics of Race* (Durham: Duke University Press, 2012), 2. See also Patricia Hill Collins, who has argued that "racism and heterosexism both require a concept of sexual deviancy for meaning." Racism pivots upon a belief in Black hypersexuality and promiscuity, while heterosexism pivots upon "the stigmatization of the sexual practices of homosexuals. The undergirding logic of these two systems views Black people as possessing excess heterosexual desire while viewing LGBT people as possessing an absence of heterosexual desire. Based upon this logic, Black people could not be homosexual or those Blacks who were homosexual were not "authentically" Black. Collins, *Black Sexual Politics*, 97–106.

75. See discussion in Ross, "Beyond the Closet," 164. Drawing upon the work of Robyn Wiegman, who has argued that in the seventeenth century "color had become the *primary* organizing principle around which the natural historian classified human differences," Marlon Ross highlights Wiegman's conclusion that the discourses of sexual development, upon which Foucault bases his theory of sexuality, point to an "uneven history" of racial and sexual development.

76. See Ross, "Beyond the Closet."

77. Murray, *Omni-Americans*, 22. The book also has an alternate subtitle "Some Alternatives to the Folklore of White Supremacy." Murray goes on to say that the "so-called Black and so-called white people of the United States resemble nobody else in the world so much as they resemble each other."

78. Murray, *Proud Shoes*, 59.

79. Ibid., 67.

80. Ibid., 66–67.

81. Ibid., 91.

82. *Ibid.*, 59.

83. Pauli Murray Letter to Peg Holmes, March 18, 1973, PMP, Box 96, Folder 1688.

84. Murray, *Proud Shoes*, 167–68.

85. Drury, "Love, Ambition, and 'Invisible Footnotes,'" 302.

86. In this regard, I find the work of Aliyyah I. Abdur-Rahman instructive. She writes, "blackness and queerness are both used to shore up whiteness; both function as its exiled and abased excesses. Both blackness and homosexuality pose a threat to whiteness in that it impedes the continuous propagation of white generations and violates the unity and integrity of the white family as the basic unit of capital acquisition and consolidation in the American political economy." *Against the Closet*, 18.

87. Muñoz, *Disidentifications*, 4, 28.

88. Murray argues in *Proud Shoes*, which is an important work of Civil War and Reconstruction history in its own right, that freedom was defined by many things for the formerly enslaved. Now these folks could own both their bodies and their souls, could move freely about the world, and could reconnect with kin who were dear to them. Tera Hunter makes a very similar argument in *To 'Joy My Freedom: Southern Black Women's Lives and Labors after the Civil War* (Cambridge: Harvard University Press, 1997).

89. Hardison, Loc 351–52 of the Kindle edition. Hardison was speaking of Murray's second memoir, *Song in a Weary Throat*, but the same Jane Crow politics apply to her negotiations of sexuality in *Proud Shoes.*

90. Watson, "Unspeakable Differences," 394–95.

91. Ibid.

Chapter 4. The Problems and Possibilities of the Negro Woman Intellectual

1. Ponchitta Pierce, "Problems of the Negro Woman Intellectual," *Ebony Magazine*, August 1966, 149.

2. Ibid., 144.

3. Ibid.

4. Harold Cruse, *The Crisis of the Negro Intellectual* (repr. New York: New York Review Books, 2005), 4–5.

5. Hedgeman, *Trumpet Sounds*. The period between 1916 and 1933 was a critical moment in the first half of the twentieth century for proclaiming the next generation of intellectual leaders. These two dates are significant because in both these years, Joel Spingarn hosted two conferences, the Amenia Conferences at his estate in upstate New York. At Amenia I, Mary Church Terrell had been one of sixty attendees invited to spend a weekend with other race leaders "thrash[ing] out their differences and unit[ing] on some definite program of work." For her, the first Amenia Conference "marked an end of old ways of attacking the race problem and the beginning of the

new." Hedgeman had been invited to Amenia II. For more on the Amenia Conferences, see Jonathan Holloway, *Confronting the Veil: Abram Harris, Jr., E. Franklin Frazier, and Ralph Bunche 1919–1941* (Chapel Hill: University of North Carolina Press, 2001) and Eben Miller, *Born along the Color Line: The 1933 Amenia Conference and the Rise of a National Civil Rights Movement* (New York: Oxford University Press, 2012).

6. Hedgeman, *Trumpet Sounds*, 62.

7. Ibid.

8. Ibid.

9. Jennifer Scanlon, *Until There Is Justice*. See also Gallagher, *Black Women and Politics in New York City* (Urbana: University of Illinois Press, 2012).

10. For a longer account of this incident, see Scanlon, *Until There Is Justice*, 164–69.

11. Hedgeman, *Trumpet Sounds*, 179.

12. Ibid., 180.

13. Ibid., 180.

14. Ibid., 188.

15. Ibid., 189.

16. Edwards, *Charisma and the Fictions*, xv.

17. Pierce, "Problems of the Negro Woman Intellectual," 144.

18. See Dorothy Sterling, *We Are Your Sisters: Black Women in the Nineteenth Century* (New York: W. W. Norton and Company, 1984), 436.

19. Pierce, "Problems of the Negro Woman Intellectual," 145.

20. Ibid., 145.

21. Ibid.

22. Ibid., 146.

23. Ibid., 145.

24. Ibid.

25. Ibid., 149.

26. Ibid., 146.

27. Ibid., 147.

28. Kennard W. Reed Jr., Letter, *Ebony Magazine*, October 1966, 14. To be fair, other male writers were more effusive in their praise. Reader Howard B. Woods wrote "it has always seemed incongruous that as we have talked endlessly of the matriarchal society within the Negro American's culture, the Negro female's dominance was constantly negated by the male, who consciously or not, fought to retain his proper status with demeaning story, song or off-color joke. It was a kind of mass male psychosis that seemed bent on undermining this steadfast and redoubtable figure who endured despite the subtle campaign." (14).

29. Pierce, "Problems of the Negro Woman Intellectual," 147.

30. Ibid., 148.

31. Ibid.

32. Ibid.

33. Shaw, *What a Woman Ought to Be*.

34. Murray, *The Autobiography*, 390.

35. Ibid., 391.

36. Ibid., 391.

37. About Collins's participation in the student takeover, Murray writes, "Patricia Hill, the only Black senior in the class and an honor student, got up immediately and left the room, saying something about 'Black solidarity.'" Murray, *The Autobiography*, 408.

38. Ibid., 394–95.

39. "Negro Youth's Dilemma," PMP, Box 84, Folder 1458.

40. Pauli Murray Letter to Mrs. Rodman, February 28, 1943, PMP, Box 83, Folder 1455.

41. Murray, *The Autobiography*, 396.

42. "Negro Youth's Dilemma," PMP, Box 84, Folder 1458.

43. Beverly Guy-Sheftall, "Where Are the Black Female Intellectuals?" in *Harold Cruse's The Crisis of the Negro Intellectual Reconsidered*, ed. Jerry Watts (New York: Routledge, 2004), 224.

44. Ibid., 223.

45. Bambara, *Black Woman*, 1.

46. Ibid., 2.

47. Ibid., 3–4.

48. Farah Jasmine Griffin, "Conflict and Chorus: Reconsidering Toni Cade's *The Black Woman: An Anthology*," in *Is It Nation Time? Essays on Black Power and Black Nationalism* (Chicago: University of Chicago Press, 2002), 122.

49. Ibid., 126.

50. Bambara, *Black Woman*, 4.

51. See Griffin, "Conflict and Chorus," and Guy-Sheftall, *Where Are the Black Intellectuals?*

52. Barbara Jordan, "Impeachment Speech," July 25, 1974, accessed May 14, 2013. http://watergate.info/1974/07/25/barbara-jordan-speech-on-impeachment.html.

53. Shirley Chisholm, "The Black Woman in Contemporary America," June 17, 1974, accessed May 14, 2013. http://americanradioworks.publicradio.org/features/sayitplain/schisholm.html.

54. Ibid.

55. Bambara, *Black Woman*, 5.

56. Ibid., 6.

57. Bambara, "On the Issue of Roles," in *Black Woman*, 123–24.

58. Ibid., 125–26.

59. Ibid., 132.

60. Ibid., 133.

61. Cooper, Voice from the South, 29.

62. Ibid., 134–35.

63. Walker, "Zora Neale Hurston," in *In Search*, 84.

64. Smith, "Sexual Politics and the Fiction of Zora Neale Hurston," in *Truth That Never Hurts*, 28.

65. Walker, "Looking for Zora," in *In Search*, 105.

Epilogue

1. Garza, "Herstory."

2. Ibid.

3. All of these women don't identify with the Black Lives Matter Movement organization. Elzie and Packnett helped cofound Campaign Zero. Carruthers and Master are part of the Chicago-based Black Youth Project 100. I am also an active participant in the Black Lives Matter New York Chapter.

4. hooks, "Black Women Intellectuals," in hooks and West, *Breaking Bread*, 153–54.

5. Dani McClain, "The White House Focuses on Women and Girls of Color with New $118 Million Dollar Initiative," *Nation*. November 16, 2015, accessed December 19, 2015. http://www.thenation.com/article/white-house-turns-toward-women-and-girls-of-color-with-new-118-million-initiative/. I participated in the White House Summit and the campaign against My Brother's Keeper.

6. Kimberlé Williams Crenshaw, Jyoti Nanda, and Priscilla Ocen, "Black Girls Matter: Pushed Out, Overpoliced and Underprotected," accessed December 19, 2015. www.aapf.org.

7. Journalist Ta-Nehisi Coates called Melissa Harris-Perry "America's foremost public intellectual" in a January 2014 column in *Atlantic*, accessed May 21, 2016. http://www.theatlantic.com/politics/archive/2014/01/the-smartest-nerd-in-the-room/282836/. Another reporter, Dylan Byers at Politico, tweeted that such an assertion undermined Coates's intellectual credibility. Byers then offered a list of all white men and one dead white woman as his idea of who did constitute actual public intellectuals. See Coates's reply, accessed May 21, 2016. http://www.theatlantic.com/politics/archive/2014/01/what-it-means-to-be-a-public-intellectual/282907/.

8. Melissa Harris-Perry, "Email to Staff," accessed May 21, 2016. https://medium.com/@JamilSmith/melissa-harris-perry-s-email-to-her-nerdland-staff-11292bdc27cb#.qspx47udn.

9. Baker, *Betrayal*, xi.

10. Ibid., 71.

11. Patterson, *Exodus Politics*, 3.

12. Patricia Hill Collins, "Black Public Intellectuals: From Du Bois to the Present," *Contexts* 4, no. 4 (2005): 25.

13. Imani Perry, "Putting the 'Public' in Public Intellectual," *Chronicle of Higher Education*, June 6, 2010.

14. Hooks and West, *Breaking Bread*, 72.

15. Wells, *Crusade for Justice*, 23–24.

16. One innovative use of Twitter and blogs together has been the creation of digital syllabi that offer reading lists to the general public about major cultural or

political events. For instance, when Beyoncé released her visual album *Lemonade* in April 2016, Candice Benbow, a writer and blogger, started the #LemonadeSyllabus, a crowd-sourced list of books, music, and films with Black feminist and womanist themes. Accessed over 100,000 times, the digital syllabus reflects the new ways that Black women are using digital tools to help Black women become, as Fannie Barrier Williams said, "students of their own social condition," accessed May 21, 2016. http://issuu.com/candicebenbow/docs/lemonade_syllabus_2016/1?e=24704410/3543401.

Selected Bibliography

Archival Collections

Pauli Murray Papers (PMP), Schlesinger Library, Radcliffe Institute, Harvard University.

Mary Church Terrell Papers (MCT), Moorland-Spingarn Research Center, Howard University.

Books and Articles

Alexander, Elizabeth. "'We Must Be about Our Father's Business': Anna Julia Cooper and the In-Corporation of the Nineteenth Century African-American Female Intellectual." *Signs* 20, no. 2 (1995): 336–56.

Baker, Jr., Houston A. *Betrayal: How Black Intellectuals Have Abandoned the Ideals of Civil Rights Era*. New York: Columbia University Press, 2008.

Bambara, Toni Cade. *The Black Woman: An Anthology*. New York: Washington Square Press, 2005.

Bay, Mia. *To Tell the Truth Freely: The Life of Ida B. Wells*. New York: Hill and Wang, 2009.

Bay, Mia, Farah J. Griffin, Martha S. Jones, and Barbara D. Savage, eds., *Toward an Intellectual History of Black Women*. Chapel Hill: University of North Carolina Press, 2015.

Butler, Judith. *Gender Trouble: Feminism and the Subversion of Identity*. New York: Routledge, 1990.

Carby, Hazel. *Race Men*. Cambridge: Harvard University Press, 1998.

———. *Reconstructing Womanhood: The Emergence of the Afro-American Woman Novelist*. New Haven: Yale University Press, 1987.

Collins, Patricia Hill. *Black Feminist Thought: Knowledge, Consciousness, and the Politics of Empowerment*. 2nd ed. New York and London: Routledge, 2000.

————. *On Intellectual Activism*. Philadelphia: Temple University Press, 2013.

Cooper, Anna Julia. *A Voice from the South*. New York: Oxford University Press, 1988.

Deegan, Mary Jo, ed. *The New Woman of Color: The Collected Writings of Fannie Barrier Williams, 1893–1918*. Dekalb: Northern Illinois University Press, 2002.

Dotson, Kristie. "Knowing in Space: Three Lessons from Black Women's Social Theory." labrys, études féministes/estudos feministas janvier/juin 2013 - janeiro/junho 2013. Available at SSRN, May 15, 2016. http://ssrn.com/abstract=2270343.

Drake, St. Clair, and Horace R. Cayton. *Black Metropolis: A Study of Negro Life in a Northern City*. New York: Harcourt, Brace, and Company, 1945.

Drury, Doreen. "Love, Ambition, and 'Invisible Footnotes' in the Life and Writing of Pauli Murray." *Souls: A Critical Journal of Black Politics, Culture, and Society* 11, no. 3 (2009): 295–309.

Drury, Doreen Marie. "Experimentation on the Male Side: Race, Class, Gender and Sexuality in Pauli Murray's Quest for Love and Identity, 1910–1960." PhD diss., Boston College, 2000.

Du Bois, W. E. B. "The Talented Tenth," in *W. E. B. Du Bois: Writings*, 842–61. New York: Library of America, 1987.

Dworkin, Ira, ed. *Daughter of the Revolution: The Major Nonfiction Works of Pauline Hopkins*. New Brunswick: Rutgers University Press, 2007.

Edwards, Erica. *Charisma and the Fictions of Black Leadership*. Minneapolis: University of Minnesota Press, 2012.

Evans, Stephanie Y. *Black Women in the Ivory Tower, 1850–1954: An Intellectual History*. Gainesville: University Press of Florida, 2008.

Ford, Tanisha C. *Liberated Threads: Black Women, Style, and the Global Politics of Soul*. Chapel Hill: University of North Carolina Press, 2015.

Foucault, Michel. *The History of Sexuality, Volume I: An Introduction*. New York: Vintage, 1990.

Fradin, Dennis Brindell, and Judith Bloom Fradin. *Fight On! Mary Church Terrell's Battle for Integration*. New York: Clarion Books, 2003.

Gaines, Kevin K. *Uplifting the Race: Black Leadership, Politics, and Culture in the Twentieth Century*. Chapel Hill: University of North Carolina Press, 1996.

Gallagher, Julie. *Black Women and Politics in New York City*. Urbana: University of Illinois Press, 2012.

Garfinkel, Harold. "Color Trouble," in *The Best American Short Stories 1941*, ed. Edward J. O'Brien. Boston: Houghton Mifflin Company, 1941.

Garza, Alicia. "A Herstory of the #BlackLivesMatter Movement," *Feminist Wire*, accessed December 19, 2015. http://www.thefeministwire.com/2014/10/blacklivesmatter-2/.

Giddings, Paula. *Ida: A Sword among Lions*. New York: Harper Collins, 2008.

————. *When and Where I Enter: The Impact of Black Women on Race and Sex in America*. New York: Quill, 1984.

Gilmore, Glenda. *Defying Dixie: The Radical Roots of Civil Rights, 1919–1950*. New York: W. W. Norton and Company, 2008.

Gore, Dayo F., Jeanne Theoharis, and Komozi Woodard, eds. *Want to Start a Revolution? Radical Women in the Black Freedom Struggle.* New York: New York University Press, 2009.

Haley, Sarah. *No Mercy Here: Gender, Punishment, and the Making of Jim Crow Modernity.* Chapel Hill: University of North Carolina Press, 2016.

Hammonds, Evelynn. "Black (W)holes and the Geometry of Black Female Sexuality," in *African American Literary Theory: A Reader,* ed. Winston Napier, 482–97. New York and London: New York University Press, 2000.

Hardison, Ayesha. *Writing Through Jane Crow: Race and Gender Politics in African American Literature.* Charlottesville: University of Virginia Press, 2014.

Harlan, Louis. *Booker T. Washington: The Wizard of Tuskegee, 1901–1915.* New York Oxford: Oxford University Press, 1983.

Harper, Frances Ellen. *Iola Leroy or Shadows Uplifted.* Boston: Beacon Press, 1987.

Harris-Perry, Melissa. *Sister Citizen: Black Women, Shame, and Stereotypes in America.* New Haven: Yale University Press, 2011.

Hedgeman, Anna Arnold. *The Trumpet Sounds: A Memoir of Negro Leadership.* New York: Holt, Rinehart and Winston, 1964.

Henderson, Mae Gwendolyn. "Speaking in Tongues: Dialogics, Dialectics, and the Black Woman Writer's Literary Tradition," in *African American Literary Theory: A Reader,* ed. Winston Napier, 348–68. New York: New York University Press, 2000.

Hendricks, Wanda. *Fannie Barrier Williams: Crossing the Borders of Region and Race.* Urbana: University of Illinois Press, 2011.

Higginbotham, Evelyn Brooks. *Righteous Discontent: The Women's Movement in the Black Baptist Church, 1880–1920.* Cambridge: Harvard University Press, 1993.

Hine, Darlene Clark. *Hine Sight: Black Women and the Re-Construction of American History.* Brooklyn: Carlson Publishing, 1994.

hooks, bell, and Cornel West. *Breaking Bread: Insurgent Black Intellectual Life.* Boston: South End Press, 1991.

Jenkins, Candice M. *Private Lives, Proper Relations: Regulating Black Intimacy.* Minneapolis: University of Minnesota Press, 2007.

Jones, Martha S. *All Bound Up Together: The Woman Question in African American Public Culture, 1830–1900.* Chapel Hill: University of North Carolina Press, 2007.

King, Deborah. "Multiple Jeopardy, Multiple Consciousness: The Context of Black Feminist Ideology," in *Words of Fire: An Anthology of African-American Feminist Thought,* ed. Beverly Guy-Sheftall, 294–317. New York: The New Press, 1995.

Matthews, Victoria Earle. "The Value of Race Literature," in *With Pen and Voice: A Critical Anthology of Nineteenth-Century African-American Women,* ed. Shirley Logan, 126–48. Carbondale: Southern Illinois University Press, 1995.

May, Vivian. *Anna Julia Cooper, Visionary Black Feminist: A Critical Introduction.* New York: Routledge, 2007.

Mayeri, Serena. *Reasoning from Race: Feminism, Law, and the Civil Rights Revolution.* Cambridge: Harvard University Press, 2011.

McGuire, Danielle. *At the Dark End of the Street: Black Women, Rape, and Resist-*

ance—A New History of the Civil Rights Movement from Rosa Parks to the Rise of Black Power. New York: Knopf, 2010.

McKittrick, Katherine. *Demonic Grounds: Black Women and the Cartographies of Struggle*. Minneapolis: University of Minnesota, 2005.

Morgan, Francesca. *Women and Patriotism in Jim Crow America*. Chapel Hill: University of North Carolina Press, 2005.

Morris, Susana M. *Close Kin and Distant Relatives: The Paradox of Respectability in Black Women's Literature*. Charlottesville: University of Virginia Press, 2014.

Mostern, Kenneth. *Autobiography and Black Identity Politics: Racialization in Twentieth Century America*. Cambridge: Cambridge University Press, 1999.

Murray, Albert. *The Omni-Americans: Black Experience and American Culture*. New York: Da Capo Press, 1970.

Murray, Pauli. "Constitutional Law and Black Women"—An Occasional Paper for the Afro-American Studies Program at Boston University, undated, PMP, Box 84, Folder 1460.

———. *Pauli Murray: The Autobiography of a Black Activist, Feminist, Lawyer, Priest and Poet*. Knoxville: University of Tennessee Press, 1989.

———. *Proud Shoes: The Story of An American Family*. Boston: Beacon Press, 1999.

———. "Why Negro Girls Stay Single," *Negro Digest*, July 1947.

Patterson, Robert J. *Exodus Politics: Civil Rights and Leadership in African American Literature and Culture*. Charlottesville: University of Virginia Press, 2014.

Perkins, Margo V. *Autobiography as Activism: Three Black Women of the Sixties*. Jackson: University Press of Mississippi, 2000.

Peterson, Carla. *Doers of the Word: African American Women Speakers and Writers in the North, 1830–1880*. Oxford: Oxford University Press, 1995.

Riggs, Marcia Y., ed. *Can I Get a Witness? Prophetic Religious Voices of African American Women: An Anthology*. Maryknoll: Orbis, 1997.

Ross, Marlon. "Beyond the Closet as Raceless Paradigm," in *Black Queer Studies: An Anthology*, ed. E. Patrick Johnson and Mae Henderson, 161–89. Durham: Duke University Press, 2005.

Scanlon, Jennifer. *Until There Is Justice: The Life of Anna Arnold Hedgeman*. New York: Oxford University Press, 2016.

Schuller, Kyla. "Taxonomies of Feeling: The Epistemology of Sentimentalism in Late-Nineteenth Century Racial and Sexual Science." *American Quarterly* 64, no. 2 (2012): 277–99.

Sexton, Jared. *Amalgamation Blues: AntiBlackness and the Critique of Multiracialism*. Minneapolis: University of Minnesota Press, 2008.

Shaw, Stephanie. *What a Woman Ought to Be and to Do: Black Professional Women Workers during the Jim Crow Era*. Chicago: University of Chicago Press, 1996.

Smith, Barbara. "Homophobia: Why Bring It Up?" in *The Truth That Never Hurts: Writings on Race, Gender, and Freedom*. New Brunswick: Rutgers University Press, 1999.

Spillers, Hortense. "Mama's Baby, Papa's Maybe: An American Grammar Book," in *American Literary Theory: A Reader*, ed. Winston Napier, 257–79. New York: New York University Press, 2000.

Tate, Claudia. *Domestic Allegories of Political Desire*. New York: Oxford University Press, 1992.

Terrell, Mary Church. *A Colored Woman in a White World*. Amherst: Prometheus Books, 2005.

Walker, Alice. *In Search of Our Mother's Gardens: Womanist Prose*. New York: Harcourt and Brace, 1983.

Watson, Julia. "Unspeakable Differences: The Politics of Gender in Lesbian and Women's Autobiographies," in *Women, Autobiography, and Theory: A Reader*, ed. Sidonie Smith and Julia Watson, 393–402. Madison: University of Wisconsin Press, 1998.

Wells, Ida B. *Crusade for Justice*. Chicago: University of Chicago Press, 1970.

———. *The Light of Truth: Writings of Anti-Lynching Crusader*, ed. Mia Bay. New York: Penguin Classics, 2014.

———. "The Requisites of True Leadership," in *Can I Get a Witness? Prophetic Religious Voices of African American Women: An Anthology*, ed. Marcia Y. Riggs, 62–67. Maryknoll, N.Y.: Orbis, 1997.

Welter, Barbara. "The Cult of True Womanhood." *American Quarterly* 18 (1966): 151–74.

White, Deborah Gray. *Too Heavy a Load: Black Women in Defense of Themselves, 1894–1994*. New York: W. W. Norton and Company, 1999.

Williams, Fannie Barrier. "The Club Movement among Colored Women of America," in *Can I Get a Witness? Prophetic Religious Voices of African American Women: An Anthology*, ed. Marcia Y. Riggs, 117–31. Maryknoll: Orbis, 1997.

———. "The Intellectual Progress of Colored Women," in *The World's congress of representative women: a historical résumé for popular circulation of the World's congress of representative women, convened in Chicago on May 15, and adjourned on May 22, 1893, under the auspices of the Woman's branch of the World's congress auxiliary*, ed. May Wright Sewall, 696–711. Chicago: Rand McNally, 1984.

Williams, Zachery. *In Search of the Talented Tenth: Howard University Public Intellectuals and the Dilemmas of Race, 1926–1970*. Columbia: University of Missouri Press, 2009.

Index

Index

BRITTNEY C. COOPER is an assistant professor of women's and gender studies and Africana Studies at Rutgers University.

Women, Gender, and Sexuality in American History

The Women's Joint Congressional Committee and the Politics of Maternalism,
1920–1930   *Jan Doolittle Wilson*

"Swing the Sickle for the Harvest Is Ripe": Gender and Slavery in
Antebellum Georgia   *Daina Ramey Berry*

Christian Sisterhood, Race Relations, and the YWCA, 1906–46
Nancy Marie Robertson

Reading, Writing, and Segregation: A Century of Black Women Teachers
in Nashville   *Sonya Ramsey*

Radical Sisters: Second-Wave Feminism and Black Liberation in
Washington, D.C.   *Anne M. Valk*

Feminist Coalitions: Historical Perspectives on Second-Wave Feminism
in the United States   *Edited by Stephanie Gilmore*

Breadwinners: Working Women and Economic Independence, 1865–1920
Lara Vapnek

Beauty Shop Politics: African American Women's Activism in the
Beauty Industry   *Tiffany M. Gill*

Demanding Child Care: Women's Activism and the Politics of Welfare,
1940–1971   *Natalie M. Fousekis*

Rape in Chicago: Race, Myth, and the Courts   *Dawn Rae Flood*

Black Women and Politics in New York City   *Julie A. Gallagher*

Cold War Progressives: Women's Interracial Organizing for Peace
and Freedom   *Jacqueline Castledine*

No Votes for Women: The New York State Anti-Suffrage Movement
Susan Goodier

Anna Howard Shaw: The Work of Woman Suffrage   *Trisha Franzen*

Nursing Civil Rights: Gender and Race in the Army Nurse Corps
Charissa J. Threat

Reverend Addie Wyatt: Faith and the Fight for Labor, Gender, and
Racial Equality   *Marcia Walker-McWilliams*

Lucretia Mott Speaks: The Essential Speeches   *Edited by Christopher Densmore,
Carol Faulkner, Nancy Hewitt, and Beverly Wilson Palmer*

Lost in the USA: American Identity from the Promise Keepers to the
Million Mom March   *Deborah Gray White*

Women against Abortion: Inside the Largest Moral Reform Movement
of the Twentieth Century   *Karissa Haugeberg*

Colored No More: Reinventing Black Womanhood in Washington, D.C.
Treva B. Lindsey

Beyond Respectability: The Intellectual Thought of Race Women
Brittney C. Cooper

The University of Illinois Press
is a founding member of the
Association of American University Presses.

University of Illinois Press
1325 South Oak Street
Champaign, IL 61820-6903
www.press.uillinois.edu